75 CLASSIC RIDES
COLORADO

75 CLASSIC RIDES
COLORADO
THE BEST ROAD BIKING ROUTES

Jason Sumner

MOUNTAINEERS
BOOKS

MOUNTAINEERS BOOKS

Mountaineers Books is the publishing division of The Mountaineers, an organization founded in 1906 and dedicated to the exploration, preservation, and enjoyment of outdoor and wilderness areas.

1001 SW Klickitat Way, Suite 201, Seattle, WA 98134
800.553.4453, www.mountaineersbooks.org

Printed in China

First edition, 2015

Copy editor: Laura Shauger
Design: Heidi Smets
Additional design and layout: Jennifer Shontz, redshoedesign.com
Cartographer: Pease Press Cartography
Cover photograph: *Quiet lonely roads and big mountain scenery are commonplace in Colorado.*
Frontispiece: *A quiet road winding through the ranchland just west of Salida*
All photographs by the author unless otherwise noted.

Library of Congress Cataloging-in-Publication Data
Sumner, Jason.
   75 classic rides, Colorado : the best road-biking routes / by Jason Sumner.
      pages   cm
   Includes index.
   ISBN 978-1-59485-858-1 (pbk)—ISBN 978-1-59485-859-8 (ebook)
1. Cycling—Colorado—Guidebooks. 2. Colorado—Guidebooks. I. Title.
   GV1045.5.C6S85 2015
   796.609788—dc23
                                                    2014030917

ISBN (paperback): 978-1-59485-858-1
ISBN (ebook): 978-1-59485-859-8

CONTENTS

Overview Map   8

Rides-at-a-Glance   10

Acknowledgments   15

Introduction   17

DENVER METRO

1. Golden Gate Canyon   31
2. Lookout Mountain   34
3. Red Rocks Cruiser   37
4. Deer Creek Canyon   40
5. Squaw Pass Road   44
6. Platte River Trail   46
7. Cherry Creek Trail   50
8. Denver City Parks   53

FRONT RANGE NORTH

9. Rist Canyon Loop   57
10. Dams Road to Pinewood Climb   60
11. Trail Ridge Road   65
12. Carter Lake   70
13. South St. Vrain Canyon   73
14. Super James Loop   77
15. Lefthand Canyon   80
16. Sunshine Canyon   84
17. Gold Hill Loop   87
18. Sugarloaf-Magnolia   91
19. Flagstaff Road   94
20. Gross Dam Loop   97
21. Boulder Bike Paths   100
22. Morgul-Bismark Loop   103

FRONT RANGE SOUTH

23. Air Force Academy Loop   108
24. Pikes Peak Greenway Trail   111
25. Garden of the Gods   115
26. Cheyenne Cañon   117
27. Pikes Peak   121

28. Arkansas River Trail 126

29. Hardscrabble Century 128

30. Highway of the Legends 133

NORTHERN ROCKIES

31. Rabbit Ears Pass 137

32. Deep Creek Steamboat Springs 140

33. Coal Mine–Oak Creek Loop 143

34. Emerald Loop 146

35. Mount Evans 149

36. Guanella Pass 153

37. Lake Dillon Loop 157

38. Copper Triangle 160

39. Glenwood Canyon 164

40. Turquoise Lake Loop 167

41. Independence Pass 170

42. Maroon Creek Road 173

SOUTHERN ROCKIES

43. Salida to St. Elmo 177

44. Salida Spinner 180

45. Crested Butte to Gunnison 183

46. Cottonwood Pass 186

47. Ohio Creek Road 189

48. North Cochetopa Pass 192

49. Black Mesa 194

50. Slumgullion Pass 197

51. Cumbres and La Manga Passes 201

SOUTHWEST COLORADO

52. Wolf Creek Pass 204

53. Ignacio–Bayfield Loop 206

54. Texas Creek Loop 210

55. Animas Valley Loop 213

56. Iron Horse Classic 216

57. Deep Creek Telluride 220

58. Lizard Head Pass 223

59. Red Mountain Pass 226

60. Mesa Verde National Park 229

61. Paradox Valley 232

WESTERN SLOPE

62. Unaweep Canyon   236

63. Fruita Farms Loop   239

64. Colorado National Monument   243

65. Little Park Road Loop   246

66. Palisade Fruit and Wine Byway   249

67. Grand Mesa   252

EASTERN PLAINS

68. South Platte River Trail   256

69. Two Time Zones, Three States   258

70. Hugo Race Loop   261

71. Pawnee Buttes Roubaix   264

72. Santa Fe Trail Triangle   268

MULTIDAY ROUTES

73. Central Summits Challenge   271

74. San Juan Scenic Skyway   275

75. Plains to Pueblos   279

Resources   285

Index   291

MAP LEGEND

———	Featured Route
- - - -	Unpaved Route
- - - - -	Route on Bike Path
·········	Route Variation
·–·–·–	Unpaved Variation
- - - - - -	Other Bike Path
══════	Freeway (Limited Access)
———	Highway
———	Secondary Road
- - - - -	Unpaved Road

S	Start (and Finish for loops and out-and-back rides)
F	Finish (for one-way rides)
→	Route Direction
↶	Turnaround Point
▼3 4	Numbered Stages in Multiday Rides
76 225	Interstate Highway
6 50 160	US Highway
7 96 135	State Route
T 213	County Road
813	Forest Road

■	Building/Point of Interest
▲	Campground
▲	Peak
⚌	Bridge
) (	Tunnel
‿	Pass
◗	Water
◖	Dam
	Park/Forest
⊢⊣	Railroad Tracks
— ·· —	State Boundary
○	Town

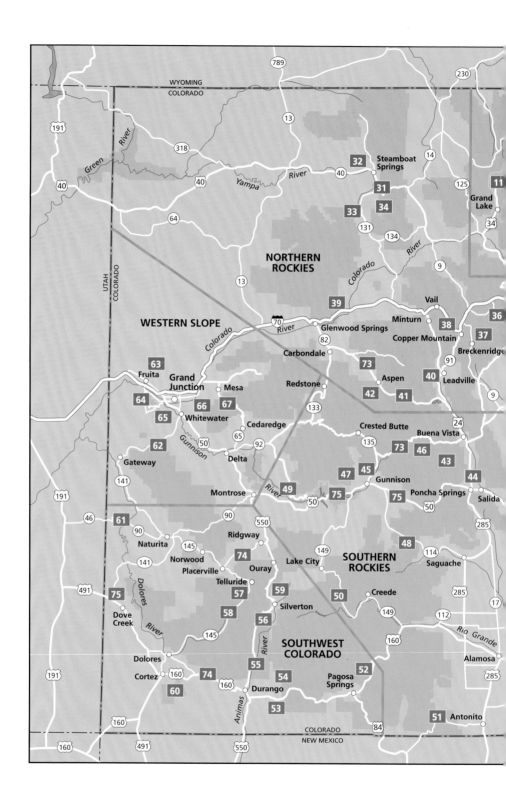

789

WYOMING
COLORADO

13

191

318

32 Steamboat
Springs

14

Green River

40

Yampa River

40

40

31

125

11

40

64

33 34

Grand
Lake

34

131

134

Colorado River

9

NORTHERN
ROCKIES

UTAH
COLORADO

13

39

Vail

36

WESTERN SLOPE

70 River

Glenwood Springs

Minturn

38

Copper Mountain

37

82

Colorado River

Carbondale

73

Breckenridge

63

Fruita

Grand
Junction

Mesa

Redstone

Aspen

40 Leadville

91

64

66 67

42 41

9

65 Whitewater

Cedaredge

133

62

50

65

92

Crested Butte

Buena Vista

24

Gateway

141

Gunnison River

Delta

135

73 46

43

191

46

61

90

Montrose

47 45

Gunnison

44

49

50 75

75 Poncha Springs

Salida

90

550

50

285

90

Ridgway

48

114

Naturita

145

74

Lake City

149

SOUTHERN
ROCKIES

Saguache

141

Norwood

Ouray

491

75

Placerville

Telluride

57

59

50

285

17

Dove
Creek

Dolores River

58

56

Silverton

Creede

149

112

Rio Grande

145

Animas River

SOUTHWEST
COLORADO

160

Alamosa

Dolores

55

52

191

Cortez 160

74 160

54

Pagosa
Springs

285

60

Durango

53

51 Antonito

160

COLORADO
NEW MEXICO

84

160

491

550

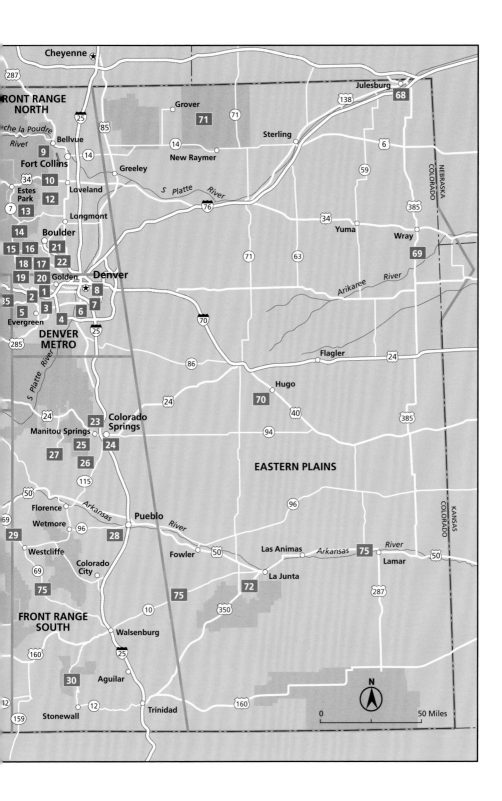

Cheyenne ★

287

FRONT RANGE
NORTH

che la Poudre
River   Bellvue

9

Fort Collins

34   10

Estes
Park   12

7   13

14   Boulder

15   16   21

18   17   22

19   20   Golden

2   1

35

5   3   6   7

Evergreen   4

DENVER
METRO

285

14   New Raymer

Greeley

S Platte River

76

25   85

14

Loveland

Longmont

8

★

25

Grover   71

71

Sterling

6

59

34   Yuma   Wray

385

71   63   69

Arikaree   River

70

86   Flagler   24

24   Hugo   70

40

94   385

Julesburg   68

138

COLORADO   NEBRASKA

EASTERN PLAINS

COLORADO   KANSAS

24   Colorado
23   Springs

Manitou Springs

25   24

27

26

115

50

Florence

69   Wetmore   96

29

Westcliffe

69

75

FRONT RANGE
SOUTH

42

159   Stonewall

Arkansas

Pueblo   River

28

Colorado
City

10   75

30   Aguilar

12   Trinidad

96

Fowler   50

Las Animas   Arkansas   River

75

Lamar

La Junta   287   50

72

350

Walsenburg

160   25

160

N

0   50 Miles

9

RIDES-AT-A-GLANCE

NO.	RIDE	DIFFICULTY RATING	DISTANCE (IN MILES)	ELEVATION GAIN (IN FEET)	TIME (IN HOURS)	POINTS OF INTEREST
1	Golden Gate Canyon	Challenging	27.8	4163	2–3½	Golden Gate Canyon State Park, city views, tough climb
2	Lookout Mountain	Moderate	9.8	1416	½–1½	Buffalo Bill's grave, city views, famous climb
3	Red Rocks Cruiser	Easy	9.4	1033	¾–1½	Red Rocks Amphitheatre, dinosaur tracks, city views
4	Deer Creek Canyon	Moderate to Challenging	34.1	4212	2–4	Pleasant Park School, cyclist rest stop, city views
5	Squaw Pass Road	Moderate to Challenging	37.5	4239	2–3	Echo Lake Lodge, Mount Evans views, Bergen Park
6	Platte River Trail	Easy	32.8	190	2–3	Downtown Denver, Confluence Park, South Platte Park
7	Cherry Creek Trail	Easy	34.5	790	2–3	Downtown Denver, Confluence Park, Cherry Creek Reservoir and State Park
8	Denver City Parks	Easy	12.6	288	1–2	City Park, Washington Park, Cheesman Park
9	Rist Canyon Loop	Challenging	46.5	5229	2½–4½	Tough climb, quiet rural roads, narrow canyon, classic loop
10	Dams Road to Pinewood Climb	Challenging	59.3	4350	3½–4½	Horsetooth Reservoir, rural roads, quiet countryside, tough climb
11	Trail Ridge Road	Epic	94.3	9976	6–10	Big Thompson Canyon, Rocky Mountain National Park, Kawuneeche Valley
12	Carter Lake	Moderate	65.6	3767	3½–5½	Rural countryside, mountain views, Carter Lake Reservoir
13	South St. Vrain Canyon	Challenging	66.2	7062	4–6	Canyon climb, Peak to Peak Highway, Brainard Lake
14	Super James Loop	Challenging	52.8	4829	3½–5½	Jamestown, high mountain views, South St. Vrain Canyon descent
15	Lefthand Canyon	Challenging	42.4	6200	3–5	Canyon climb and descent, mountain views, historic town of Ward
16	Sunshine Canyon	Moderate	11.3	1800	¾–1½	Indian Peaks views, Eastern Plains views
17	Gold Hill Loop	Moderate	21.3	3192	1½–2½	Historic church, dirt road climb, town of Gold Hill
18	Sugarloaf-Magnolia	Challenging	28.1	5321	2–4	Two tough climbs, Boulder Creek Path, mountain views
19	Flagstaff Road	Moderate	12	2173	1–2	City views, famous climb, Sunrise Circle Amphitheater
20	Gross Dam Loop	Challenging	53.3	6342	4–6	Gross Reservoir, Wondervu, Peak to Peak Highway, Eldora ski area

NO.	RIDE	DIFFICULTY RATING	DISTANCE (IN MILES)	ELEVATION GAIN (IN FEET)	TIME (IN HOURS)	POINTS OF INTEREST
21	Boulder Bike Paths	Easy	14.2	281	1–2	Boulder Creek, Valmont Bike Park, views of the Flatirons
22	Morgul-Bismark Loop	Moderate	20.5	1276	1–2	Famous race route, mountain views, giant wind turbines
23	Air Force Academy Loop	Moderate	14	1130	¾–1½	Air Force Academy campus, plains views, famous cycling circuit
24	Pikes Peak Greenway Trail	Easy to Moderate	41	909	3–4	Pikes Peak, Fountain Creek, Monument Creek, downtown Colorado Springs
25	Garden of the Gods	Easy	5.8	729	½–1	Stunning red rock formations, Pikes Peak views
26	Cheyenne Cañon	Moderate	11	1697	1–2	Narrow canyon climb, rushing creek and waterfall, city views
27	Pikes Peak	Epic	38.8	7175	3–6	14,115-foot summit, massive views, historic setting
28	Arkansas River Trail	Easy	28.2	912	2–3	Arkansas River, famous outdoor mural, Lake Pueblo State Park
29	Hardscrabble Century	Epic	105.1	7672	5–8	A supermax prison, Wet Mountain Valley, Royal Gorge bridge, Skyline Drive
30	Highway of the Legends	Challenging	44.2	5260	3½–5	Dakota Sandstone stone wall, Spanish Indian Peaks, Cucharas Mountain Resort
31	Rabbit Ears Pass	Challenging	32	2967	2½–3½	Yampa River Core Trail, huge valley views, Lake Catamount
32	Deep Creek Steamboat Springs	Moderate	39	1970	2–3	Elk River, Mount Zirkel views, scenic gravel roads
33	Coal Mine–Oak Creek Loop	Challenging	51.2	3655	3½–5	Quiet country roads, Stagecoach State Park, Old Brooklyn neighborhood
34	Emerald Loop	Moderate	28	1883	1½–2½	Emerald Mountain, scenic gravel roads, Yampa River
35	Mount Evans	Epic	55.2	7132	4–6	14,130-foot summit, massive mountain views, highest paved road in the United States
36	Guanella Pass	Challenging	50	7185	3–5	Historic Georgetown, scenic seasonal road, mountain views
37	Lake Dillon Loop	Easy to Moderate	32	1537	1½–3	Lake Dillon, Frisco, Swan Mountain
38	Copper Triangle	Challenging to Epic	79.3	6952	4½–6½	Copper Mountain ski area, Vail Pass, Camp Hale
39	Glenwood Canyon	Easy	32.7	896	2–3	Colorado River, Hanging Lake, bighorn sheep
40	Turquoise Lake Loop	Moderate	23.3	2341	1½–2½	Leadville, mountain views, Turquoise Lake

NO.	RIDE	DIFFICULTY RATING	DISTANCE (IN MILES)	ELEVATION GAIN (IN FEET)	TIME (IN HOURS)	POINTS OF INTEREST
41	Independence Pass	Challenging	37.2	3120	2–4	Continental Divide, Aspen, view of Mount Elbert
42	Maroon Creek Road	Moderate	22.2	2056	1½–2½	Maroon Bells, Aspen, Stein Meadow overlook
43	Salida to St. Elmo	Challenging	62.4	4100	3½–5½	Mount Princeton Hot Springs, historic ghost town
44	Salida Spinner	Easy	17.6	584	1–2	Arkansas River, mountain views, Franz Lake
45	Crested Butte to Gunnison	Moderate	67.4	2872	3½–5	Taylor River, Almont, Mount Crested Butte
46	Cottonwood Pass	Challenging to Epic	68.2	4452	4–6	Continental Divide, Taylor Park, amazing views
47	Ohio Creek Road	Easy	31.9	746	1–2	Gunnison River, valley and mountain views
48	North Cochetopa Pass	Challenging	62	2979	3½–5	Cochetopa Dome, mountain views, quiet road
49	Black Mesa	Challenging	83.5	7205	5–7	Blue Mesa Reservoir, Gunnison River, Crawford, Black Canyon
50	Slumgullion Pass	Epic	102.3	8120	7–9	Lake San Cristobal, Rio Grande River, Creede
51	Cumbres and La Manga Passes	Epic	95.8	6220	5½–7½	Historic railroad, New Mexico, incredibly varied scenery
52	Wolf Creek Pass	Challenging	47	4100	3–5	Continental Divide, Pagosa Hot Springs, San Juan River
53	Ignacio–Bayfield Loop	Challenging	72.2	3637	4–6	Animas River, varied terrain, distant mountain views
54	Texas Creek Loop	Moderate	42.4	4221	3–5	Durango, gravel roads, valley views
55	Animas Valley Loop	Easy	27.1	841	1–2	Animas Valley, Bakers Bridge, Trimble Hot Springs
56	Iron Horse Classic	Challenging	47.5	5812	3–5	Historic and scenic route, Silverton, high mountain scenery
57	Deep Creek Telluride	Moderate	28.7	2687	1½–3	San Miguel River, Deep Creek Mesa, great valley and mountain views
58	Lizard Head Pass	Challenging	55.4	5203	3–5	Lizard Head Peak, Trout Lake, Wilson Peak
59	Red Mountain Pass	Challenging	69.2	6190	4–6	Ouray Hot Springs, Million Dollar Highway, Silverton
60	Mesa Verde National Park	Moderate to Challenging	53	5310	3–5	American Indian ruins, desert scenery, beautiful roads
61	Paradox Valley	Challenging	79.2	5323	4–6	Dolores River, old Bedrock store, Utah, Paradox Valley
62	Unaweep Canyon	Challenging	88.5	5589	5–7	Geologic mystery, Gateway, beautiful canyon

NO.	RIDE	DIFFICULTY RATING	DISTANCE (IN MILES)	ELEVATION GAIN (IN FEET)	TIME (IN HOURS)	POINTS OF INTEREST
63	Fruita Farms Loop	Easy	37	835	1½–3	Valley views, Fruita, quiet rural roads
64	Colorado National Monument	Moderate to Challenging	39.5	3518	2½–4	Spectacular scenery, Colorado River, famous cycling route
65	Little Park Road Loop	Moderate to Challenging	26.3	2937	1½–3	Views of Grand Valley and Colorado National Monument, tough climb
66	Palisade Fruit and Wine Byway	Easy	23.2	695	1–2	Mount Garfield, Colorado River, orchards and vineyards
67	Grand Mesa	Epic	68.2	6747	4½–7½	Scenic and Historic Byway, Powderhorn ski area, massive views
68	South Platte River Trail	Easy	19.4	156	1–2	Historic loop, Colorado Welcome Center, South Platte River
69	Two Time Zones, Three States	Challenging	88	2918	4½–6	Kansas, Nebraska, quiet roads, Eastern Plains views
70	Hugo Race Loop	Moderate	80	1823	3½–5	Rural roads, Eastern Plains views, town of Karval
71	Pawnee Buttes Roubaix	Epic	56.5	1649	5–8	Pawnee Buttes, gravel roads, Eastern Plains views
72	Santa Fe Trail Triangle	Easy	32	505	1½–2½	Quiet rural roads, Eastern Plains views
73	Central Summits Challenge	Epic	234.4	16,104	2–4 days	Multiple high mountain passes, two Continental Divide crossings, massive Aspen grove
74	San Juan Scenic Skyway	Epic	226	17,030	2–4 days	Multiple high mountain passes, Ouray Hot Springs, Silverton, Durango
75	Plains to Pueblos	Epic	515	27,236	6–9 days	East–west cross-state route, mountains, valleys, desert, solitude

With your purchase of this book, you also get access to our easy-to-use, downloadable cue sheets:

» Go to our website: www.mountaineersbooks.org/BikeCO
» Download a complete set of mileage cue sheets for all 75 rides in this book.
» When you open the document on your computer, enter the code "C0C0R0AD" when prompted.

It's our way of thanking you for supporting Mountaineers Books and our mission of outdoor recreation and conservation.

Wherever you ride, spending quality time with friends is one of cycling's great joys.

ACKNOWLEDGMENTS

Though my name appears on the front of this book, credit and thanks must be spread all over Colorado and beyond. So many people helped out, gave advice, offered route suggestions, posed for photos, went on bike rides, and generally lent the support and friendship that made this project a reality.

Thanks for the hospitality Emily McCormack, April Prout-Ralph, Kierra Skinner, Mistalynn Meyeraan, Rachel Zerowin, Anne Klein, Cathy Wiedemer (and Moots), Katy Schneider, Nikki Inglis, Chelsy Murphy, Gaylene Ore, Bonnie and Danny, and the Van Buskirks.

Thanks for the expert route beta Jon Cariveau, Greg Ralph, Todd Wells, Mary Monroe, Travis Brown, John Hodge (the map master), Patrick O'Grady, Mark Gouge, Chandler Smith (and his Ride the Rockies crew), Chris Johnson, Brian Holcombe, Dave Wiens, Sydney Fox, Ross Schnell, Anthony Carcella, Addi Cantor, Michael Shea, Matt Beaudin, Greg Brophy, Scott Christopher, and Kervin Quinones.

Thanks for coming along for the ride Dave Walker, Zack Vestal, Dave LeFevre, Whitney Rogers, Neal Rogers, KP, KB, LZ, Zac Rudolph, Ben Delaney, Garren Watkins, Jeff Kerkove, Fred Guy, and everyone else on the USC Cycling team.

Thanks to Ira and the RoadBikeReview/Mtbr crew for giving me the leash to pursue this project, and to the fine folks at Mountaineers Books for bringing the book to life.

Thanks to Mom for passing on (some of) her masterful writing skills. Thanks to Dad for instilling a sense of adventure (and perhaps a little stubbornness). Thanks to Margie, Mike, Luca, and Evie for allowing me to set up Book HQ Crested Butte, feeding me, and not worrying too much. And most of all, thanks and love to my beautiful, patient, supportive, and all-around amazing wife, Lisa. Without you, this book wouldn't have happened.

Venturing above timberline is an integral part of the Colorado cycling experience.
Ride up Pikes Peak to sample the lack of oxygen along its skyscraping road.

INTRODUCTION

I wasn't always a cyclist or a cycling writer. My post-college career started with a job on the sports desk at the local newspaper in Boulder. My beat was high school anything. The long-term goal was to cover the Broncos. Then on a quiet summer news day, my boss gave me a choice. Work in the office answering phones, he said, or head to Niwot. "There's some sort of bike race going on. Maybe you can find a story." I went to Niwot. It changed my life.

One bike racing story made me the paper's bike racing reporter, which led to a job at a bike racing magazine, which turned me into a cyclist. Becoming a cyclist meant exploring my home state in ways I never had before. Fifteen years and thousands of miles later, I get to share that state with you. We're both lucky. Colorado is a great place to ride bikes.

In the 300 or so pages that follow are details of seventy-five amazing rides (and dozens of route variations). Some crawl up mighty peaks. Others carve through towering red rock canyons. A few amble along rippling rivers. Two traverse national parks. Another crosses a 1200-foot-high bridge. Many simply roll easily, giving you time to feel the breeze in your face and the sun on your skin. It's a cliché, but there really is something for everyone.

Of course, Colorado being bisected by the Rocky Mountains, there's an emphasis on climbing. There are two paved roads in North America that rise above 14,000 feet. Both are detailed in this book. Want to climb the world's largest flat-top mountain? Grand Mesa, Ride 67. Want to cross the Continental Divide? North, central, or south? There are choices in every region. More interested in ancient American Indian ruins and spectacular desert panoramas? Meet Mesa Verde National Park. Prefer sandstone spires and Grand Valley views? Colorado National Monument is the place to pedal.

How about following the wheel tracks of the famed Coors Classic bike race, 1986 world road cycling championships, or USA Pro Challenge? Start on the Peak to Peak Highway, spin a lap of the Air Force Academy campus, and then finish with back-to-back climbs over Cottonwood Pass and Independence Pass. I could go on, but why spoil all the fun of discovering it for yourself? Read on, then ride on. I hope you enjoy the journey.

GETTING STARTED

If you're holding this book in your hands, you've likely done at least some riding beyond bike path beer runs or cruiser spins to the movie theater. If you're brand-new to the sport, congratulations. In my humble opinion, riding a bike is the single greatest way to exercise, spend time with friends, and explore the world around us. Studies have shown that cycling improves concentration and memory function, reduces stress, and generally makes us happier and healthier.

But there is more to riding a bike than what you learned as a kid. Even basic skills, such as shifting gears, braking, and cornering, are loaded with subtle nuance. So how do you learn these finer points, as well as more advanced techniques, such as countersteering and riding in a pace line? Practice is the short answer. Like most things in life, the more you ride the better cyclist you'll become. Of course, finding mentors helps too. Colorado is packed with all manner of clubs, teams, and various other cycling organizations. Check the appendix in the back of this book for a list of local clubs and teams.

Bike shops are another valuable resource. Many offer free seminars that teach basic safety, riding, and maintenance skills. Call (or surf) around, and you're sure to find something going on in your area. And of course, nearly limitless information is available online. Check out websites, such as the *Bicycling* magazine site and RoadBikeReview .com, which include myriad how-to articles that can help you advance your current skills and learn new ones.

RIDING ETIQUETTE AND SAFETY

Being a competent cyclist goes beyond setting personal records or dropping your riding buddies on the local throw-down climb. We all have a responsibility to be good citizens of the road, both for our own safety and the safety of those around us. In Colorado, bicyclists and motorists have equal rights and responsibili-

ties, starting with obeying all traffic signs and signals, riding with (not against) traffic, and staying off pedestrian sidewalks. By law two bicyclists may ride side by side when doing so does not impede vehicle traffic. Otherwise, ride single file to allow vehicles to pass. When you're riding curvy canyon roads without bike lanes or shoulders, play it safe. Ride single file.

Don't dart through traffic like a New York City bike messenger. Instead aim to be smooth and predictable. Signal turns using traditional signals (arm out or arm pointing up) or simply point where you intend to go. Always try to establish eye contact with drivers. Never assume they see you or that you have the right-of-way. And keep a close eye on parked cars—and their doors. Wher-

Within the pages of this book are multiple routes that ascend above tree line into the clouds, including this testing push to the summit of Mount Evans, the highest paved road in North America.

There's no wrong time to ride bikes in Colorado. But it's hard to argue with fall when the leaves are ablaze in their golden glow.

ever you're riding, be courteous and share. Whether on a road or multiuse path, ride as far right as is safe, and always warn others before you overtake them. A pleasant "hello" or "on your left" does the trick. If you're riding early in the morning or after dark, wear reflective clothing and mount a headlight and taillight somewhere on your bike or body.

Many of these same rules apply to riding in a group. Be predictable, not jerky. Accelerate and brake smoothly. Point out obstacles, call out cars, and always keep your eyes on the road ahead. Don't just stare at the wheel in front of you. If you're riding in a rotating pace line (in which cyclists rotate through a

line, taking turns riding up front, then peeling off and drifting to the back), don't overlap wheels with the rider in front of you, and always maintain a steady pace. Just because it's your turn to take a pull at the front doesn't mean upping your effort by 200 watts. And relish the fact that when you fall back in line, you'll be working about 30 percent less than if you were riding all alone.

Even if you're on a quiet, rural road, don't fall asleep at the proverbial wheel. Gravel, glass, potholes, rocks, railroad crossings, and cattle guards can all ruin your day if you're not paying attention. Stay loose, stay focused, and have fun.

As the famous quote from JFK goes, "Nothing compares to the simple pleasure of a bike ride."

THE BIKE

If you're in the market for a new bike or thinking about upgrading, figure out your budget before you roll into your local bike shop. (Yes, shop locally. It will save a lot of headaches in the long run.) Also remember that non-negotiable items, such as a helmet, padded cycling shorts, cycling shoes, clipless pedals, and some basic repair tools, will add at least a few hundred dollars to your bottom line.

When it comes time to choose a bike, focus on fit. No matter what parts or color your new two-wheeler is, if it doesn't fit, you won't ride it. Start with a test ride. Are you comfortable? Can you imagine hours of pain-free pedaling? Or does your back start throbbing before you're out of the parking lot?

Many bike makers offer what's called endurance geometry. I like to call it normal-people geometry. Without delving too deeply into the minutiae, it means you'll be able to pedal in a more upright relaxed position, which translates to less chance of back, shoulder, and neck aches.

Once you've narrowed your choices, comparison shop for parts. You may find that one bike is equipped with a better drivetrain or lighter wheels. Also consider gearing options. Unless you're planning to race the local criterium circuit, opt for a compact crankset, which will make it easier to spin up steep hills but won't leave you totally spun out on the descent. Finally, ask the shop to help fine-tune your on-bike position. Many shops will include basic fit adjustments with the purchase price, setting the saddle height and helping you choose the right stem length.

Before each ride, do a quick safety check. Are your brakes working properly, or do you need new brake pads? Does the chain need lube? Are the tires properly inflated? Periodically check all your bike's bolts to assure none have loosened. Then grab on-road essentials: a spare tube, a pump or CO_2 inflation device, and a multitool. And of course, make sure you know how to use them. It's tough to change a flat tire if you don't know how to take your wheel off. Practice in the garage, not on the side of the highway.

After every couple rides, give your bike a bath and lube the chain, which helps maintain proper drivetrain function. If you're mechanically inclined, swap on new cables and housing once or twice a year. Otherwise, take it back to the shop where you bought it and get it tuned up at the beginning of each cycling season.

THE RIDER

Give your body the same care you give your bike. Lather on sunscreen, then put on the proper cycling kit. The notion of padded cycling shorts may seem foreign at first. But trust me, your backside will thank you. If you're headed out for an all-day affair, mix a little chamois cream into the equation. It takes a little getting used to, but again, it works. If you're not comfortable in a full Lycra getup, more and more apparel companies are offering high-performance casual wear that looks like "normal" clothing but is designed for real bike riding. Personally, I'm a function over fashion guy, but to each his own.

Whatever you slip on, make sure it has some secure pockets, then stuff those pockets with just-in-case gear. I can't stress enough how fast Colorado's summertime weather can change, especially in the mountains. Pack a pair of light gloves, a beanie, knee warmers, and a rain jacket. They won't take up much space and can make the difference between riding home or huddling under a tree waiting for your significant other to pick you up. Round out your getup with a pair of sunglasses (bug and sun protection) and a helmet. Always wear a helmet. Period.

FUELING

Your car needs gas. Your body needs food and drink. For rides under an hour, a topped-off water bottle is all you need as long as you didn't skip your last meal. If you plan on being out longer, carry food, or stop to eat along the way. A simple rule of thumb is to ingest one bottle (16 ounces) of water, one bottle (16 ounces) of an electrolyte-infused sports drink, and 30–60 grams of carbohydrates per hour of exercise.

What you eat and drink is entirely a matter of personal choice. I don't mind slurping down gooey gel packs, but others would just as soon eat dirt. Bottom line, you need to experiment and figure out what works for you. After a long ride, it's critical to eat (or slurp a protein-laden recovery drink) within thirty minutes to help switch your metabolism from a breaking-down state to a rebuilding state. Also, be sure to get a good night's rest. Sleep is the body's natural recovery mechanism.

GRAVEL GRINDING

If you follow the cycling world with even casual interest, you've surely heard mention of the phenomena that is gravel road riding. Thanks to advances and changes in road bike technology (disc brakes, through-axles, wider tires, and greater tire clearance),

and a new breed of cyclist looking to explore beyond the confines of paved roads and concrete bike paths, the definition of what road bikes and road bikers are capable of has greatly expanded. The movement is reflected in this book via multiple mixed-surface rides. The idea of riding off-pavement may seem intimidating at first, but the trade-off is virtually traffic-free roads that lead deep into quiet countryside, past forests and meadows, and even across high mountain passes. Many of my personal favorite rides include time on dirt.

If you opt to take the road less traveled, consider swapping on a set of wider tires, which help smooth the ride and increase

The Colorado cycling calendar is packed with all manner of events, from hotly competitive pro and amateur races, to casual rides of varying difficulty and distance. Pictured here is the route between Telluride and Cortez, day one of the 2013 Ride the Rockies, an annual weeklong bike tour.

traction. Most road bikes are specced with 23-millimeter-wide tires but can handle 25-millimeter or even 28-millimeter. Before your ride, pull on a pair of cycling gloves for extra cushioning. On the road, stay relaxed and keep your body weight evenly distributed. This helps maintain rear-wheel traction. Also, try pushing a larger gear, which will smooth out the ride and increase your control. Finally, remember to constantly scan for hazards and brake gently. It's much easier to skid and lose control when riding on a loose surface. But with a little practice, you'll soon be comfortable pedaling off the beaten path.

2013 FLOODS

In September 2013, severe flooding struck Boulder and Larimer counties, damaging dozens of roadways and bridges, including some featured prominently in this guidebook. In many cases, repairs and reconstruction had begun by spring 2014 and were slated to be completed by the end of that year. However, ongoing construction, variable road surface conditions, and additional closures are possible into 2015 and beyond. I have provided alternative routes when possible, but please check with the appropriate agency (detailed in each ride description) for the latest updates.

TEN ESSENTIALS

Unlike in life, there are absolutes in cycling. Here are ten preride checks and items that should be part of any cycling excursion.

1. Bike check: Properly inflate your tires, lube your chain, and check your brakes.
2. Helmet: Put it on. Leave it on. It could save your life.
3. Basic repair tools: Always carry a spare tube, inflation device, and small multitool.
4. Food and drink: Cycling takes fuel. Don't forget yours.
5. Extra clothing: Storms brew quickly. Hope for the best; be prepared for the worst.
6. Sun protection: The sun's rays are intense, especially in the mountains. Protect yourself.
7. ID: If something goes wrong, help those who are helping you by carrying identification.
8. Phone: Great for calling for help, and a handy navigation tool (mapping apps optional).
9. Lights: Even a small blinking light on your seatpost will help motorists spot you.
10. Plan: Know where you're going and how you're getting there.

HOW TO USE THIS BOOK

No two people will use this book the exact same way, but the core elements at your disposal begin with the regional map and rides-at-a-glance chart. They're a good place to start just to get your bearings. Find a region or route that interests you, then flip to the appropriate page. There you'll find detailed ride descriptions that begin with an elemental sketch of what you can expect: how hard, how long, how far, how much climbing, and the best time of year to tackle it. That's followed by directions to the ride's start point and some basic information on road conditions. Finally, I've done my best to paint a picture of the experience. In the end, my goal is to inform and inspire.

DIFFICULTY

"How hard is that ride?" It's a question you hear all the time. The only absolutely correct answer is "It depends." It depends on your fitness level, the weather, wind, temperature, how much time you have. One person's

It's obvious why this road is called the Peak to Peak Highway. Roll far enough north and you'll end up in Rocky Mountain National Park.

la-di-da lunch hour spin is another's Sisyphean stone. So while my four-tier rating system (Easy, Moderate, Challenging, and Epic) will give you an outline of what to expect, you must also consider your own circumstances before deciding if that ride on this day is the right one for you.

Of course, the other way to find out is to simply get out there and pedal. In the end, that's what cycling is all about. Generally speaking, though, each ride's rating is based on distance and elevation gain, with extra credit for high elevation, tricky descents, or time on unpaved roads. Finally, if a ride's general rating isn't what you're looking for,

check for a route variation at the end of the description. Often there are easier and harder options.

» **Easy** rides are typically less than 25 miles, have little or no climbing, and can be knocked out in a couple hours. Many of these rides are on bike paths or roads with little traffic, wide shoulders, or both. Many are also perfectly suitable for children and beginners.

» **Moderate** rides feature increased distance (usually in the 35- to 50-mile range), greater elevation gain (2000–4000 feet), or both. Someone with a decent level of fitness and cycling experience will see these rides as solid workouts, but not overly taxing. Figure at least a couple hours of saddle time.

» **Challenging** rides account for the largest number of routes in this book. These have sustained climbs and distances in the 50- to 80-mile range. If you don't have at least a solid fitness base and intermediate-level skill set, perhaps steer clear of these until you feel more capable and confident.

» **Epic** ride is a tag reserved for a very select group (Pikes Peak, Mount Evans, Grand Mesa, Trail Ridge Road, and the like). Expect big mileage, huge climbs, and possibly extended time on unpaved roads. You can't simply roll out of bed and decide to tackle one of these rides. Planning and preparation are key.

I've also split the difference in a handful of instances, listing rides as "Easy to Moderate" or "Challenging to Epic," which means that they simply fall somewhere in between the outlined ratings listed above.

TIME

Estimating ride time is yet another hugely subjective measure. Tour de France pros can tick off 30 miles per hour with an energy bar in one hand. Beginning riders may struggle to keep the speedometer in double figures. Most of us fall somewhere in between. Each ride has a predicted time range (two to three hours, five to seven, etc.), which is based on average speeds of 10 miles per hour on the low end and around 18 miles per hour at the high end. Adjustments are made for routes with exceptionally steep climbs, ultra-high altitude, or extended dirt road sections. Of course, this does not account for long lunch stops, coffee breaks, flat tire fixes, or bonks. Adjust accordingly.

DISTANCE

Route distances were determined using a Garmin GPS device, online mapping tools,

or both. I opted not to use hundredths in my calculations, which meant rounding up or down from time to time. All that said, expect to sometimes encounter subtle differences between my numbers and numbers from your chosen mileage-measuring device. But if you follow the mileage log—and pay careful attention to noted landmarks, street signs, summits, etc.—you'll get where you intended to go.

ELEVATION GAIN

As anyone who's tracked elevation during bike rides knows, discrepancies are the norm, not the exception. Mount the same model GPS device on two bikes, send them on the same route at the same time of day, then download the data to the same place, and it's still unlikely that the total elevation measures will match. Close is really the best you can hope for.

The figures in this book are an amalgamation of data collected with a Garmin GPS unit, downloaded to online mapping services Strava and Ride with GPS, and then massaged with a little meet-in-the-middle smoothing. The final output is a best guess that will give you at least a fair idea of what's to come when you head out the door and up the road.

Note that rides with minimal or no elevation gain do not have elevation profiles.

BEST SEASONS

Three times I've signed up for the Iron Horse Bicycle Classic held annually on Memorial Day weekend (see Ride 56). One year I took off my arm warmers about an hour into the ride from Durango to Silverton and never put them back on. Another year, my prerace warm-up jacket became my all-day barely-warm-enough jacket. The year after that, the race was cancelled due to snow. Point being, while Colorado enjoys an inordinate number of sunny days per year, its weather is also notoriously unpredictable—especially in the mountains. Warm sunny days can quickly turn cold, wet, and windy. Some summers you can keep time by the arrival of afternoon thunderstorms (and sometimes hail).

Generally speaking, rides along the Front Range, around Denver, in the Southwest, and on the Western Slope are possible from April to October. Sometimes the season is longer, sometimes shorter. Farther into the mountains, you'll likely need to wait until late spring or even early summer. But it all depends on the spring snowpack. Several routes in this book include roads that are closed six to seven months each year. Bottom line, use the guidelines outlined here as a starting point. But remember that they are only a starting point. Always check the weather before you go.

ROAD CONDITIONS

Memorize the phrase "The shoulder comes and goes, but traffic is usually light," and you'll know the road conditions for most rides in this book. The same goes for the condition of the pavement, which is generally fair with occasional potholes, cracks, and/or seams. In all but a few cases, I've avoided high traffic roads (no interstates, only a handful of US highways). But with Colorado being the tourist hot spot that it is, occasionally

Wildlife sightings are common in Colorado. This pair of mountain goats was unperturbed as I pedaled past on the way to the summit of Mount Evans.

Years ago, the famed Coors Classic pro race roared through Colorado National Monument in what was dubbed the Tour of the Moon stage. Today, an amateur event with that same name spins through this red rock wonderland at a much more casual pace.

sharing these wonderful backroads with campers, RVs, or loaded-down minivans is simply part of the game. To enjoy cycling, you must learn to live with traffic.

GETTING THERE

For all those people without a GPS-outfitted smartphone, these directions are for you. Everybody else, simply note the actual starting point, which in most cases is near a city park where parking is free, and restrooms and water are readily available.

BEST OF THE BEST

In no particular order, here are my top five rides in a variety of categories. These lists are highly subjective. Ask me again tomorrow, and I'd probably give different answers. I love them all.

FAMILY RIDES

These outings are ideal for beginners or even some children.

Cherry Creek Trail (Ride 7): If you live in—or visit—Denver, this multiuse path in the heart of the city is a must-do experience.

Denver City Parks (Ride 8): Three parks, one ride. What more could you ask for?

Boulder Bike Paths (Ride 21): Spin from downtown along the Boulder Creek Path to the famed Valmont Bike Park.

Arkansas River Trail (Ride 28): Get an up-close look at the world's largest outdoor mural.

The Pikes Peak Greenway Trail runs through the heart of Colorado Springs and may someday be part of a larger trail system that runs the length of the state, connecting New Mexico in the south to Wyoming up north.

Glenwood Canyon (Ride 39): Trace the shores of the Colorado River on a bike path beneath towering walls of sandstone and sedimentary rock.

BEST SCENERY
There's a reason it's called colorful Colorado.

Trail Ridge Road (Ride 11): Trek through the heart of spectacular Rocky Mountain National Park on the highest paved through-road in the country.

South St. Vrain Canyon (Ride 13): Roll toward the foothills of the Rockies on a ser-

pentine canyon road, then traverse the famed Peak to Peak Highway and climb to Brainard Lake for stunning Indian Peaks views.

Black Mesa (Ride 49): Stare into the abyss of Black Canyon and spin past glimmering aspen groves, but rarely see a car.

Lizard Head Pass (Ride 58): See the inspiration for the Coors logo, the famed Lizard Head Peak, plus lakes, rivers, and historic Telluride.

Colorado National Monument (Ride 64): Take in towering red rock spires, deep canyons, and immense Grand Valley views.

BUCOLIC FLATS

These rides have little or no climbing and plenty of good scenery.

Salida Spinner (Ride 44): Enjoy quiet country roads, views of the Collegiate Peaks, and nearly three hundred days of sunshine per year.

Ohio Creek Road (Ride 47): Take a spin in cowboy country along a broad valley where cattle graze in the shade of towering cottonwoods.

Animas Valley Loop (Ride 55): Roll north along the Animas River, cross famed Bakers Bridge, then return beneath sheer red rock walls.

Palisade Fruit and Wine Byway (Ride 66): See Colorado wine country from the seat of a bike, stopping at orchards and vineyards along the way.

Santa Fe Trail Triangle (Ride 72): Go for a spin in the state's far northeast corner, learning a little history along the way.

LUNCHERS

These beautiful rides (usually) take two hours or less.

Flagstaff Road (Ride 19): Boulder's most famous climb is easily accessible and can even be knocked out in an hour if you're feeling good.

Cheyenne Cañon (Ride 26): Just west of downtown Colorado Springs, this short but steep climb is the locals' go-to workout when time is tight.

Emerald Loop (Ride 34): Smooth country roads and scenic gravel road grinding make this short loop a Steamboat Springs noontime staple.

Turquoise Lake Loop (Ride 40): Trace the initial miles of the famed Leadville Trail 100 mountain bike race while looping a scenic mountain lake.

Maroon Creek Road (Ride 42): Roll from downtown Aspen to the base of the spectacular Maroon Bells on a road with restricted motorized traffic.

Cycling in its purest form is the simple joy of discovering what's around the next bend.

(PARTIALLY) OFF-ROAD ADVENTURES

These gravel grinders lead off the beaten path.

Gold Hill Loop (Ride 17): Roll out of downtown Boulder on a bike path, then grind up a moderate dirt road climb to the tiny town of Gold Hill.

Pikes Peak Greenway Trail (Ride 24): Bisect the heart of Colorado Springs, then leave the city behind on this path that vacillates between smooth pavement and crushed gravel.

Deep Creek Steamboat Springs (Ride 32): Explore the dirt roads northwest of Steamboat Springs, with great views of Mount Zirkel and the surrounding wilderness.

Salida to St. Elmo (Ride 43): Spin past Mount Princeton (and Mount Princeton Hot Springs), then roll the out-and-back dirt road to St. Elmo, a well-preserved ghost town.

Texas Creek Loop (Ride 54): A Durango-area classic that starts on pavement, then traverses a series of gravel road rollers and one seriously tough climb.

TOUGHEST CLIMBS

Colorado is full of roads that head uphill. These are some of the most challenging.

Pikes Peak (Ride 27): Gain more than 7000 feet in less than 40 miles—and top out above 14,000 feet. Ouch . . .

Mount Evans (Ride 35): The grades aren't as steep as those of Pikes Peak, but this is America's highest paved road (peak elevation 14,130 feet).

Cottonwood Pass (Ride 46): Climb above 12,000 feet to the Continental Divide—and do it on 13.7 miles of dirt road.

Slumgullion Pass (Ride 50): Average gradient: 7 percent, with numerous pitches above 10 percent. Total elevation gain: 2600 feet. Peak elevation: 11,530 feet. Enough said.

Red Mountain Pass (Ride 59): Known alternatively as the "Million Dollar Highway" and one of the "world's most dangerous roads," this "skyscraper" from Ouray to Silverton is relentless.

A NOTE ABOUT SAFETY

Safety is an important concern in all outdoor activities. No guidebook can alert you to every hazard or anticipate the limitations of every reader. Therefore, the descriptions of roads, trails, routes, and natural features in this book are not representations that a particular place or excursion will be safe for your party. When you follow any of the routes described in this book, you assume responsibility for your own safety. Under normal conditions, such excursions require the usual attention to traffic, road and trail conditions, weather, terrain, the capabilities of your party, and other factors. Keeping informed on current conditions and exercising common sense are the keys to a safe, enjoyable outing.

—*Mountaineers Books*

DENVER METRO

One of the first major metropolitan areas to embrace bike sharing, Denver is always near the top of the list when cycling-friendly cities are ranked. From Confluence Park in the heart of downtown, you can roll almost any direction via bike path. If you're looking for a bigger challenge, head west to the nearby base of the Rocky Mountains, where myriad climbing options await. Or better yet, connect the two. It's possible to get out of the city and into the hills without riding in traffic.

1 GOLDEN GATE CANYON

Difficulty:	Challenging
Time:	2–3½ hours
Distance:	27.8 miles
Elevation gain:	4163 feet
Best seasons:	Spring through fall
Road conditions:	Narrow shoulder on majority of route. Steady, fast-moving traffic on Golden Gate Canyon Rd. Rough, broken pavement from mile 8.1 to 10.6. Very steep, mile-long descent starting at mile 9.6.

GETTING THERE: From downtown Golden, head southwest on 12th St. Take first right onto Washington Ave.; go right on SR 93. Then take a left onto Golden Gate Canyon Rd., and park on the side of the road (no restrooms or water).

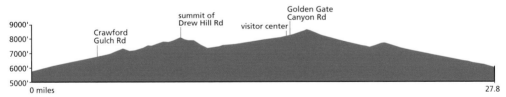

Warning: If you are a nervous descender, have brakes of questionable reliability, and/ or don't like riding on rough pavement, do not ride this route. There's a 2.5-mile section of bumpy, occasionally broken pavement on Drew Hill Road, and near the end of that section is a very steep, mile-long descent—also with bumpy, broken pavement.

Instead, ride straight out Golden Gate Canyon Road to the Golden Gate Canyon State Park Visitor Center (about 13 miles one-way), do an out-and-back trip into the park for additional mileage, or just turn around and head back the way you came. Aside from the narrow shoulder and steady traffic on Golden Gate Canyon Road, this is a perfectly nice ride with some stiff climbs, fast and fun descents, and a lot of pretty scenery.

However, if you're the adventurous type who is willing to endure a little rugged terrain

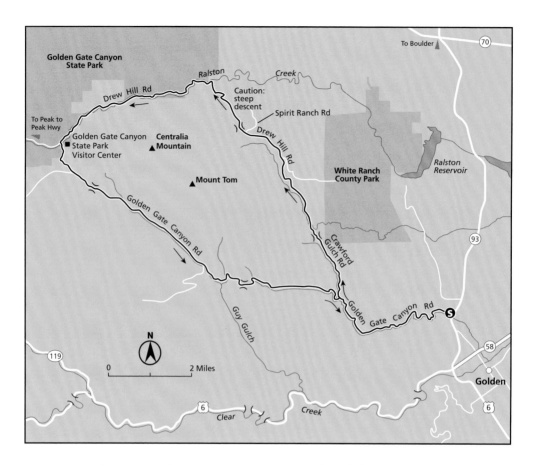

to avoid spending extended time on a busy road with a narrow shoulder, read on.

This ride comes courtesy of my wife, Lisa, who after getting tired of the high traffic volume on Golden Gate Canyon Road, decided to do some exploring. The end result is a great string-and-balloon route that gets you off Golden Gate Canyon Road during most of the climbing. Like most cyclists I know, she'd rather be going downhill on a busy road.

This ride starts from the intersection of State Route 93 and Golden Gate Canyon Road. There's a handful of pull-off parking spots just west of SR 93. The climbing starts right away, but the grade is gentle, never more than 6 percent for the first 4 miles. Mile 4 is also where you leave the bustle of Golden Gate Canyon Road, turning right onto

Crawford Gulch Road. This road is blissfully quiet, which is the no. 1 reason to head this way.

Reason no. 2 is a fantastic—and tough—stair-stepping climb that has a few of those drawn-out stretches where you can see long ribbons of pavement. I know some cyclists prefer to have their pain parceled out one short switchback at a time. But I've always loved being able to see what's coming.

As you get closer to the top, the grade backs off, and the heretofore pine tree–lined road opens up, revealing rolling green meadows, grazing horses, and long-distance views back toward Denver. This is also where the road surface turns rough. It's still paved; it's just not very good pavement.

The summit of what's now called Drew Hill

With its close proximity to Denver, Golden Gate Canyon is a popular weekend destination for cyclists. But head out during the week and you just might have the road to yourself.

Road (though you never turned) is just shy of 9 miles into the ride at the intersection with Spirit Ranch Road. Catch your breath, have a drink, and then prepare for the aforementioned adventurous descent. On the cycling-centric social sharing website Strava, this segment is affectionately known as "Oh Shit!!!" But if you take your time, keep your speed in check, and watch out for broken pavement, it's not that big a deal.

At the bottom, around mile 10.6, normal pavement returns, as you slowly climb toward the Golden Gate Canyon State Park Visitor Center. This mellow, 4.5-mile stretch of Drew Hill Road is the southern border of this

12,000-acre state park that has 35 miles of hiking and mountain biking trails.

At mile 15, you arrive at the park's visitor center and the intersection with Golden Gate Canyon Road. Inside are bathrooms, water, and a cool topographical scale model of the park. Outside is a small pond teeming with giant rainbow trout.

From here, turn left onto Golden Gate Canyon Road, and head back to your car. This section starts with a gradual, mile-long climb that takes you to the route's high point at 8735 feet. After that it's almost all downhill, except for one short climb that winds around a pair of tight switchbacks.

MILEAGE LOG

0.0   From SR 93, head west on Golden Gate Canyon Rd.
4.0   Right on Crawford Gulch Rd.
7.6   Road becomes Drew Hill Rd.
8.9   Caution on the steep descent
15.0   Arrive at Golden Gate Canyon State Park Visitor Center
15.1   Left on Golden Gate Canyon Rd.
27.8   Finish the ride at the intersection of SR 93

2 LOOKOUT MOUNTAIN

Difficulty:	Moderate
Time:	½–1½ hours
Distance:	9.8 miles up-and-back
Elevation gain:	1416 feet
Best seasons:	Spring through fall (possible year-round)
Road conditions:	Narrow to nonexistent shoulder, but usually light, slow-moving traffic.

GETTING THERE: Ride starts at Beverly Heights Park, a few miles west of downtown Golden at 2151 Lookout Mountain Rd. From downtown Golden, head south on Washington Ave., then take a right on 19th St. Follow it for a mile, then continue on Lookout Mountain to the park on your right (free parking and porto-johns).

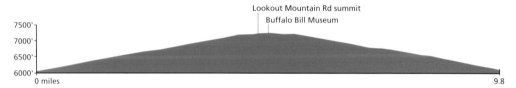

At less than 10 miles round-trip, the climb and descent of Lookout Mountain Road is one of the shortest rides in this book. But as you can see from the profile (and guess from the name), it is by no means easy. With an elevation gain of 1416 feet in less than 5 miles, the Lookout Mountain ascent is one of the top cycling draws in the Denver Metro area. On any weekend day, when the road is dry and the sun is shining, expect to see dozens of cyclists winding their way up the dozen switchbacks that lead to the summit at 7350 feet.

You can start this ride from just about anywhere in Golden (or even ride over from Denver), but I'm only detailing the heart of the climb, which starts as Lookout Mountain Road. The unofficial starting point is where the road passes between a pair of large rock pillars marked with a sign on the left that reads, "Entering Denver Mountain Parks." Just before the pillars is Beverly Heights Park, which has free parking and porto-johns.

From there it's all uphill for 4.7 miles with an average grade right at 5 percent. Top riders can crest the climb in less than 17 minutes, and in 2006, pro rider Tom Danielson set the record of 16:02.

Unless you're feeling the need to suffer, back off a little, find a spinnable gear, and enjoy the great long-distance views, which are dominated by stunning panoramas of Golden, Denver, and the distant Eastern Plains. Nearby landmarks include the sprawling Coors Brewery (look for the big red sign), the Colorado School of Mines campus (the athletic fields are easy to spot), and the school's distinctive white "M" perched on the hillside above Lookout Mountain Road. Each fall, incoming School of Mines freshmen must carry a 10-pound rock from campus up to the giant "M" and coat the symbol with fresh white paint. Four (or more) years later, graduating seniors return to the "M" to retrieve their rocks.

You'll also spot North Table Mountain

and South Table Mountain, which straddle the Coors plant. Back in the late 1990s, shoe and apparel maker Nike had a deal in place to open a giant corporate campus on top of South Table Mountain, but the deal fell through when the state didn't offer enough economic incentives.

After twisting through three tight switchbacks that offer great views of Clear Creek Canyon to the northeast, the road straightens out for about a mile, before curling back on itself four more times as it heads into the trees.

The grade is much shallower from here to the top, which for our purposes is the sign for Buffalo Bill's grave on the right side of the road at mile 4.7. This is also where the annual Lookout Mountain Hill Climb race ends, earning the event its nickname "Pillar to Post" because it starts at the stone pillars and ends at this signpost.

You can turn around here and head back to your car (mind your speed on the sharp turns). Or go right and up the short climb to the Buffalo Bill Museum and Grave. There's a great 270-degree lookout point here where you can spot snowcapped Rocky Mountains to the northwest, the Boulder Flatirons to the north, and more yawning views of Golden, Denver, and the Eastern Plains.

There's also a gift shop that sells snacks and drinks. And of course, you can visit the

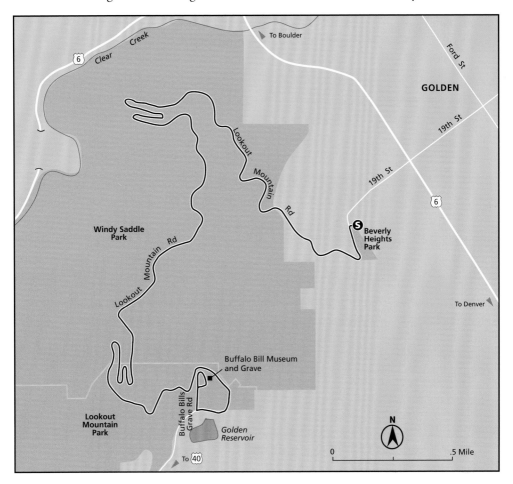

gravesite of the famous Wild West entertainer, who at his request was buried here after his death in 1912.

Route variation: If you just can't bear the thought of riding an out-and-back, this route can be done as a 15.5-mile loop. When you reach the top of the climb, continue on Lookout Mountain Road for 2.7 miles until you reach US Highway 40. Turn left and follow US 40 downhill for 5.4 miles to the intersection of Heritage Road. Follow Heritage for 1 mile to the intersection of 6th Avenue, then go left on 6th, jumping on the bike path that parallels this busy road. In 1.3 miles, go left on 19th Street, and follow it uphill back to Beverly Heights Park.

MILEAGE LOG

0.0	Start at Beverly Heights Park
0.0	Left onto Lookout Mountain Rd.
0.1	Pass side-by-side stone pillars, signaling official start of climb
4.7	Arrive at Buffalo Bill sign
4.7	Right up to Buffalo Bill Museum and Grave
4.9	Arrive at museum and overlook

Loop option:

4.7	**Continue west on Lookout Mountain Rd.**
7.4	**Left on US 40**
12.8	**Left on Heritage Rd.**
13.8	**Left on 6th Ave. joining bike path**
15.1	**Left on 19th St.**
15.4	**Return to Beverly Heights Park**

5.0	Head back down Lookout Mountain Rd.
9.8	Finish at Beverly Heights Park

During the 5-mile ascent of Lookout Mountain, you'll gain almost 1500 feet—and be treated to world-class views of Golden, Denver, and the far-off Eastern Plains.

3 RED ROCKS CRUISER

Difficulty:	Easy
Time:	¾–1½ hours
Distance:	9.4 miles
Elevation gain:	1033 feet
Best seasons:	Spring through fall (possibly winter)
Road conditions:	Mix of lightly traveled roads, bike paths, and bike-only road.

GETTING THERE: Ride starts on Morrison Rd. in downtown Morrison. From downtown Denver, head west on SR 6, then exit onto I-70 west toward Grand Junction. A mile later, take exit 260 for SR 470 east toward Colorado Springs. In 4.4 miles, take Morrison Rd. exit, and head west into Morrison for on-street parking and services.

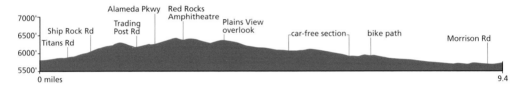

Ask a Coloradoan to list the state's most truly singular experiences, and you'll almost certainly hear about the Red Rocks Amphitheatre. The famed outdoor concert venue has been hosting musical acts since the 1940s, and has been the site of some of music's most famous performances. (Who can forget the mystically foggy 1983 music video of U2's "Sunday Bloody Sunday." Don't know what I'm talking about? YouTube it.)

But Red Rocks is much more than a music venue. I remember gleefully heading out to the park as a grade-schooler to hike and play among the red sandstone formations, including Creation Rock and Ship Rock, which together form the towering side walls of this 9450-seat venue that's been dubbed the world's only naturally occurring acoustically perfect amphitheater. Besides great hiking and mountain biking trails, Red Rocks Park has a small spiderweb of quiet roads that are perfect for a quick spin or a kid-friendly excursion.

For the sake of creating a loop, start this ride in nearby Morrison, a quaint little town with several funky gift shops and a great Mexican restaurant. Pedal west on Morrison Road, which soon becomes State Route 74. At the 0.6-mile mark, turn right onto Titans Road, which is the park's no. 4 entrance. (You'll pass the sign for no. 3 just before you get here.)

Now the full majesty of this natural wonderland comes into view, as the Great Plains converge with the Rocky Mountains in a place that was originally known as Garden of the Angels. At mile 1.0, turn left onto Ship Rock Road, and continue the gradual climb toward the actual Ship Rock.

At mile 1.6, just as you reach the crest of this road, there's a steep access ramp on the left. As long as there's not an event in progress, you can literally pedal right up to the stage. Just note that this up-and-back will add about a half mile to your mileage total.

Once you're back down, continue on Ship Rock Road to the intersection with Trading

Post Road, then turn left. A half mile later, go left onto Alameda Parkway, which leads up above the venue, where you can look down on the stage and see downtown Denver in the distance. There are also bathrooms and a restaurant here if you or the kids need a break or a snack.

Now head back down Alameda, and take a quick left on Plains View Road. This is another short up-and-back section that offers more ranging views of the park, the plains, and the Denver skyline.

Once you've soaked in the scenery, spin back down Plains View Road, go left on Alameda, and roll downhill to entrance no. 1 at the intersection with County Road 93. If you're running short on time or the kids are getting tired, turn right and head down CR 93. You'll be back in Morrison in minutes.

But if you still have some gas—and are interested in dinosaurs—pedal across the road, and continue up the other side of Alameda Parkway. This 1.5-mile section, known as Dinosaur Ridge, is closed to cars and has several interpretive sites displaying ancient fossils and footprints.

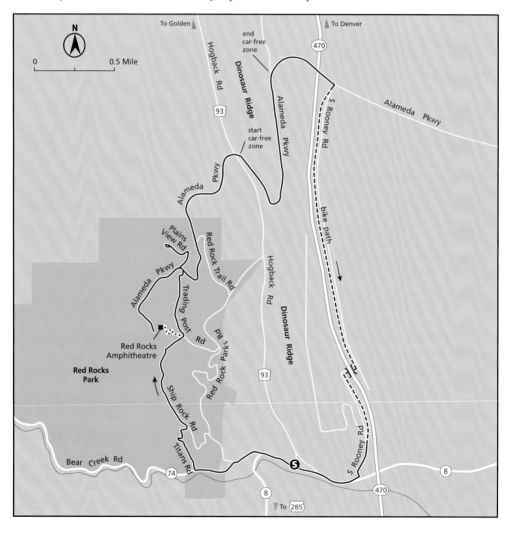

Red Rocks Park was once known as Garden of the Angels. It's easy to see why.

After a half mile of gentle uphill pedaling, the road swings around and descends northward. At mile 6.1, you leave the car-free zone, continuing on Alameda as it crosses above SR 470. On the other side, turn right onto the bike path that parallels South Rooney Road and follow it back to Morrison Road. Turn right and the starting point is a half mile ahead.

MILEAGE LOG

0.0	Head west on Morrison Rd. (SR 74)
0.6	Right on Titans Rd., no. 4 entrance of Red Rocks Park and Amphitheatre
1.0	Left on Ship Rock Rd.
1.6	Left on Trading Post Rd.
2.0	Left on Alameda Pkwy. (up-and-back section)
3.1	Left on Plains View Rd. (up-and-back section)
3.7	Left on Alameda Pkwy.
4.7	Leave Red Rocks Park, cross CR 93, and continue on Alameda Pkwy. (car-free section)
6.1	Leave car-free section and stay right, continuing on Alameda Pkwy.
6.5	Just after crossing over SR 470, turn right onto bike path parallel to S. Rooney Rd.
8.3	Cross back underneath SR 470, continuing on bike path
8.7	Exit bike path and merge onto S. Rooney Rd., continuing south
8.9	Right on Morrison Rd.
9.4	Return to starting point in downtown Morrison

4 DEER CREEK CANYON

Difficulty:	Moderate to Challenging
Time:	2–4 hours
Distance:	34.1 miles
Elevation gain:	4212 feet
Best seasons:	Early spring to late fall
Road conditions:	Minimal shoulder on majority of ride, but entire route on lightly traveled roads.

GETTING THERE: Ride starts at intersection of S. Wadsworth Blvd. and W. Deer Creek Canyon Rd. in Littleton. From downtown Denver, take I-25 south to exit 209B for US 6 west. Go 3.2 miles west on US 6, then exit onto SR 121 south (S. Wadsworth Blvd.). Go 12.6 miles south, then turn right onto W. Deer Creek Canyon Rd. (free parking on both sides).

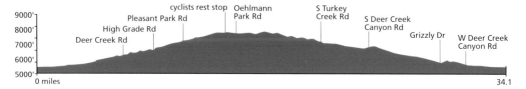

Don't be surprised if during sunny summer weekends you see more bikes than cars in Deer Creek Canyon, arguably the most popular cycling route in south metro Denver. This hilly, 34.1-mile route on quiet mountain roads is a diverse affair, with tough sustained climbing, swoopy fun descents, smooth pavement, great views, and one of the best cyclist rest stops in the state (more on that in a minute).

Unfortunately, Deer Creek Canyon also sees occasional strife between the residents who drive these canyon roads and the cyclists who ride here. Over the years, there have been isolated incidents of aggressive motorists honking and buzzing riders, as well as bad apple cyclists ignoring the single-file law or even urinating in inappropriate places. (Nearly all the land along this route is private property.)

Bottom line: If you ride Deer Creek Canyon, behave. Some drivers will never accept that cyclists have equal rights on the road. But

adding fuel to the fire by riding two abreast in single-file zones or not holding it until you get to a proper restroom just makes the situation worse. If the need arises, there's a porta-potty at the South Valley Park trailhead on your right at mile 3.1 and at the rest stop at mile 13.8.

Okay, off the soapbox and onto the route description. This ride starts at the intersection of South Wadsworth Boulevard and West Deer Creek Canyon Road, which is about 18 miles south of downtown Denver and is accessible by bike via the Platte River Trail (Ride 6).

From here, head west on West Deer Creek Canyon Road. There's an ample shoulder during the first 6 miles, as you gradually climb away from civilization and into this peaceful canyon lined by towering walls of reddish sandstone.

At mile 6.2, you reach the intersection of Deer Creek Road and what's left of the tiny

Deer Creek Canyon is arguably the most popular Denver-area ride thanks to its smooth pavement, stiff climbs, and relative tranquility.

prospecting town of Phillipsburg, where the infamous Alfred Packed (the Colorado cannibal) lived after his release from prison in the early 1900s.

Turn left. The shoulder is narrow to non-existent through here, but traffic is light. The grade remains shallow for the ensuing 2 miles, then gets steeper just as you transition onto High Grade Road. The next 4.5 miles are the toughest, gaining 1300 feet rapidly as you twist through switchbacks that hang on the edge of a steep, tree-covered hillside.

At mile 10.7, stay straight on what becomes Pleasant Park Road. Soon the road levels out, as you make your way onto the top of a rolling plateau. It's beautiful country up here, meadows of wavy grass, horse ranches, mountain cabins, and lodgepole pines blending in a tapestry of rural tranquility.

At mile 13.8, you'll arrive at the aforementioned rest stop, which is on the right side of the road just past the historic Pleasant Park School (built in 1894). Here you'll find a porta-potty, bike rack, a half dozen shaded picnic tables, and several coolers that from May to October are stocked with water, hydration drinks, energy snacks, and even a bottle of ibuprofen.

It's an honor system operation, so take what you need, and then drop some money in the cash box. The rest stop is maintained by the Pleasant Park Grange, which also tends to the school and surrounding land. Once you're refreshed, continue along Pleasant Park Road to mile 14.5, then turn right on Oehlmann Park Road (look for the giant barn with a green roof). The next 3 miles are ever-rolling, as the road changes names to Snowy Trail,

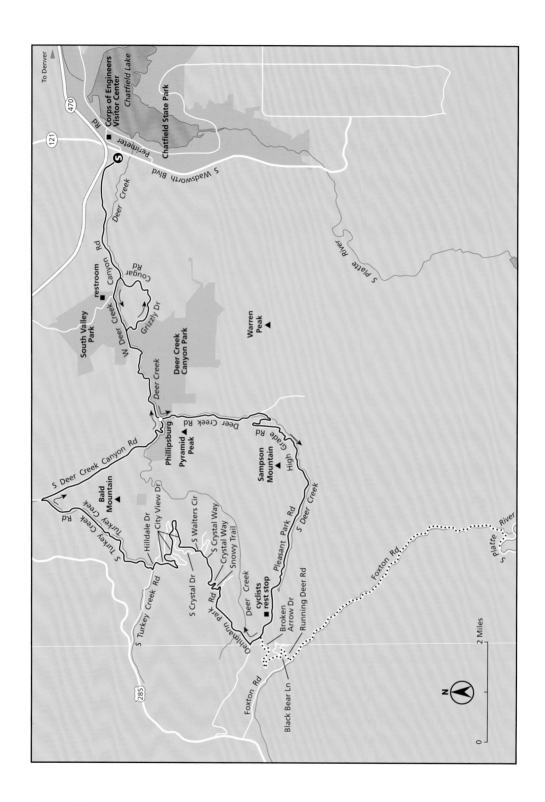

To Denver

470
121

Corps of Engineers Visitor Center

Chatfield Lake

Chatfield State Park

Perimeter Rd

restroom

S Wadsworth Blvd

Deer Creek

S Platte River

Cougar Rd

Canyon Rd

Grizzly Dr

W Deer Creek

South Valley Park

Warren Peak

Deer Creek

Deer Creek Canyon Park

Deer Creek Rd

Phillipsburg

Pyramid Peak

Sampson Mountain

High Grade Rd

Deer Creek Rd

S Deer Creek Canyon Rd

Bald Mountain

City View Dr

Hilldale Dr

S Walters Cir

S Crystal Way

Crystal Way

Snowy Trail

Pleasant Park Rd

S Deer Creek

Turkey Creek Rd

S Turkey Creek Rd

S Crystal Dr

Crystal Park Rd

Oehlmann Park Rd

Deer Creek

cyclists rest stop

Broken Arrow Dr

Running Deer Rd

Foxton Rd

S Platte River

Foxton Rd

Black Bear Ln

285

N

2 Miles

0

Crystal Way, and then South Crystal Way. In every case, simply stay on the main road to stay on the prescribed route.

At mile 17.4, turn right at the fork, joining South Walters Circle, and then take the next left onto City View Drive. The ensuing 3 miles are almost all downhill. And yes, there are great views of Denver—and an occasional glimpse of the snowcapped Rockies.

At mile 20.7, turn right onto South Turkey Creek Road, continuing gradually downhill, before making a sharp right onto South Deer Creek Canyon Road at mile 23.8. A short climb gives way to another long downhill that returns you to the intersection of Deer Creek Road and West Deer Creek Canyon Road. Go left and it's a straight shot back to the starting point. Or you can add on a little extra climbing—and great sightseeing—by spinning up to Deer Creek Canyon Park. (Trust me, it's worth it.)

At mile 29.4, turn right onto Grizzly Drive, roll up to the park (restrooms and water), and then continue looping around to the left, passing a handful of McMansions,

and then turning left on Cougar Road at mile 30.6. This drops you back to West Deer Creek Canyon Road. A little over three miles later, you're done.

Route variation: To reach the Deer Creek Canyon route from Denver via the Platte River Trail, take the C-470 East Trail into Chatfield State Park, then follow the park's perimeter road around the west side of the reservoir. Turn right at the sign for the Corps of Engineers Visitor Center, head up the hill, bear left at the fork, and then roll past the visitor center to the intersection of South Wadsworth Boulevard and West Deer Creek Canyon Road.

For extra climbing, add the 16-mile Foxton Road out-and-back. At mile 14.3, turn left off Pleasant Park Road onto Broken Arrow Drive. Then take a left on Black Bear Lane, a right on Running Deer Road, and finally a left onto Foxton Road. From here it's a rapid 6.2-mile descent down to the South Platte River. Splash some water on your face, then buckle up for the nasty climb back to Pleasant Park Road.

MILEAGE LOG

0.0	From intersection of S. Wadsworth Blvd. and W. Deer Creek Canyon Rd., head west on W. Deer Creek Canyon Rd.
6.2	Left onto Deer Creek Rd.
8.3	Stay straight on High Grade Rd.
10.7	Stay straight on Pleasant Park Rd.
13.8	Arrive at the cyclists rest stop
	Foxton Rd. option:
14.3	**Left onto Broken Arrow Dr.**
15.5	**Left on Black Bear Ln.**
15.7	**Right on Running Deer Rd.**
16.0	**Left on Foxton Rd.**
22.2	**Turn around at Platte River Rd.**
30.3	**Left onto Pleasant Park Rd. to rejoin main route**
14.5	Right onto Oehlmann Park Rd.
16.0	Left onto Snowy Trail
16.2	Right onto Crystal Way
17.0	Stay straight on S. Crystal Way
17.4	Right onto S. Walters Circle

17.5	Left onto City View Dr.
18.2	Left at fork, continuing on City View Dr.
18.9	Stay straight, continuing on City View Dr.
19.5	Right, continuing on City View Dr.
20.0	Right, continuing on City View Dr.
20.6	Left onto Hilldale Dr.
20.7	Right onto S. Turkey Creek Rd.
23.8	Right onto S. Deer Creek Canyon Rd.
29.4	Right onto Grizzly Dr.
30.6	Left onto Cougar Rd.
31.2	Straight on W. Buckhorn Rd.
31.3	Right on W. Deer Creek Canyon Rd.
34.1	Return to start

5 SQUAW PASS ROAD

Difficulty:	Moderate to Challenging
Time:	2–3 hours
Distance:	37.5 miles out-and-back
Elevation gain:	4239 feet
Best seasons:	Spring to fall
Road conditions:	Smooth pavement and ample shoulder on majority of ride. Some sections have dedicated bike lane.

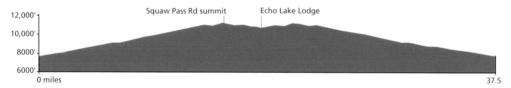

GETTING THERE: Ride starts from the Bergen Park near Evergreen. From downtown Denver, take I-25 north to I-70 west, continue west for 23 miles, and then take exit 252 for SR 74 (Evergreen Pkwy.). After 3 miles, turn left on CR 65, and park will be on your right. Free parking and restrooms.

Some will argue that Squaw Pass is simply "the other road" to get to the base of Mount Evans (Ride 35). And technically they're right. While the traditional route to the top of North America's highest paved road embarks farther west from Idaho Springs, you can also access that monstrous climb via Squaw Pass Road.

In my mind, though, it deserves to stand alone. Not only is the ride up Squaw Pass Road a testing 18.7-mile grind that gains nearly 3400 feet, the trip back down is one of the best descents in the state. The majority of the road surface is silky smooth, traffic is usually light, and there's nary a sharp turn.

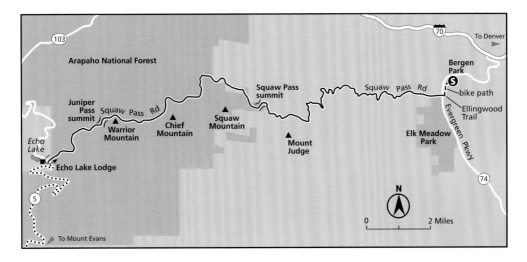

Heck, there's even a dedicated bike lane along a portion of this recently repaved road.

The ride starts from Bergen Park, 3 miles southwest of Interstate 70. From there, jump on the bike path that heads south out of the park, paralleling Evergreen Parkway. Less than a half mile later, turn off the path, and go right onto Ellingwood Trail, then cross Evergreen Parkway, and start rolling up Squaw Pass Road. That's it for routefinding—but the work is far from over. For the next hour or two, you'll be heading uphill nearly the entire time, making your way to the high point at 11,154 feet.

The climb starts gently, as you cruise past a wide-open meadow, its tall prairie grass waving

The ride up Squaw Pass takes riders past wide-open prairie on its way into the high mountains that form the eastern flank of the Rockies.

in the wind. But a mile later the grade pitches up to near 5 percent, and the thick forest closes in around you. And so it goes for most of the next dozen miles, just you, the trees, and the climb in front of you. It's peaceful and painful.

It's also worth noting that this climb is really two in one, with Squaw Pass leading into Juniper Pass. But because the road traverses a ridgeline rather than going up and over these mountains, it feels like one continuous climb with a slight respite in between. Technically, the summit of Squaw Pass is around mile 9, with the summit of Juniper Pass coming at mile 15. Between these two points, the views finally start to open up, and you get a sense of just how high you've come. Up ahead you can see the summit of Mount Evans and the faint outline of the road that can get you there.

From the top of Juniper Pass, either turn around and head back, or follow the prescribed route downhill for 3 more miles to Echo Lake Lodge, where you can grab a snack and top off your bottles. The return trip starts with a mellow 3-mile climb that gains a shade under 500 feet. After that it's nearly all downhill, as you swoop down this fabulous descent back to the start point in Bergen Park.

Route variation: The obvious add-on is to tackle the proverbial whole enchilada, and pedal the additional 14.5 miles to the summit of Mount Evans (Ride 35) via State Route 5. Just know this is not an excursion that should be taken lightly.

MILEAGE LOG

0.0	Head south out of Bergen Park parking area, picking up bike path parallel to Evergreen Pkwy. (SR 74)
0.4	Follow bike path to left, then turn right onto Ellingwood Trail
0.5	Go straight across Evergreen Pkwy. and onto Squaw Pass Rd.
18.7	Reach turnaround point at Echo Lake Lodge
	Mount Evans option:
	18.7 Turn left on SR 5 to Mount Evans
	33.2 Reach Mount Evans summit
	47.7 Right onto Squaw Pass Rd., rejoining main route
37.5	Return to starting point

6   PLATTE RIVER TRAIL

Difficulty:	Easy
Time:	2–3 hours
Distance:	32.8 miles out-and-back (longer options)
Elevation gain:	190 feet
Best seasons:	Spring to fall (possible in winter)
Road conditions:	Entire route on paved multiuse trail. Trail, especially close to downtown Denver, can be congested during weekends and commuting hours.

From the Platte River Trail, catch ranging views of numerous Mile High City landmarks, including the skyscrapers of downtown Denver.

GETTING THERE: Ride starts at Confluence Park, just east of the REI flagship store in downtown Denver. From I-25 southbound, take exit 212C, turn right on 20th St., left on Central St., left on 15th St., and then right on Platte St. Just after REI, there is a small free parking lot on left side of what becomes Water St. From I-25 northbound, take exit 211 for 23rd St., then make a slight right onto Water St., and parking lot is 0.3 mile ahead on right. If lot is full, there are metered and pay-lot options nearby.

To see Denver in all its grandeur (and grime) head downtown, then pedal south on the Platte River Trail. This dead-flat, 16.4-mile stretch of multiuse path traces the banks of the South Platte River, while delivering a sundry assault of sights and sounds that collectively exemplify the Mile High City and its suburbs—both good and bad.

Along the way are landmark views of Elitch Gardens amusement park, Sports Authority Field, and the city's downtown skyscrapers. You'll also get up-close looks at often-congested Interstate 25 and the biggest gravel pit I've ever seen. The noise level, as you'd expect from a trip through the guts of a major city, is representative of the scenery.

Fortunately, this path includes extended stretches of pristine—and quiet—natural beauty as well. The latter half winds by idyllic gardens, shimmering lakes, and nature preserves alive with soothing birdsong. And if you arrive at the end of the trail and wish to continue, hop on the C-470 Trail and roll into scenic Chatfield State Park, which is crisscrossed by bike trails and cycling-friendly roads. You can also link up with Deer Creek Canyon (Ride 4).

Like the Cherry Creek Trail ride (Ride 7), this route starts at Confluence Park, another municipal landmark. Denver was officially founded here in 1858. Besides historical significance—and fabulous people-watching—

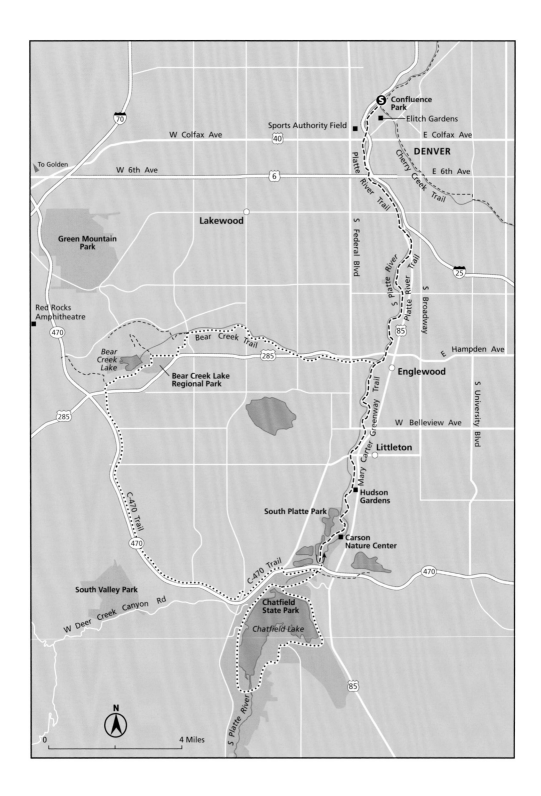

the park offers easy access to the adjacent 100,000-square-foot REI store, which has a full-service bike shop and a Starbucks. Restrooms are on the second floor.

Head south on the Platte River Trail, which is marked by mileage signs that count upward. Within the first mile, you'll pass the amusement park (across the river on your left), the Denver Broncos' stadium (ahead on the right), and the Children's Museum (one of my favorite childhood haunts).

Soon though, the scenery takes a turn for the industrial. The next 5 miles are where people work, not live or play. But the cacophony of capitalism eventually fades. There's a lovely little park with a pond around mile 6, and at mile 7 the path crosses a bridge with a great view of the river.

The next 5 miles are a back-and-forth battle between industry and nature, a park here, a giant parking lot there. At mile 9, you pass a large movie cinema on the right, then turn left and cross the river. Going straight puts you on the Bear Creek Trail, which runs west to the small town of Morrison near Red Rocks (Ride 3).

This is also where the Platte River Trail changes names to the Mary Carter Greenway Trail. In the early 1990s, Carter played an integral role in getting the trail built, as well as revitalizing what was once a heavily abused river corridor.

From mile 10 to 16, you'll pass the aforementioned gravel pit (mile 10), but also the Hudson Gardens botanical park (mile 13, restrooms and water), the 600-acre South Platte Park nature preserve (mile 14), and the Carson Nature Center (mile 14.8, more restrooms and water).

The last 2 miles of trail are arguably the best. Out here, the racket of the city is banished for good, as the path cuts through cottonwood stands and wetlands, and past a quintet of small lakes. It's hard to believe the mania of downtown is just an hour spin back in the other direction.

Route variations: Continue south for an out-and-back into Chatfield State Park via bike paths and bike-friendly roads. For a longer ride, roll to the end of the Platte River Trail and Mary Carter Greenway Trail, then take the C-470 Trail west about 9 miles to Bear Creek Lake Regional Park. In the park, turn right onto the Bear Creek Trail, heading east. It's 14.2 miles back to the intersection with the Platte River Trail, and then another 9 miles to downtown Denver (total distance about 50 miles).

MILEAGE LOG

0.0	From Confluence Park in downtown Denver, head south on Platte River Trail
0.6	Stay right, continuing on Platte River Trail
0.7	Stay left, continuing on Platte River Trail
2.5	Cross bridge, continuing on Platte River Trail
3.6	Cross bridge, continuing on Platte River Trail
5.8	Cross bridge continuing on Platte River Trail
7.0	Cross bridge continuing on Platte River Trail
9.0	Left at fork, cross bridge, then right onto Mary Carter Greenway Trail
9.7	Straight through roundabout, then right across bridge, continuing on Mary Carter Greenway Trail
10.5	Bear right, continuing on Mary Carter Greenway Trail
10.8	Straight, continuing on Mary Carter Greenway Trail
12.7	Left, crossing bridge and continuing on Mary Carter Greenway Trail
13.0	Pass Hudson Gardens

13.4	Straight through roundabout
14.8	Pass South Platte Park and Carson Nature Center
15.0	Bear right, crossing bridge and continuing on Mary Carter Greenway Trail
15.1	Left at fork, continuing on Mary Carter Greenway Trail
16.4	Reach turnaround point at end of Mary Carter Greenway Trail
32.8	Return to start

7 CHERRY CREEK TRAIL

Difficulty:	Easy
Time:	2–3 hours
Distance:	34.5 miles out-and-back
Elevation gain:	790 feet
Best seasons:	Early spring to late fall (possible year-round)
Road conditions:	Entire route on paved multiuse trails, save for short portion of Cherry Creek State Park loop, where traffic is light and slow-moving.

GETTING THERE: Ride starts at Confluence Park, just east of the REI flagship store in downtown Denver. From I-25 southbound, take exit 212C, turn right on 20th St., left on Central St., left on 15th St., and then right on Platte St. Just after REI, there is a small free parking lot on left side of what becomes Water St. From I-25 northbound, take exit 211 for 23rd St., then make a slight right onto Water St., and parking lot is 0.3 mile ahead on right. If lot is full, there are metered and pay-lot options nearby.

Top five quintessential Denver experiences: climb to the 13th step of the State Capitol (it's exactly a mile high), see a Colorado Rockies baseball game at Coors Field, eat a green chile–smothered burrito, drink a local microbrew, and ride a bike on the Cherry Creek Trail—not necessarily in that order.

This popular multiuse path is flat enough for novices and kids, but long enough to carve out a decent evening workout. It's also a great way to see the city (or leave it behind) without worrying about traffic. Between downtown Denver and Cherry Creek State Park (12 miles), you'll never once roll rubber on road as you venture out of downtown and into the city's well-heeled southern suburbs. The only real hazard is other users. The path can get congested, especially on summer weekends.

This ride starts at Confluence Park, where the South Platte River and Cherry Creek converge, and the site of Denver's founding in 1858. Panning for gold was the main draw back then. Today, it's people-watching. You'll also encounter a 100,000-square-foot REI flagship store, which includes a bike shop and Starbucks lest you need repairs, tools, or fuel.

Pick up the path on the east bank of the Platte, and begin the very gradual (if not imperceptible) climb away from downtown. At mile 1.0, look left to spot "The Dancers," a pair of 50-foot-high white humanoid statues cavorting in front of the Denver Performing Arts Center. At mile 4.3, skirt the southern edge of the Cherry Creek shopping district. Two miles later pass Four Mile Historic Park, an old stagecoach stop that includes the old-

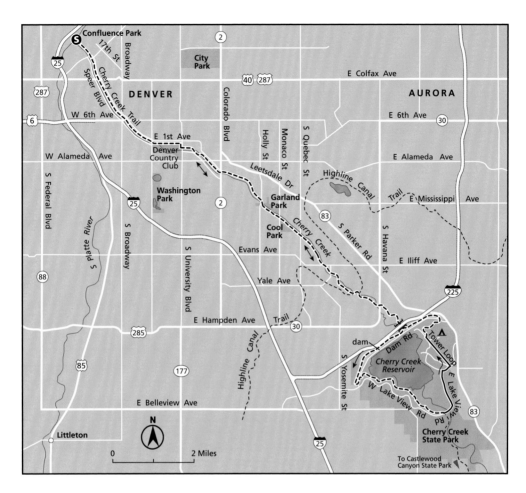

est structure in the Denver metro area (built in 1859).

After another half dozen miles of easy spinning comes the route's only real climb, a short but steep grind from the Interstate 225 underpass to the top of the Cherry Creek Reservoir Dam. On the way up, at mile 12.1, turn right on what will become a counter-clockwise loop of Cherry Creek State Park. At mile 14.2, cross Dam Road, and rejoin the Cherry Creek Trail, heading into the park (free for cyclists).

Inside this 4,200-acre swath of serenity, you'll find water, restrooms, and a lot of shady spots to rest and take in the scenery. On a clear day, you can see Pikes Peak looming in

the south, Longs Peak in the northern sky-line, and downtown Denver in between. The park is also home to a large wetlands preserve, swimming beach, and the area's longest running cycling time-trial series, held Wednesday evenings in April and May.

Follow the path about halfway around the lake, then exit left onto East Lake View Road at mile 17.2. Complete the park loop by turning right at mile 18.4 to stay on East Lake View Road, going left onto Tower Loop 0.2 mile later, and finally picking up the Camp-ground Trail on your right at mile 19.9 (look for the cluster of RVs).

At mile 20.7, turn left onto the Parker Road Trail, then cross Dam Road and rejoin

The Cherry Creek Trail runs through the heart of Denver, making it exceptionally popular with all manner of cyclists.

the Cherry Creek Trail. A mile later stay right at the fork, which sends you back underneath the I-225 underpass and onward back to downtown Denver.

Route variation: For a longer ride, stay on the Cherry Creek Trail instead of turning onto East Lake View Road at mile 17.2. The path continues south away from Denver for another 20 miles before ending in the wooded hills of Castlewood Canyon State Park. Have a look around and then spin back to downtown.

Another longer option is to add a portion of the Highline Canal Trail, which intersects the Cherry Creek Trail at mile 10.4 (just after you pass the Cherry Creek Country Club golf course on your left when heading away from downtown). This well-shaded path is far less traveled than the Cherry Creek Trail, and offers great views of the city, the mountains, and the sprawling estates of Denver's well-to-do. The entire Highline Canal Trail is about 40 miles long, running from Aurora in the north to Highlands Ranch in the south.

0.0	From Confluence Park in downtown Denver, head south on Cherry Creek Trail
10.3	Right at fork to stay on Cherry Creek Trail
10.4	Left at fork to stay on Cherry Creek Trail
12.1	Right at fork, following Cherry Creek Trail to west side of dam
14.2	Cross Dam Rd., entering Cherry Creek State Park
14.3	Rejoin Cherry Creek Trail, on far side of intersection
17.2	Left onto East Lake View Rd.
18.4	Right continuing on East Lake View Rd.
18.6	Left on Tower Loop
19.9	Right on Campground Trail
20.7	Left on Parker Road Trail
20.9	Cross Dam Rd. and rejoin Cherry Creek Trail
21.8	Right at fork
34.5	Return to start at Confluence Park

8 DENVER CITY PARKS

Difficulty:	Easy
Time:	1–2 hours
Distance:	12.6 miles
Elevation gain:	288 feet
Best seasons:	Year-round
Road conditions:	Entire route on bike paths, roads with designated bike lanes, or marked shared lane roads.

GETTING THERE: Ride starts from main parking lot of Denver Museum of Nature and Science at 2001 Colorado Blvd. From the north, take I-25 south to I-70 (exit 214), then I-70 east to Colorado Blvd. south (exit 276-B). Go 2 miles south on Colorado Blvd., then turn right at 22nd Ave. From the south, take I-25 north to Colorado Blvd. (exit 204). Go 5 miles north on Colorado Blvd., then turn left at 22nd Ave. Free parking, restrooms, and water.

Within Denver, there are more than 200 parks and 350 miles of bike paths, bike lanes, and shared lanes roads ("sharrows"). Here's a family-friendly spin that links three of the city's best-known parks via a 100 percent bike-friendly route through the heart of Colorado's capital.

The ride starts from the main parking lot of the Denver Museum of Nature and Science in the northeast corner of City Park. From here, roll counterclockwise around the perimeter of Denver's largest park, passing between Ferril Lake and the back side of the zoo, before turning south and exiting the park by crossing 17th Avenue and continuing onto the City Park Esplanade bike lane. A block later turn right onto 16th Avenue, which has a designated bike lane running all the way to

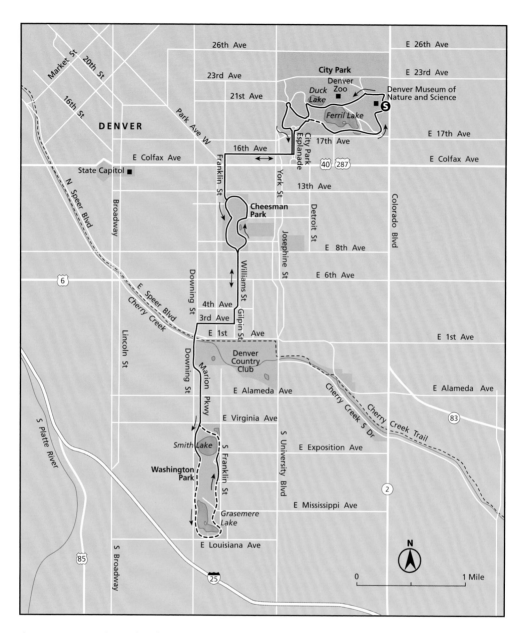

downtown. Don't go that far, though; instead turn left on Franklin Street at mile 2.4. This is a sharrow street, meaning cyclists can take the full lane.

A half mile later, enter Cheesman Park, turning right at the fork. (Look right and you'll see the rolling path where I learned to ride a bike.) Continue around the perimeter of this park, exiting the south end by turning right onto Williams Street. This, too, is a designated bike route. Look for the "D11" signs, which indicate the road is part of Denver's expansive bike route grid system, where networks of broad, quiet residential streets conducive to cycling provide connections between schools, city services—and parks!

Denver's 350 miles of bike paths, bike lanes, and shared lane roads make it one of the most bicycling-friendly cities in the United States.

Continue following the D11 signs, jogging south past the swanky Denver Country Club and on to Washington Park. Bear right at the park entrance, this time making a full counterclockwise loop (2.2 miles), passing a pair of placid lakes and returning to where you entered the park. Now retrace your route, spinning up the bike lane on Marion Park-

way, passing back by the country club, and reentering Cheesman Park. Go right here to complete the loop you started earlier, passing the impressive stone Cheesman Pavilion along the way.

Next exit the north end of Cheesman, heading back to City Park via Franklin Street, 16th Avenue, and the City Park Esplanade.

Once you're back in City Park, take the first right out of two roundabouts, which will point you around the southern perimeter of the park, finishing your final loop. Now head over to the plaza below the museum, and take in one of the best views in the city, with Ferril Lake, the downtown skyline, and the snowcapped peaks of the Rockies all spread out before you.

MILEAGE LOG

0.0	From Denver Museum of Nature and Science main parking lot, head west (toward mountains and downtown) on park's main road between Denver Zoo and Ferril Lake
1.0	Left just after passing Duck Lake
1.1	First right out of roundabout
1.4	Fourth right out of roundabout
1.6	First right out of roundabout, then exit City Park, crossing 17th Ave., continuing on the City Park Esplanade
1.8	Right onto 16th Ave.
2.4	Left onto Franklin St.
2.9	Right into Cheesman Park
3.4	Exit Cheesman Park, turning right onto Williams St.
3.9	Slight right onto 4th Ave., then immediate left onto Gilpin St.
4.1	Right onto 3rd Ave.
4.5	Left onto Downing St., joining bike path
4.8	Left onto Marion Pkwy., continuing on bike path
4.9	Exit bike path, and continue on Marion Pkwy.
5.4	Enter Washington Park, and bear right at fork
5.9	Stay right at fork, continuing counterclockwise loop of park's perimeter
7.6	Take a right out of park, and rejoin Marion Pkwy.
8.2	Rejoin bike path, turning right onto Downing St.
8.6	Right onto 3rd Ave.
8.9	Left on Gilpin St.
9.0	Right onto 4th Ave., then immediate left on Williams St.
9.5	Reenter Cheesman Park, then bear right, and follow park's perimeter
10.3	Exit park, turning right onto Franklin St.
10.7	Right on 16th Ave.
11.3	Left on City Park Esplanade
11.5	Cross 17th Ave., reenter City Park, then take first right out of roundabout
11.7	Take first right out of roundabout, and continue around park's perimeter
12.6	Return to Denver Museum of Nature and Science

FRONT RANGE NORTH

No region of Colorado boasts a larger concentration of high-quality road riding than the swath of land between Fort Collins in the north and Boulder down south. Challenge yourself with menacing climbs, spin through bucolic countryside, trace scenic reservoir shores, or go really big and set out for Rocky Mountain National Park's spectacular Trail Ridge Road, peak elevation 12,183 feet.

9 RIST CANYON LOOP

Difficulty:	Challenging
Time:	2½–4½ hours
Distance:	46.5 miles
Elevation gain:	5229 feet
Best seasons:	Early spring to late fall
Road conditions:	Shoulder comes and goes, but entire route on secondary highways and quiet rural roads. In 2013, portions of CR 27 (a.k.a. Buckhorn Rd./Stove Prairie Rd.) suffered severe flood damage. Closures, construction, and variable road surface conditions possible into 2015 and beyond. Check www.larimer.org/flooding2013 for the latest updates.

GETTING THERE: Ride starts at Lions Park at 2319 N. Overland Trail in Laporte, a suburb of Fort Collins. From downtown Fort Collins, go north on N. College Ave. (US 287), then after leaving downtown area and winding to the west, stay left at fork, continuing on US 287 Business (CR 54G) toward Laporte. In Laporte, turn left on N. Overland Trail (CR 21). Park is a half mile ahead on the right. Free parking, restrooms, and water.

The epicenter of Colorado's famed craft beer scene (ten microbreweries within city limits), Fort Collins is also an ideal launching point for great road rides. The spectacular Rist Canyon Loop is among the best. With one monster climb, several scenic canyons, and extended time along the tranquil but testing shores of Horsetooth Reservoir, this route has it all.

The ride starts at Lions Park in the northwest corner of the city next to the Cache la Poudre River. After less than a half mile on North Overland Trail, you turn right onto Bingham Hill Road and leave the city behind. You also get your first taste of climbing, as you roll up toward Claymore Lake and the rolling summit of Bingham Hill.

A quick descent, and then a quick right and left put you on Rist Canyon Road. Now the real climbing begins. Over the next 11 miles you'll gain a shade under 3000 feet,

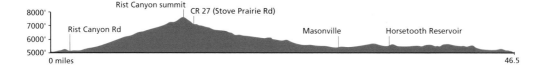

grinding up a climb that averages 5 percent and is steepest near the top. Pacing is key.

The climb starts out fairly shallow, winding through open grassland and past ranches and alfalfa fields. Soon, though, the evergreen-lined canyon closes in and the road tilts upward. The grade is reasonably steady the rest of the way, save for a few short flat stretches. Occasionally the trees recede, revealing distant views of the Mummy Range or a crumbling shack clinging to the hillside. Charred remains of the 2012 High Park forest fire (87,000 acres and 259 homes burned) are everywhere. A series of tight switch-backs—right, left, and left again—signal the final approach to the summit. The last few hundred yards are the toughest, with pitches steeper than 15 percent.

Now take a drink, and make sure your brakes are in good working order. The next mile and a half is basically dead-straight downhill. You'll have no problem exceeding the posted 25-mile-per-hour speed limit. Fifty's not out of the question.

At the base of the descent, turn left onto County Road 27 (Stove Prairie Road) to commence the ever-rolling southern leg, which dips and turns as you descend into narrow,

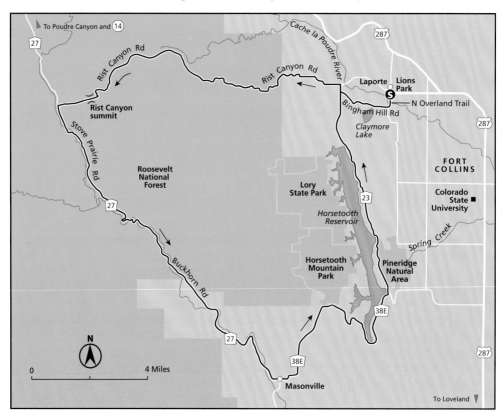

Just a few miles outside Fort Collins, you'll find yourself surrounded by quiet countryside and stunning natural beauty such as these red sandstone canyon walls just east of the small town of Masonville.

rock-walled Buckhorn Canyon, and then emerge for the final approach to Masonville at mile 29.2 (food and water).

Just outside Masonville, you bend back to the north, passing through another small canyon before climbing two gentle hills that bring you to the southern tip of Horsetooth Reservoir. At the second summit, stop at the overlook on the left for a sprawling view of the 6.5-mile artificial lake that's held in place by a quartet of earthen dams.

Three miles ahead you'll cross the first of those dams. Expect the word *damn* to come to mind. On the far side of each is a precipitously steep hill, three in total, each about a half mile long. It's 5 tough miles from the start of the first climb to the summit of the last.

From the top of that final climb, spy Horsetooth Dam on your left. Three miles ahead you'll return to the intersection of CR 23 and Bingham Hill Road. Turn right here,

and head back to the start at Lions Park. Then go find yourself one of those craft beers. You earned it.

Route variation: If CR 27 through Buckhorn Canyon is closed or in poor condition, try the Rist Canyon–Poudre Canyon route, a 42-mile loop with approximately 3600 feet of climbing. From Lions Park, follow the Rist Canyon Loop route for 14.8 miles to the intersection of Rist Canyon Road and CR 27 (Stove Prairie Road). Turn right here, then turn right again in 5 miles, joining State Route 14 for its descent through the Poudre River Canyon (busy on weekends, narrow shoulder). At mile 36.2, turn right onto US Highway 287 south. A mile later, turn right onto CR 54E, and a half mile after that, turn left onto CR 25E. This leads to the intersection of Rist Canyon Road. Turn left here, then right on CR 23 and backtrack over Bingham Hill Road to the start.

0.0   From Lions Park, turn right onto N. Overland Trail
0.2   Right onto Bingham Hill Rd.
2.1   Right onto CR 23
2.4   Left onto Rist Canyon Rd.
13.4   Reach summit of Rist Canyon Rd. climb
14.8   Left onto CR 27 (Stove Prairie Rd.)
       Poudre Canyon option:
       14.8   Right onto CR 27 (Stove Prairie Rd.)
       19.8   Right onto SR 14
       36.2   Right onto US 287
       37.2   Right onto CR 54E
       37.7   Left onto CR 25E
       38.7   Left onto Rist Canyon Rd.
       39.3   Right onto CR 23
       39.5   Left onto Bingham Hill Rd.
       41.5   Left on N. Overland Trail
       42.0   Return to start at Lions Park
18.4   Continue straight on CR 27 (now Buckhorn Rd.)
29.2   Arrive in Masonville, then continue straight, merging onto CR 38E
33.2   Straight, continuing on CR 38E
37.1   Left onto CR 23 (S. Centennial Dr.)
38.7   Left, continuing on CR 23 (S. Centennial Dr.)
44.4   Right on Bingham Hill Rd.
46.2   Left onto N. Overland Trail
46.5   Return to start at Lions Park

10   DAMS ROAD TO PINEWOOD CLIMB

Difficulty: Challenging
Time: 3½–4½ hours
Distance: 59.3 miles (shorter options)
Elevation gain: 4350 feet
Best seasons: Early spring to late fall (possible in winter)
Road conditions: Shoulder comes and goes, but majority of route on secondary highway
                   and quiet county roads. In 2013, portions of CR 29 along this route
                   suffered severe flood damage. Construction and closures are possible
                   into 2015 and beyond. Check www.larimer.org/flooding2013 for the
                   latest updates. If this road is closed, simply stay on CR 27 all the way to
                   the intersection of US 34, then go right on US 34, and left on CR 29
                   to continue on main route. (Detour shortens route by 0.7 mile.)

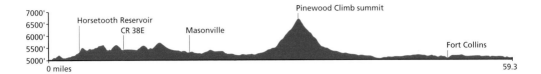

GETTING THERE: Ride starts at Lions Park at 2319 N. Overland Trail in Laporte, a suburb of Fort Collins. From downtown Fort Collins, go north on N. College Ave. (US 287), then after leaving downtown area and winding around to the west, stay left at fork, continuing on US 287B (CR 54G) toward Laporte. In Laporte, turn left on N. Overland Trail (CR 21). Park is a half mile ahead on the right. Free parking, restrooms, and water.

All by itself, the rolling road along Horsetooth Reservoir's eastern shore is cycling nirvana, a blessed mix of wide shoulders, smooth pavement, punchy climbs, and superb scenery. But tip to tail, it's just a shade longer than 7 miles, which is why most rides along the "damn dams" road are combined with longer, more arduous outings. In this case, County Road 23 serves as a warm-up for an even bigger challenge, the daunting Pinewood Reservoir climb (also known as Pole Hill Road or Rattlesnake Ridge, depending on who you talk to).

The ride starts at Lions Park, which abuts the Cache la Poudre River a few miles northwest of downtown Fort Collins. Roll out of the parking area, and turn right onto North Overland Trail, then make your next right onto Bingham Hill Road. Almost immediately you're in quiet countryside, grinding up the first few hundred feet of what will eventually be more than 4300 feet of climbing.

A left turn at mile 2.1 puts you on CR 23 and commences your journey up and over a trifecta of short but tough reservoir dam climbs that featured prominently in the 2012 USA Pro Challenge bike race. The pros tackled them going the other direction—and at a dramatically rapid pace. I suggest taking it easy and enjoying the view, which is especially good in early morning when the lake and surrounding rock outcroppings are bathed in the soft light of sunrise.

At mile 9.4, turn right on CR 38E, which traces the reservoir's southern tip before launching into two more tough but short ascents. Once you are over the top, it's flat-road sailing for the next 5.5 miles, as you drop into a small red rock canyon, pass through the small town of Masonville, and then turn south onto CR 27. Through here it's nothing but farm fields, big sky, and the occasional horse, cow, or ranch house.

At mile 19.5, turn right onto CR 29 for the last of this route's "easy" ascents, the gentle roll up past the Emissaries of Divine Light, a commune of sorts, which has led some locals to dub this the "Cult Climb." Whatever you call it, this is beautiful, quiet country. By mile 21 the road is flat again, as you roll around the eastern perimeter of Green Ridge Glade Reservoir, then continue south across the Big Thompson River and through the US Highway 34 intersection.

Two miles later, turn right onto Pole Hill Road (CR 18E), and prepare to suffer. After a gradual start, the Pinewood Reservoir climb bares its teeth, gaining nearly 1200 feet in 3 miles. The gradient averages 8 percent, with the final half mile hovering above 10 percent. At the summit, cool off in the shade, check out the distant mountain views, then flip around and head back the way you came.

At the base of the climb, turn left onto CR 29, then either retrace your route through Masonville and on to Horsetooth Reservoir,

Among the toughest ascents along Colorado's Front Range, the Pinewood Climb gains nearly 1200 feet in 3 miles and is steepest near the summit.

or mix it up and head east toward Loveland for a flat spin home. If you choose the latter, go right on CR 20, then follow the turn-by-turn below, jogging northward to Taft Hill Road, which runs through the Cathy Fromme Prairie Natural Area on its way into Fort Collins.

At mile 51.6, turn left onto CR 38E, then turn right onto the Fossil Creek Trail a mile later. The trail entrance is directly across from the intersection of Red Fox Road. Continue on the trail as it changes names to Spring Creek Trail, then exit into the parking lot on the west side of Cottonwood Glen Park at mile 53.3. If you're still on the trail when it

turns east, you've gone too far.

Now pedal north to the end of the parking lot, which dumps you onto North Overland Trail. From here it's a winding 5.8 miles back to the start point at Lions Park.

Route variations: For more climbing and about 4 extra miles in the saddle, drop down the far side of the Pinewood climb, and continue past Pinewood Reservoir to the start of the private road section. Turn around here, and ascend this more gentle approach to rejoin the main route.

Extend the ride even farther by adding the Carter Lake climb. Turn right on CR 31 after coming back down the Pinewood

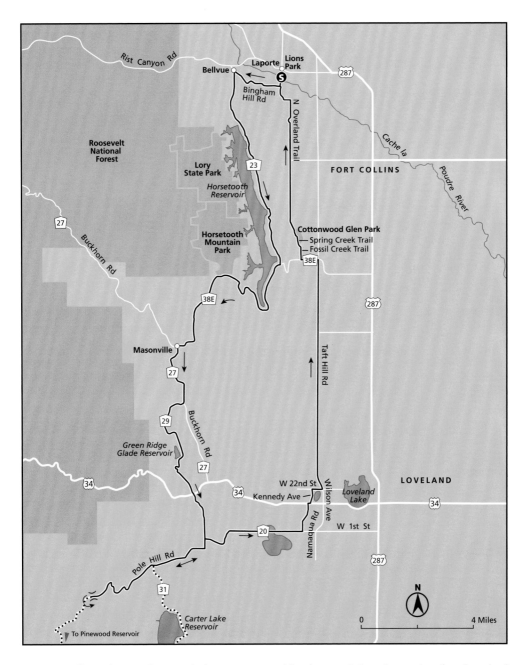

ascent. Follow this road around the eastern edge of Carter Lake, then head downhill on CR 8E, turn left on CR 23, left on CR 12, and finally right on CR 29, which will lead you back to the main route. This option adds about 12.5 miles and a few hundred feet of climbing.

Finally, for a shorter ride that includes the rolling run along Horsetooth Reservoir, follow the prescribed route until mile 9.4, then turn left on CR 38E, which leads back into Fort Collins. After winding your way down the hill, pick up the Fossil Creek Trail on your left across from the intersection of Red Fox Road, and follow the main route back to Lions Park. Total distance is about 18 miles.

MILEAGE LOG

0.0	From Lions Park, turn right onto N. Overland Trail
0.2	Right onto Bingham Hill Rd.
2.1	Left onto CR 23
7.9	Continue on CR 23 (S. Centennial Dr.)
9.4	Right on CR 38E
17.2	Arrive in Masonville, left onto CR 27 (Buckhorn Rd.)
19.5	Right on CR 29

Flood closure variation:

19.5	**Straight on CR 27**
22.5	**Right on US 34**
23.2	**Left onto CR 29, rejoining main route**
26.0	Right onto Pole Hill Rd.
31.7	Reach Pinewood Climb summit

Extra climbing option:

31.7	**Continue west, descending Pole Hill Rd.**
33.7	**Turn around, return to summit, and rejoin main route**
31.7	Head east back down Pole Hill Rd.

Carter Lake add-on option:

35.3	**Right onto CR 31**
40.3	**Left onto CR 8E**
43.3	**Left onto CR 23**
44.9	**Left onto CR 12**
46.6	**Right onto CR 29 to rejoin main route**
37.3	Left on CR 29
37.6	Right onto CR 20 (W. 1st St.)
41.5	Left onto Namaqua Rd.
42.5	Right on US 34
42.6	Left onto Kennedy Ave.
43.2	Right onto W. 22nd St.
43.6	Left onto Wilson Ave. (Taft Hill Rd.)
46.1	Stay straight on Taft Hill Rd.
51.6	Left onto CR 38E
52.5	Right onto Fossil Creek Trail
53.0	Stay straight on Spring Creek Trail
53.3	Left off trail into parking lot
53.4	Continue north heading along west side of Cottonwood Glen Park
53.5	Straight onto N. Overland Trail
58.1	Left continuing on N. Overland Trail
58.3	Right continuing on N. Overland Trail
59.3	Return to start at Lions Park

11 TRAIL RIDGE ROAD

Difficulty:	Epic
Time:	6–10 hours (with shorter options)
Distance:	94.3 miles
Elevation gain:	9976 feet
Best seasons:	Late spring to fall (road closed in winter)
Road conditions:	Trail Ridge Road is typically closed from mid-October to Memorial Day, but dates vary based on snowpack. Check Rocky Mountain National Park's website or CoTrip.org for current status. During summer weekends, Trail Ridge Road is very busy and drivers are often distracted by the scenery. Be vigilant and do this ride on a weekday if possible. Shoulder along entire route comes and goes, but most of ride is on lesser traveled highway or county roads. A 1-mile stretch on CR 22H is hard-packed gravel road. Cyclists must pay a $10 entrance fee for Rocky Mountain National Park at Fall River Visitor Center.
	In 2013, portions of CR 29, 22H, and 43 suffered severe flood damage. Closures, construction, and variable road surface conditions are possible into 2015 and beyond. Check www.larimer.org /flooding2013 and CoTrip.org for the latest updates.

GETTING THERE: Ride starts at Lions Park at 2319 N. Overland Trail in Laporte, a suburb of Fort Collins. From downtown Fort Collins, go north on N. College Ave. (US 287), then after leaving the downtown area and winding around to the west, stay left at fork, continuing on US 287 Business (CR 54G) toward Laporte. In Laporte, turn left on N. Overland Trail (CR 21), and park will be a half mile ahead on the right. Free parking, restrooms, and water.

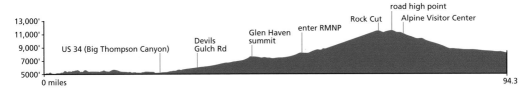

First, a few important caveats. Number one, this ride does not have to be nearly as hard as I've made it. The most common approach to tackling Trail Ridge Road is to park at the Beaver Meadows Visitor Center (2.7 miles west of Estes Park on US Highway 36), then spin an up-and-back to Rocky Mountain National Park's Alpine Visitor Center. This is a fabulous and difficult 43-mile round-trip with loads of spectacular scenery, roughly 4600 feet of climbing, and a peak elevation of 12,183 feet.

I've opted to spin a longer yarn both to outline a true epic and to work in Big Thompson Canyon, whose absence would have made this guide incomplete, but whose near-term status is tenuous due to the extensive 2013 flooding damage detailed in the road conditions above. That's why I did not include it as a separate ride.

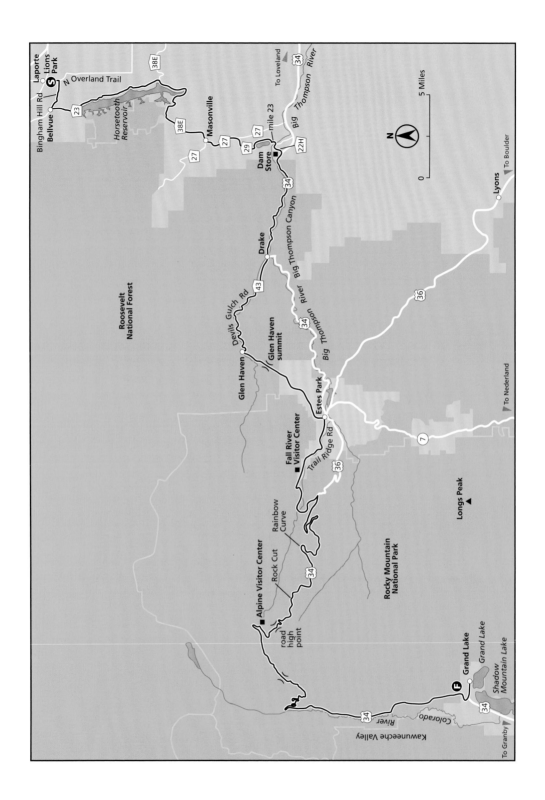

Laporte
Lions Park
Bingham Hill Rd
Bellvue
N Overland Trail
38E
23
Horsetooth Reservoir
38E
Masonville
27
27
29
27
mile 23
Dam Store
22H
To Loveland
34
Big Thompson River
34
Drake
Big Thompson Canyon
43
Devils Gulch Rd
River
34
Roosevelt National Forest
Glen Haven summit
Glen Haven
Big Thompson River
Estes Park
Fall River Visitor Center
Trail Ridge Rd
36
7
To Nederland
To Boulder
Lyons
36
Longs Peak
Rainbow Curve
Rock Cut
34
Trail Ridge Rd
Alpine Visitor Center
road high point
Rocky Mountain National Park
Grand Lake
Grand Lake
Shadow Mountain Lake
34
34
Colorado River
Kawuneeche Valley
To Granby

N

0   5 Miles

Few rides in Colorado—or anywhere else—are as breathtaking as the trip up and over Trail Ridge Road inside Rocky Mountain National Park. (Dave Epperson)

Finally, know that cycling above tree line in Colorado can be tricky business. Warm sun-splashed days can quickly turn cold, wet, and windy. Check the weather, bring adequate gear, get an early start, and don't let hubris be your guide. Getting caught in a thunderstorm at 12,000 feet is not fun, and can be downright dangerous if lightning's around. Even if the weather remains favorable, 20-degree temperature swings between the park entrance and the road's summit are not uncommon.

Okay, on to the fun part—riding a bike from Fort Collins up and over the highest continuously paved road in the United States, which happens to be inside one of America's greatest national parks. The first 23 miles of this ride mimic the Dams Road to Pinewood Climb (Ride 10) and are the perfect warm-up for the big climbing ahead.

From Lions Park, turn right onto North Overland Trail, then right onto Bingham Hill Road. At the next intersection, go left onto County Road 23, which leads along the eastern shore of Horsetooth Reservoir, and on to the small town of Masonville. Now head south on CR 27, then right onto CR 29. (If CR 29 is still closed, remain on CR 27 until you reach the intersection of US 34, then go right to pick up the main route.)

At mile 23, after crossing a short bridge just below the Big Thompson River Power

Plant, immediately turn right from CR 29 onto CR 22H, a mile-long stretch of hard-packed gravel road that reduces your highway time.

Next turn right onto US 34, and immediately roll past the historic Dam Store and into the Narrows section of Big Thompson Canyon, where towering rock walls cast long shadows on the road and river below. Here too is where the climbing begins. You'll be going uphill for most of the next 46 miles.

Seven miles up canyon, you reach the small town of Drake and the intersection with CR 43 (Devils Gulch Road). Go right onto CR 43, beginning your spin up one of my all-time favorite roads. Most people passing through this area remain on US 34 toward Estes Park, leaving the road less traveled to its handful of residents and lucky cyclists.

Moderate climbing for 8 miles along the North Fork of the Big Thompson River brings you to the tiny town of Glen Haven, and more importantly the Glen Haven General Store, home to the world's best cinnamon roll. Just make sure to give yourself time to digest it before you continue. The next 2.5 miles are nasty, with an imposing straight ramp followed by a quartet of steep switchbacks. The summit (elevation 7966 feet at mile 42) reveals a panoramic view of the Estes Valley and a half dozen skyscraping peaks. Take a deep breath. You're headed up there.

Ten rolling miles later, stop at the Fall River Visitor Center to top off your bottles, then pay to enter the park. Your Trail Ridge Road odyssey has officially begun. It's 20 miles and 4000 feet to the top. The gradient hovers around 4 percent. Figure at least two hours of uphill pedaling.

The opening miles wind through the mountain meadows and ponderosa pine of the montane ecosystem. Deer, elk, or even moose may be spotted trolling for food among vibrant fields of wildflowers. Next comes the subalpine (9000–11,400 feet) where spruce and fir crowd the landscape, and thin wooden

poles alert plow drivers of the road's edge. In springtime, fifteen-foot-tall snowbanks are commonplace. Take a break at the Rainbow Curve overlook (mile 63), and soak in views of the Mummy Range and Horseshoe Park.

Next is the approach to tree line where wind-sculpted shrubs seem to crawl along the ground. Then reach the alpine ecosystem where plant life—and oxygen—are sparse, but the Rocky Mountain scenery is sublime. Snowcapped peaks extend in every direction. Thickets of stubby tundra cling to the ground. You might even see a bighorn sheep.

At mile 67.5, you'll approach what appears to be the ascent's end, at Rock Cut (elevation 12,142 feet). Alas, it's a false summit. Soon the road drops away to the base of Iceberg Pass, where the true final climb begins. Wind your way up through a pair of sweeping switchbacks, past the Lava Cliffs overlook, and finally to the Trail Ridge Road high point (elevation 12,183 feet). Don't bother looking for a sign. There isn't one.

Two miles ahead lies the Alpine Visitor Center, where food, drink, and warmth await. Fuel up, rest up, then exult in the final mostly downhill 20 miles. Along the way you'll cross the Continental Divide, skirt the headwaters of the Colorado River, then settle into the marshy Kawuneeche Valley for the southerly spin to Grand Lake, a quaint touristy town that wraps around the shores of Colorado's largest natural lake. It's a great spot to relax for a day or two. And after this ride, you'll definitely be ready to relax.

Route variation: Trail Ridge Road is also accessible from Boulder. The most common and straightforward approach is to pick up US 36 on the north end of the city, then follow it to Estes Park (33 miles) and continue west into Rocky Mountain National Park. Alternatively, you can avoid the often busy stretch of US 36 between Lyons and Estes Park by taking State Route 7 instead, which adds about 13 miles.

For a ride that starts in Boulder and

includes Big Thompson Canyon, follow the Carter Lake route (Ride 12) for 24.3 miles. Instead of turning left on CR 8E, continue 1.6 miles north, then turn left on CR 12. Follow this west then north, as it changes to CR 29, then intersects US 34 at mile 32.5. Turn left onto US 34, and proceed to the main route.

The first half of the Boulder–Big Thompson Canyon combination is also part of the fantastic Cinnamon Roll Century Loop that starts and ends in Boulder. After reaching the Glen Haven summit, drop into Estes Park instead of going up Trail Ridge Road. From Estes Park, pick up State Route 7 southbound. Twenty miles later turn right onto SR 72. Then follow SR 72 10.5 miles to Ward and Lefthand Canyon Drive (Ride 15), which leads back to Boulder. The reason I didn't include this approximately 110-miler with 8500 feet of climbing as a separate ride was the uncertainty around CR 43.

MILEAGE LOG

0.0	From Lions Park, turn right onto N. Overland Trail
0.2	Right onto Bingham Hill Rd.
2.1	Left onto CR 23
7.9	Right at fork, continuing on CR 23 (S. Centennial Dr.)
9.4	Right on CR 38E
17.2	Arrive at Masonville
17.5	Left onto CR 27 (Buckhorn Rd.)
19.5	Right onto CR 29

If CR 29 is closed for construction:

19.8	**Remain on CR 27 to intersection of US 34**
22.8	**Right onto US 34 to rejoin main route**
21.3	Stay left, continuing on CR 29
23.0	Cross short bridge, then immediate right onto CR 22H (start of gravel road)

If CR 22H is closed for construction:

23.0	**Follow CR 29 to US 34, then turn right to rejoin main route**
23.9	Right onto US 34 (end of gravel road)
31.7	Right onto CR 43 (Devils Gulch Rd.), toward Glen Haven

If CR 43 is closed for construction:

31.7	**Stay on US 34 into national park, and rejoin main route**
42.0	Reach summit of Glen Haven climb
45.8	Stay left, continuing on CR 43
46.6	Right onto US 34 (Wonderview Ave.)
48.4	Continue on US 34 (Fall River Rd.)
50.8	Pass Fall River Visitor Center
51.2	Enter Rocky Mountain National Park
55.0	Right, continuing on US 34
67.5	Pass Rock Cut summit
70.3	Pass Trail Ridge Road high point
72.2	Reach Alpine Visitor Center
92.5	Exit Rocky Mountain National Park
92.9	Pass Kawuneeche Visitor Center
94.3	Finish at Grand Lake

12 CARTER LAKE

Difficulty:	Moderate
Time:	3½–5½ hours
Distance:	65.6 miles
Elevation gain:	3767 feet
Best seasons:	Early spring to late fall (possible in winter)
Road conditions:	Majority of route travels on rural roads with ample shoulder.

GETTING THERE: Ride starts at intersection of Yarmouth Ave. and Broadway St. in north Boulder. From downtown Boulder, head 3 miles north on Broadway to Yarmouth. Free on-street parking. Adjacent commercial center includes popular coffee shop and one of city's best local bike shops.

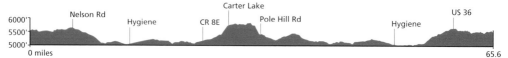

What's the easiest way to spot a Boulder-based pro cyclist tuning up for the year ahead? Show up for the early-season Carter Lake group ride, which rolls from the Gateway Fun Park in north Boulder on Saturdays at 10:00 AM. This ride usually gets going in January (weather permitting), attracting upward of fifty riders for what's essentially a 65-mile simulated race. Get dropped and you'll be riding home alone.

If you'd rather not spend three and a half hours drooling on your top tube, skip the head-banging shenanigans, and take on this classic springtime ride at a more casual pace. The trip to Carter Lake (it's actually a reservoir) is a mostly flat affair on rural roads with great views of the Rockies and one punchy hill near the turnaround point.

The route starts from the Amante Coffee Shop on Broadway, the most popular north-end meet-up locale for the city's large cyclist populace. From here, head north on Broadway, then left on US Highway 36. This two-lane highway can be a little busy on the weekends, but the shoulder is plenty wide.

At mile 6.1, turn right onto Nelson Road, a quiet, rolling stretch of rural tarmac that's representative of the rest of the ride, which wiggles northward via North 65th Street, St. Vrain Road, and North 75th Street, passing horse farms, hay fields, and open prairie along the way.

Around mile 14.5, you pass through the small town of Hygiene, your last chance to top off bottles before the Carter Lake summit at mile 31. In between are a handful of stiff rollers, but mostly it's easy spinning to the base of the ride's lone climb of significance, which comes around mile 25.

And even this ascent is nothing serious. The hardest section is about 2 miles with a modest 400 feet of elevation gain. Up top you'll get your first look at 3-mile-long Carter Lake, a popular spot for boating, fishing, and general summertime frolicking.

Keep spinning northward along the shoreline and across three dams until you reach the Carter Lake Marina, which has food, drink, and restrooms and typically opens for the season on April 1. There's also a small general

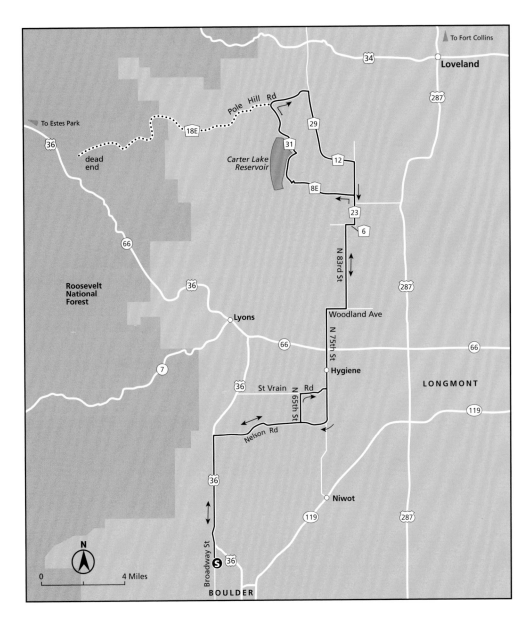

store another half mile up the road, but it too is only open during the spring and summer months.

Once you are rehydrated, continue north on County Road 31, dropping down the back side of the reservoir to Pole Hill Road (CR 18E) at mile 32.7. Go right here, then right again on CR 29, which will point you south-

ward back to Boulder. From here, retrace your route, save for a slight variation after passing back through Hygiene that I included in the mileage log and map just to mix things up.

There are actually numerous ways to connect Boulder with North 75th Street, this route's first essential road. Other alternatives include US 36 to State Route 66 to North

Even in the middle of winter, it's often possible to pedal to the tranquil shores of Carter Lake.

75th Street; US 36 to Hygiene Road to North 75th Street; and US 36 to St. Vrain Road to North 75th Street. I prefer the US 36 to Nelson Road to North 75th Street option because it means less highway time.

Route variation: If you want to shorten the route, simply turn around at the top of the Carter Lake climb and come back the way you came, which subtracts 9 miles. Or extend the ride by 7 miles, and add the brutal Pinewood Reservoir Climb by turning left at Pole Hill Road (CR 18E). From there, it's 3.5 miles to the summit on an ascent that averages 8 percent. From the summit, turn around and rejoin the main route.

Carter Lake can also be accessed from Fort Collins. One popular hilly, 49-mile loop heads south out of town on Taft Hill Road, which becomes Wilson Avenue as it enters Loveland. From Loveland, go right on 14th Street (CR 18), left on CR 21, right on CR 14, left on CR 23, and finally right on CR 8E, the same road the Boulder route uses for its final approach to Carter Lake.

Climb up to the reservoir, trace the shoreline heading north, then drop down the back side, turning right on Pole Hill Road (CR 18E). Two miles later, turn left on CR 29, which takes you past the Green Ridge Glade Reservoir before merging with Buckhorn Road and heading into the small town of Masonville.

From Masonville, join the Rist Canyon route (Ride 9), following CR 38E around the south end of the Horsetooth Reservoir, before turning left on South Centennial Drive, which runs along the lake's eastern shore. Finally, go right at the intersection of Dixon Canyon Road, which drops back into Fort Collins.

MILEAGE LOG

0.0	From intersection of Yarmouth Ave. and Broadway St., head north on Broadway
0.5	Left on US 36
6.1	Right onto Nelson Rd.
10.5	Left onto N. 65th St.
12.0	Right onto St. Vrain Rd.

13.4	Left onto N. 75th St.
17.5	Right onto Woodland Rd.
18.3	Left onto N. 83rd St.
20.3	Continue on CR 23E
22.4	Right onto CR 6
22.8	Continue onto CR 23
23.8	Left onto CR 23
24.3	Left onto CR 8E
27.8	Right onto CR 31

Shorter option:

28.1 Reach top of Carter Lake climb, retrace route back to Boulder

32.7	Right onto Pole Hill Rd. (CR 18E)

Longer option:

32.7 Left on Pole Hill Rd.

36.4 Reach Pole Hill Rd. summit, turn around, and rejoin main route

34.7	Right onto CR 29
38.0	Continue onto W. CR 12
39.8	Right onto CR 23
41.8	Right to stay on CR 23
43.0	Left on CR 6
43.2	Left onto CR 23E
45.2	Continue onto N. 83rd St.
47.3	Right onto Woodland Ave.
48.3	Right onto N. 75th St.
53.8	Right onto Nelson Rd.
59.5	Left onto US 36
65.1	Right onto Broadway St.
65.6	Return to start at intersection of Yarmouth Ave. and Broadway St.

13 SOUTH ST. VRAIN CANYON

Difficulty:	Challenging
Time:	4–6 hours
Distance:	66.2 miles (or 55.6 without Brainard Lake add-on)
Elevation gain:	7062 feet
Best seasons:	Spring to fall
Road conditions:	Ample shoulder on US 36, but it comes and goes along rest of route. Watch for cracks, seams, and potholes on Brainard Lake Rd. In 2013, portions of Lefthand Canyon Dr. suffered significant flood damage. Lefthand reopened in early 2014, but ongoing repairs may result in delays or sections of rough road. Check www.BoulderCounty.org /flood/roads for the latest updates.

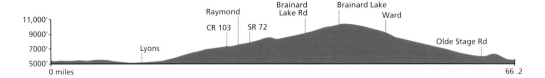

GETTING THERE: Ride starts at intersection of Yarmouth Ave. and Broadway St. in north Boulder. From downtown Boulder, head 3 miles north on Broadway to Yarmouth. Adjacent commercial center has a good coffee shop and one of city's best local bike shops. Free on-street parking.

Rare is the case when one road deserves completely separate uphill and downhill ride descriptions. But South St. Vrain Canyon, along with its various connectors, is such a superb cycling experience that an exception must be made. The uphill route is detailed here; check out Ride 14 to learn about the descent.

From the north end of Boulder, head out of town via Broadway to US Highway 36 westbound. This is one of the busiest thoroughfares along the foothills. But fortunately, we're talking cyclists, not cars. Riders from all over the Front Range flock to this gently rolling road with its wide shoulder and ranging high plains views.

After 11 miles of easy spinning (unless there's a headwind), turn left, continuing on US 36 as it rolls into Lyons, a quaint artsy community with several bike shops and abundant food and drink options. On the far side of town, turn left again, joining State Route 7 (South St. Vrain Drive). Now the fun begins, as you quickly trade civilization for the tranquility of a beautiful red rock canyon.

The climbing begins as the road winds its way up the South St. Vrain Creek drainage, passing through a series of towering granite-walled narrows, water rushing by on your left. The grade here is never too steep (4 percent on average). But you'll be going uphill for most of the next 10 miles, gaining 1870 feet along the way.

At mile 24.7, duck off the highway again, turning left onto County Road 103 (Riv-erside Drive) toward the tiny town of Raymond. Two miles ahead is the old Raymond Store, a great spot to regroup, refill your water bottles, and grab a snack. The fresh popcorn is salty and delicious. Make sure to check out the cash register. It's at least a century old.

From Raymond, continue up CR 103, which soon intersects SR 72, better known as the Peak to Peak Highway. Resume climbing, as you pass by the turnoff for the aptly named Peaceful Valley Campground, then continue upward to mile 31.5. The road levels out for about 3 miles, then pitches up again for the final grind to the Brainard Lake turnoff. You'll know you're close when you pass the Mill Site Inn on your right.

Now it's decision time. Either turn right onto Brainard Lake Road and pedal up to the Brainard Lake Recreation Area (elevation 10,300 feet), or skip the 10.6-mile out-and-back, and go left on Nelson Street down to Ward. The climb gains about 1300 feet, but is fairly mellow (3–4 percent with a few flat sections). I don't always go up. But on a sunny day, it's one of the best alpine lake and high mountain overlooks in the state—and admission is free for cyclists.

After lapping the lake, spin back to SR 72, and drop down to Ward, another tiny mountain town with an old general store that's cyclist friendly. The homemade chocolate chip cookies are to die for. The coffee isn't bad either.

Once you've recuperated, continue down-

This classic Boulder-area ride includes a side trip to Brainard Lake, which offers majestic views of the lake and the distant Indian Peaks Wilderness.

hill on what becomes Lefthand Canyon Drive (the same road you ascend and descend during Ride 14). Aside from a hard left about 2.5 miles down the road, this is a no-brakes-needed, non-technical descent all the way to the intersection of James Canyon Drive. Just remember that this road was badly damaged by the 2013 flood, so you may encounter rough patches or construction zones.

From the James Canyon Drive intersection, continue down Lefthand for another 2.5 miles, then turn right onto Olde Stage Road. Up ahead is one last bit of work, a punchy 1.2-mile climb that averages 6 percent and will likely feel much tougher because you already have 60 miles in your legs. Once over the top, you're home free. Spin down Olde Stage to the intersection with Lee Hill Drive, then follow Lee Hill to Broadway, and turn right. The start point is two blocks ahead on your left.

Route variation: You can skip the Olde Stage climb by staying on Lefthand Canyon Drive all the way to US 36, and then retrace the outbound route back to Boulder. Alternatively, for a slightly tougher finishing climb, turn right onto Lee Hill Drive at mile 57.9, and follow it all the way to Broadway.

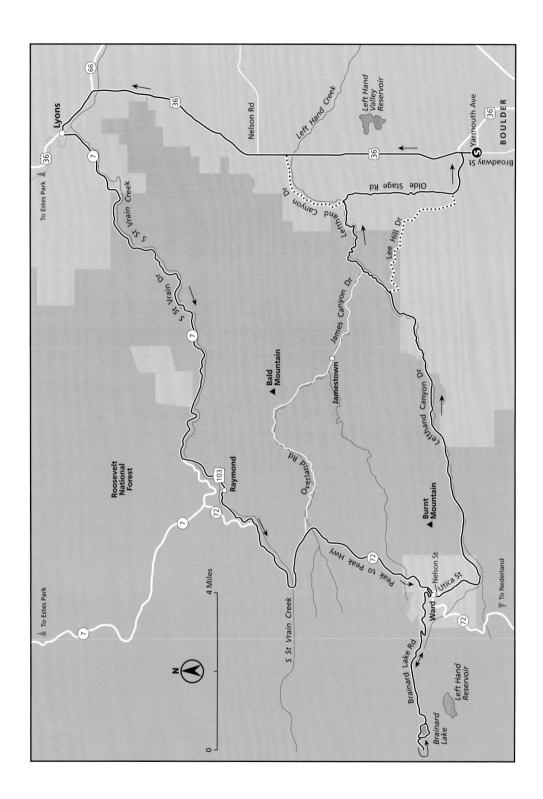

0.0	From intersection of Yarmouth Ave. and Broadway St., head north on Broadway
0.5	Left onto US 36
11.2	Left continuing on US 36 (SR 66)
12.4	Arrive in Lyons
12.5	Left onto Main St. (US 36)
12.8	Left onto 5th Ave. (SR 7)
24.7	Left onto Riverside Dr. (CR 103) toward Raymond
26.9	Arrive in Raymond
27.0	Left at fork continuing on Riverside Dr. (CR 103)
28.6	Left onto SR 72 (Peak to Peak Highway)
36.5	Right onto Brainard Lake Rd.
41.2	Right at fork beginning lap of Brainard Lake
42.4	Finish lap of lake, stay right heading back to SR 72
47.1	Right onto SR 72
47.2	Left at "Post Office" sign onto Utica St. toward Ward
47.5	Arrive in Ward
47.6	Continue downhill on Utica St., which becomes Lefthand Canyon Dr.
58.8	Right at intersection continuing on Lefthand Canyon Dr.
61.5	Right onto Olde Stage Rd.
64.6	Stay straight merging onto Lee Hill Dr.
65.9	Right onto Broadway St.
66.2	Return to start

14 SUPER JAMES LOOP

Difficulty:	Challenging
Time:	3½–5½ hours
Distance:	52.8 miles (shorter options)
Elevation gain:	4829 feet
Best seasons:	Spring to fall
Road conditions:	Good shoulder on US 36 and SR 72 and 7; intermittent elsewhere. Overland Dr. section includes 2.1 miles of gravel road. In 2013, portions of Lefthand Canyon Dr. and James Canyon Dr. suffered severe flood damage. Closures, construction, and variable road surface conditions are possible into 2015 and beyond. Check www.bouldercounty.org/flood/roads for the latest updates.

GETTING THERE: Ride starts at intersection of Yarmouth Ave. and Broadway St. From downtown Boulder, head 3 miles north on Broadway to Yarmouth. Free on-street parking. Adjacent commercial center has popular coffee shop and one of city's best local bike shops.

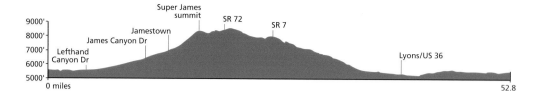

Like so many Boulder-area bike routes, the Super James Loop is packed with options. Want something easy? Head north out of Boulder, roll on US Highway 36 to Lefthand Canyon Drive, then spin up to Jamestown. It's 13.6 miles one-way, with about 1500 feet of gentle climbing through a lovely little canyon. Return the way you came, or tack on the Olde Stage Road climb, which bumps up your elevation gain another 500 feet. Both are perfect weekday outings when time is short.

Want to go farther? Good. The full Super James Loop is as good as it gets. Ample warm-up, killer climb in the middle, then a brief unpaved adventure leading to majestic high mountain scenery and one of the best descents around. Whatever your flavor, pedaling begins with easy spinning along the wide shoulder of US 36. Five miles in, say good-bye to sweeping vistas of the Eastern Plains and hello to the gentle Lefthand Canyon ascent. Figure an hour to Jamestown, ninety minutes max.

Along the way you'll get an up-close look at the lingering aftermath of the devastating 2013 floods that washed away roads, swamped cars, and destroyed dozens of homes. Nearby Lefthand Creek and James Creek changed channels, rerouting through yards and across

The menacing Super James climb is among the toughest ascents in Boulder County, with several sustained pitches above 10 percent and very little shade.

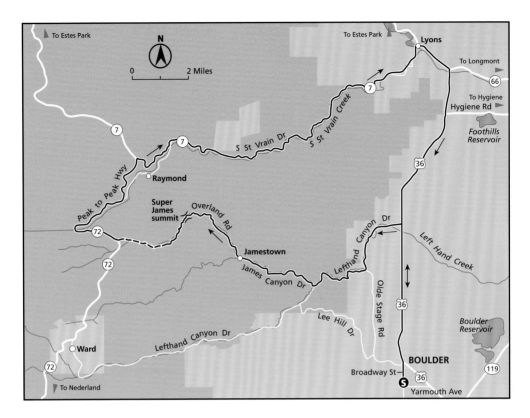

driveways. It was a stunning testament to the power of Mother Nature, but also of our ability as humans to cope and rebuild.

Once you're in Jamestown, it's decision time. Easy ride or extended adventure? There's no wrong answer, but if you have the time, why not take on the challenge? Just west of Jamestown the Super James climb (as locals call it) begins; this 3.6-mile can of whoopass gains 1600 feet and averages 8 percent. If you don't have a compact crankset, I suggest you get one. This is no place for a 39-tooth chainring unless your last name is Nibali, Contador, or Froome.

This shadeless climb starts gradually. But a half mile up, it's game on with little relief. The worst part? Several long straight stretches that mess with your legs—and your mind. I've never felt good on this climb—only happy when it was done. Less than a mile past the Super James summit, the pavement ends but

not the climbing. The next 2 miles are littered with tough rollers, as you grind over gravel toward the Peak to Peak Highway (a.k.a. State Route 72). Turn right here, rolling back onto tarmac and up yet another short climb.

At mile 21, your hard work is finally rewarded. On the right a sign warns of the upcoming steep descent. Up ahead jagged gray granite peaks fill the western skyline. It's a hallmark Rocky Mountain view. The next 5 miles pass in a blink, as you plummet through aptly named Peaceful Valley, then zip up the short climb to the SR 7 intersection.

A left here leads to Estes Park. Instead, head downhill on South St. Vrain Drive (SR 7), the same road you ascend in Ride 13. It's tough to say which direction is better, but it's hard to find fault with a 14-mile descent with smooth pavement, a decent shoulder, gentle radius turns, and a perfect Goldilocks grade—not too steep, not too shallow . . . just right.

Throw in a handful of über-scenic box canyon stretches, and you really can't ask for more.

Mile 40 brings you to Lyons. Grab a drink and snack, then wiggle out of town and pick up US 36 eastbound for the rolling 13-mile run back to Boulder. This time sweeping Eastern Plains views will be on your left, and with any luck, the wind will be at your back.

MILEAGE LOG

0.0	Head north on Broadway St.
0.5	Left onto US 36
5.3	Left onto Lefthand Canyon Dr.
10.5	Straight at fork, merging onto James Canyon Dr.
13.6	Arrive in Jamestown and merge onto Overland Dr.
17.2	Reach summit of Super James climb
18.0	Start gravel road section
20.1	Right onto SR 72 (Peak to Peak Highway) and end of gravel road section
25.8	Right onto SR 7 toward Lyons
40.0	Arrive in Lyons
40.1	Right on US 36 (SR 66 and Broadway)
40.3	Right, continuing on US 36 (SR 66)
41.6	Right, continuing on US 36
52.4	Right onto Broadway St.
52.8	Return to start

15 LEFTHAND CANYON

Difficulty:	Challenging
Time:	3–5 hours (shorter options)
Distance:	42.4 miles
Elevation gain:	6200 feet
Best seasons:	Spring to fall
Road conditions:	Shoulder width varies, but these very popular cycling roads have minimal traffic. Potholes on descent of Deer Trail Rd. and Linden Dr. The Bow Mountain climb includes a 1.5-mile section of dirt road. In 2013, portions of Lefthand Canyon Dr. suffered severe flood damage. Closures, construction, and variable road surface conditions are possible into 2015 and beyond. Check www.bouldercounty.org/flood/roads for the latest updates.

GETTING THERE: Ride starts at the intersection of Yarmouth Ave. and Broadway St. in north Boulder. From downtown Boulder, head 3 miles north on Broadway to Yarmouth. Free on-street parking. Adjacent commercial center includes a popular coffee shop and one of city's best local bike shops.

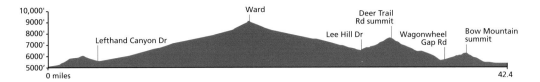

First, a word of warning. This ride doesn't have to be as hard as I've made it. If you're looking for the path of least resistance but still want to pedal up Lefthand Canyon to the old mining town of Ward, leave north Boulder on US Highway 36, pedal northwest about 5 miles, turn left on Lefthand Canyon Drive, and go about 16.5 miles up this quiet, creek-lined canyon that only gets truly steep in the last 1.5 miles. Then grab a snack in Ward, turn around, and spin back the way you came. It's a great ride.

But if you'd rather skip the highway and test yourself against five of Boulder County's toughest climbs, try this somewhat circuitous route.

In either case, the riding starts at the intersection of Broadway Street and Yarmouth Avenue where there's a popular coffee shop and ample on-street parking. If you happen to pass through on the weekend, you'll witness cycling's version of Grand Central Station, with two-wheeled enthusiasts coming and going constantly. I've met friends for rides here at least one hundred times.

Once hellos are done and espresso has been downed, continue north on Broadway for a block, then turn left onto Lee Hill Drive. This takes you west out of Boulder, before intersecting with Olde Stage Road. Either option eventually dumps you onto the main route in Lefthand Canyon, but I prefer to start with

A pit stop in the quirky town of Ward is your reward for climbing up Lefthand Canyon.

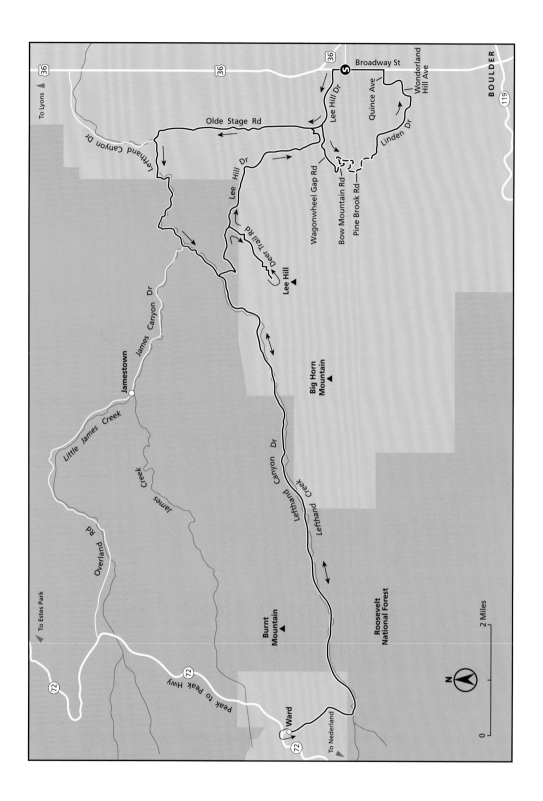

Olde Stage because it's a little more forgiving at this early juncture. For a half mile, you'll be grinding up grades near 10 percent. Then the road levels, save for a short kick near the summit.

Now descend the back side of Olde Stage Road, intersecting with Lefthand Canyon Drive about a mile later. Go left and start climbing again, albeit on a much more gradual grade. The 14-mile ascent to Ward is arguably the area's busiest bike route. On sunny summer weekends, you'll think you've stumbled onto a gran fondo.

At mile 7.3, turn left, continuing on Lefthand Canyon Drive. Going straight would put you on James Canyon Drive, which takes you to the small town of James-town and on to the grueling Super James climb (Ride 14).

The remainder of the Lefthand climb is fairly mellow, save for the final 1.5 miles, which are marked by a sharp right turn known locally as the "Turn of Events." It's here where friendly group rides often morph into pseudo races.

Near the top of this final ascent is a spring on the right side of the road. Top off your bottles here, or keep climbing for another half mile to "downtown" Ward and the Utica Street Market General Store and Full Spectrum Fiber Arts (I kid you not).

Inside you'll find water, hydration drinks, coffee, homemade cookies, and yes, fiber arts. Outside is a porta-potty and small patio with comfortable chairs. It's a great place to relax and recover.

Just up the road is the Peak to Peak Highway (State Route 72), with access to Nederland to the south, Estes Park and Lyons to the north, and spectacular Brainard Lake due west (Ride 13).

But this route heads down now. Aside from a sharp left at the bottom of the nasty climb you just came up, this is basically a no-brakes descent. If there's a headwind, you may even have to pedal. Ten miles down the road, take the 90-degree right turn onto Lee Hill Drive and immediately start climbing. This stair-stepping grind was part of the 2012 USA Pro Challenge bike race, and for good reason: In just 1.3 miles you gain nearly 500 feet, with an average grade of 7.1 percent. The worst comes early, though. The final mile to the summit is mostly flat.

Now comes the first bonus climb, the 1.5-mile up-and-back on Deer Trail Road, average grade 10 percent. Turn around where it becomes dirt. Back at Lee Hill Drive, go right and descend to the Olde Stage Road intersection. Near the bottom, watch out for the pair of tight switchbacks.

Turn right here, continuing down Lee Hill Drive. If you're ready for another espresso, pedal back to Broadway Street and the start point. For one final bonus climb (why not?), turn right on Wagonwheel Gap Road, follow it for about a mile, then turn left on Bow Mountain Road, and head up this gradual 1.5-mile dirt ascent that's no problem on a road bike unless it's rained recently.

Up top merge onto Linden Drive, and descend back toward Boulder. Just as Linden flattens out, go left on Wonderland Hill Avenue, and follow it to its end. Then take a right on the bike path, and connect with Quince Avenue. Continue east for two blocks, then go left on Broadway. In less than a mile you'll be back at the start.

MILEAGE LOG

0.0   Head north on Broadway St. from intersection with Yarmouth Ave.
0.3   Left onto Lee Hill Dr.
1.6   Continue straight, merging onto Olde Stage Rd.
4.7   Left on Lefthand Canyon Dr.

7.3	Left at fork, staying on Lefthand Canyon Dr.
18.3	Arrive in Ward and turn around
29.0	Right onto Lee Hill Dr.
30.3	Right on Deer Trail Rd.
31.8	Summit of Deer Trail Rd. climb and turnaround point
33.3	Right onto Lee Hill Dr.
36.5	Right, continuing on Lee Hill Dr.
36.8	Right onto Wagonwheel Gap Rd.
37.8	Left onto Bow Mountain Rd. Begin gravel road section
38.6	Right onto Pine Brook Rd.
39.3	Left onto Linden Dr. End gravel road section
39.4	Stay left, continuing on Linden Dr.
41.0	Left onto Wonderland Hill Ave.
41.7	Right on bike path, merging onto Quince Ave.
41.9	Left on Broadway St.
42.4	Return to start

16 SUNSHINE CANYON

Difficulty:	Moderate
Time:	¾ –1½ hours
Distance:	11.3 miles
Elevation gain:	1800 feet
Best seasons:	Spring through fall
Road conditions:	Smooth pavement, narrow shoulder, and minimal traffic.

GETTING THERE: From downtown Boulder, head north on Broadway St., then turn left on Mapleton Ave. Pass through the intersection of 4th St., then park just ahead at the Mount Sanitas trailhead at 501 Sunshine Canyon Dr. Free on-street parking and parking lot on left (no water).

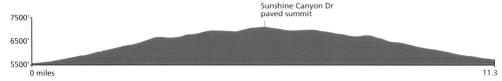

On paper this ride doesn't look too taxing. It's less than a dozen miles and can be knocked out in under an hour if you have some spring in your legs. But the Sunshine Canyon climb should not be taken lightly, especially on hot days. As the name suggests, there's not much shade along this scenic stretch of road that exits Boulder from its west flank and climbs nearly 2000 feet into the foothills of the Rockies.

But don't be scared away by the heat—or all that uphill pedaling. This is one of the best

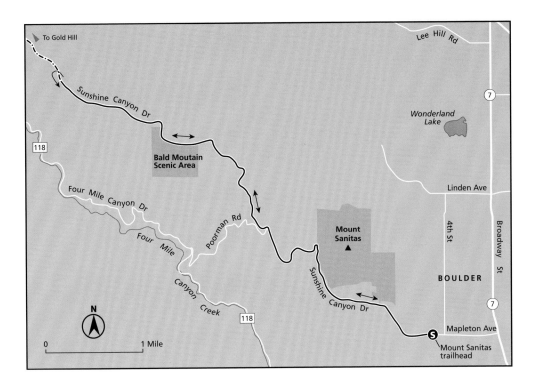

climbs among many Boulder-area ascents, offering a mix of punishing steep pitches, gradual uphill grinds, tranquil flats, short downhills, and, of course, a lot of great views. And that's just on the way up.

The trip down on this out-and-back route is a ripping fast descent with only a few tight turns. Just be on the lookout for the occasional unsuspecting deer, and be wary of traction-robbing gravel, which sometimes builds up in the turns when the road hasn't been swept in a while.

The start point is the parking area at the Mount Sanitas trailhead (the start of one of Boulder's best hikes). There are free parking spaces along both sides of the road just past the Boulder Center for Sports Medicine, as well as a parking lot a few hundred yards farther west.

Once you're on your bike, routefinding is simple: Head west—and up! There are no turns on this ride. The Sunshine Canyon climb starts gradually, gaining only 300 feet in the first mile. Here, and for most of the climb, the shoulder is narrow. But the road is lightly traveled.

Things start getting interesting around the 1.7-mile mark, when the road swings sharply left, and pitches above 9 percent. But the pain is temporary, as this first steep grade relents after only a few hundred feet. You're not out of the woods, though. Just past the intersection with Poorman Road, 2.5 miles into the ride, Sunshine kicks again, this time much harder.

The ensuing 0.75-mile stretch is the ride's toughest, doling out a steady diet of 10-plus percent ascending with ramps as steep as 13 percent. This is typically where men and boys part ways during the Sunshine Canyon Hill Climb race held annually in early June.

The road soon flattens and even heads downhill briefly before kicking up again. But the worst is behind you, as the ensuing handful of uphill pitches is in mostly in the 6 to 7 percent range.

After some tough tree-lined climbing, Sunshine Canyon Drive opens up to reveal sprawling views of the distant Indian Peaks.

As you continue climbing, you'll begin to notice the lingering effects of 2010's Fourmile Canyon Fire, which scorched nearly 6200 acres and destroyed 169 homes, a state record at the time. About two dozen of those homes were along this stretch of Sunshine Canyon Drive.

On a more upbeat note, along this same stretch of road you get your first sprawling views of the distant Indian Peaks Wilderness. On clear early spring days, the contrast between brilliant blue sky and snowcapped mountains is profoundly beautiful.

There's one final kick around the 5.2-mile mark before the grade lets off again as you roll past a "Pavement Ends" sign and County Road 83 on your right. The end of the pavement is the traditional turnaround point. Now shift into your big ring and begin the mad dash down.

Route variation: If you're feeling spry or just want to continue exploring, keep rolling uphill. Road bikes do just fine on this usually well-graded road, which climbs for another 3.4 miles before reaching its high point at 8400 feet. Along the way, you'll pass the former home of one Tyler Hamilton, a retired professional cyclist who both admitted to doping during his racing career and helped lift the lid on the nefarious deeds of disqualified Tour de France champion Lance Armstrong.

From there, it's less than a mile downhill to the tiny town of Gold Hill, population 230. There's a small general store on the main drag that sells refreshments and snacks. Once your fuel stores are topped up, either pedal back the way you came, drop down Fourmile Canyon (which eventually leads to downtown Boulder), or continue west on Gold Run Road. The latter choice means another 7 miles on dirt before you run into State Route 72 (Peak to Peak Highway).

0.0   From Mount Sanitas trailhead, head west on Sunshine Canyon Dr.
5.6   Reach end of pavement and turn around
       Gold Hill extension option:
       5.6   Continue uphill on Sunshine Canyon Dr.
       9.0   Reach Sunshine Canyon Dr. summit
       9.4   Arrive at Gold Hill and turn around
11.3   Finish at Mount Sanitas trailhead

17 GOLD HILL LOOP

Difficulty:	Moderate
Time:	1½–2½ hours
Distance:	21.3 miles
Elevation gain:	3192 feet
Best seasons:	Spring to fall
Road conditions:	Initial bike path section includes 1.4-mile stretch of crushed gravel. Minimal shoulder on Four Mile Canyon Dr., but traffic is light. In 2013, portions of Four Mile Canyon Dr. and Gold Run Rd. suffered severe flood damage. Construction, variable road surface conditions, and additional closures are possible into 2015 and beyond. Check www .bouldercounty.org/flood/roads for the latest updates. Prior to flood damage, this route included a 7-mile gravel road section; may be longer or shorter following reconstruction. Take caution on downhill dirt section of Sunshine Canyon Dr.—steep, tight turns with areas of loose gravel.

GETTING THERE: Ride starts at Boulder's Eben G. Fine Park at 101 Arapahoe Ave. From the intersection of Broadway and Pearl streets, head two blocks south on Broadway, then turn right onto Arapahoe Ave. Park is 0.8 mile ahead on right. Free parking, restrooms, and water.

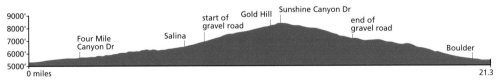

The ingredients of the perfect two-hour ride? Easy access, great scenery, quiet roads, and at least one stiff climb and one rollicking descent. The Gold Hill Loop qualifies on all fronts.

The ride starts under the cottonwood canopy of Eben G. Fine Park, just minutes from downtown Boulder. Pick up the Boulder Creek Path here, heading west away from the city and into Boulder Canyon. This popular

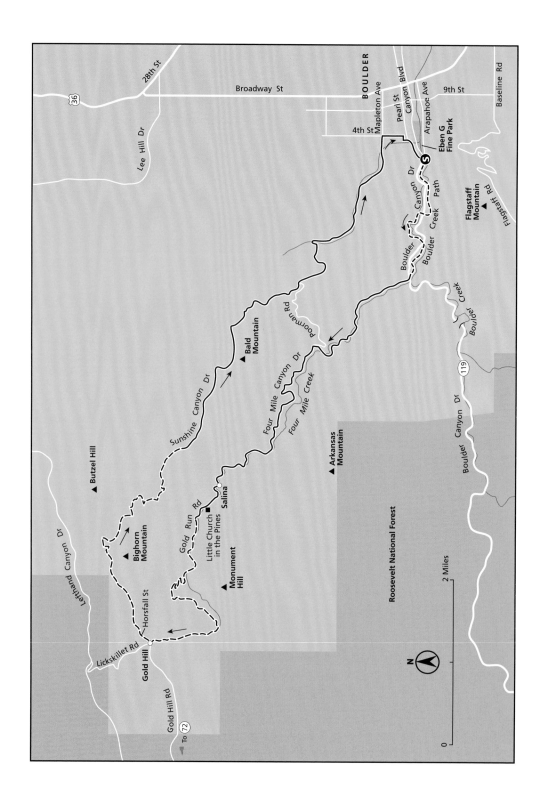

BOULDER

28th St

Broadway St

36

Lee Hill Dr

Mapleton Ave

Pearl St

Canyon Blvd

9th St

Baseline Rd

4th St

Arapahoe Ave

Eben G
Fine Park

S

Canyon Dr

Boulder Creek Path

Flagstaff
Mountain

Flagstaff Rd

Boulder Creek

Poorman Rd

Boulder Canyon Dr

119

Bald
Mountain

Sunshine Canyon Dr

Four Mile Canyon Dr

Four Mile Creek

Arkansas
Mountain

Boulder Creek

Butzel Hill

Gold Run Rd

Salina

Little Church
in the Pines

Monument
Hill

Roosevelt National Forest

Lefthand Canyon Dr

Bighorn
Mountain

Horsfall St

Lickskillet Rd

Gold Hill

Gold Hill Rd

To 72

N

2 Miles

0

The Gold Hill Store is a great spot to top off water bottles and grab a snack. Try the amazing homemade baked goods.

multiuse path is paved for the first mile, then turns into crushed gravel. It's no problem on a road bike—and keeps you off busy Boulder Canyon Drive, which parallels the path and creek.

At mile 2.2, the path ends near a couple of porta-potties. Carefully cross Boulder Canyon Drive, and begin the tranquil spin up Four Mile Canyon Drive. Aside from a paltry shoulder, this is a fabulous cycling road— smooth pavement, a playful stair-stepping climb, and minimal traffic.

Stay right at Salina Junction (mile 7.1), merging onto Gold Run Road, named after the nearby creek that yielded the bounty that started all these gold references back in the 1850s. This community is one of many affected by the September 2013 floods.

Here too is where the toughest climbing begins. With few exceptions, you'll be grinding uphill for the next 4.3 miles, including 3.5 on dirt. Your elevation gain is around 1600 feet. Average gradient is 8 percent. On the way, you'll pass the historic Little Church in the Pines, which was built in 1902 and miraculously survived the recent floods. (Check out salinachurch.blogspot.com to see the stunning images.)

Just up the road from the church, the pavement ends, and you continue on dirt. Like the Four Mile Canyon climb, this ascent stair-steps, kicking hard, then backing off, then kicking again. A tightly spaced set of three switchbacks signals that the hardest part is done.

Two miles later you reach Main Street in Gold Hill. The prescribed route turns right here. But if you have time, detour one block west to the old Gold Hill Store and Café, grab a homemade chocolate chip cookie, and relax on the front porch for a few minutes.

Now head back to the east climbing to a rounded summit (elevation 8455 feet). The road, now called Sunshine Canyon Drive, flattens out for a mile or so, then begins the precipitous plummet back to Boulder. This gravel descent can be a little sketchy in spots, so take your time and enjoy the sweeping valley views.

Pavement returns at mile 14.8, but you continue to descend for another 5.6 miles on the same stretch of road highlighted in Ride 16. At mile 20.4, you return to Boulder. Go right on 4th Street, then wiggle through the west Pearl Street neighborhood, recon-nect with the bike path, cross under Boulder Canyon Drive, and roll back into Eben G. Fine Park

Route variation: Like many Boulder area rides, this route has a super version, meaning longer and harder. After reaching Gold Hill, turn left, continuing on Gold Hill Road for an additional 7.1 miles of scenic dirt road climbing. At the Peak to Peak Highway (State Route 72) intersection, turn right and head 3.5 miles north to the right-hand turnoff for Nelson St. toward Ward. From Ward, descend Lefthand Canyon Drive, then turn right on Lee Hill Drive.

Boulder is 6 miles ahead with more climbing in between. In Boulder, go south on Broadway Street, then turn right on the Iris Avenue bike path, and left on 9th Street, which will take you past Canyon Boulevard to the Boulder Creek Path. Turn right onto the bike path. Eben G. Fine Park is a half mile ahead. Total distance is about 42 miles with 4884 feet of climbing.

MILEAGE LOG

0.0   From Eben G. Fine Park, head west on Boulder Creek multiuse path
1.0   Bike path turns into crushed gravel
2.2   Exit bike path, cross Boulder Canyon Dr., and head north on Four Mile Canyon Dr.
7.1   Right at fork onto Gold Run Rd.
7.8   Begin gravel road section
11.0 Reach Gold Hill, and right on Horsfall St.
      Super Gold Hill option:
      11.0   Left on Gold Hill Rd.
      18.1   Right onto SR 72, end gravel road section
      21.6   Right onto Nelson St.
      22.0   Pass through Ward, descend Lefthand Canyon Rd.
      32.4   Right onto Lee Hill Dr.
      38.4   Right onto Broadway St.
      40.2   Right onto bike path across from Iris Ave.
      40.4   Left onto 9th St.
      41.9   Pass Canyon Blvd. intersection, then right onto Boulder Creek Path
      42.3   Return to Eben G. Fine Park
11.2 Continue straight on Sunshine Canyon Dr.
11.4 Reach ride high point

14.8	End of gravel road section; continue straight on Sunshine Canyon Dr.
20.4	Return to Boulder
20.5	Right onto 4th St.
20.7	Right onto Spruce St.
20.8	Left onto bike path
20.9	Right onto Pearl St.
21.0	Right onto bike path
21.2	Follow bike path under Boulder Canyon Dr.
21.3	Return to Eben G. Fine Park

18 SUGARLOAF-MAGNOLIA

Difficulty:	Challenging
Time:	2–4 hours
Distance:	28.1 miles
Elevation gain:	5321 feet
Best seasons:	Spring to fall
Road conditions:	Shoulder varies, but majority of route on lightly traveled secondary roads. Portion of ride on multiuse path that has some sections of crushed gravel. Short tunnel on Boulder Canyon Dr.

GETTING THERE: Ride starts from Eben G. Fine Park at 101 Arapahoe Ave. in Boulder. From the intersection of Broadway and Pearl streets in downtown Boulder, head two blocks south on Broadway, then turn right onto Arapahoe Ave. Park is 0.8 mile ahead on right. Free parking, restrooms, and water.

If you want to start an argument between Boulder-area cyclists, ask them, "What's the hardest climb in the county?" They will invariably answer Sugarloaf Road or Magnolia Road, but good luck finding a consensus beyond that. Both are downright nasty, each lasting just shy of 5 miles with average gradients above 8 percent.

Magnolia evangelists will point to the climb's punishing early switchbacks, which routinely punch above 14 percent, leaving overgeared riders at a near standstill. Supporters of Sugarloaf will highlight the ascent's relentless pitch; it's not quite as steep as Magnolia's, but it's more consistent, offering little time for recovery. This route includes both climbs so that you can decide for yourself.

The ride starts at Eben G. Fine Park at 101 Arapahoe Avenue, just west of downtown Boulder. From here, take the Boulder Creek Path west into Boulder Canyon. This is one of the busiest multiuse paths in the city, so

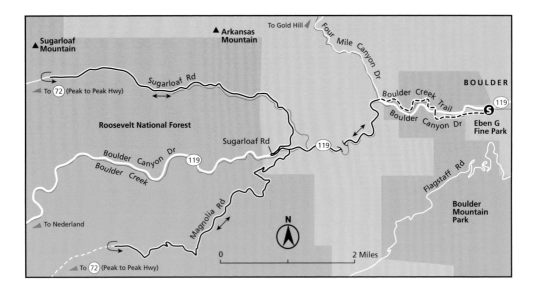

be cautious and courteous. At mile 2.3, the path ends. Turn left onto Boulder Canyon Drive. Once upon a time, this scenic, cliff-lined road was a hallmark of the Coors Classic bike race. But it's so busy today that most cyclists avoid it unless they're trying to get somewhere else.

In this case, that somewhere else is the right-hand turn for Sugarloaf Road at mile 4.7. (You can also start with the Magnolia Road climb, which is 4.4 miles up the canyon on your left. But for whatever reason, I like to begin with Sugarloaf—less backtracking and, in my mind, a fraction easier.)

Right from the start, Sugarloaf hits you hard and rarely lets up. The 4.7-mile, 1900-foot grind averages 8 percent with sustained pitches above 10 during the climb's first half mile, in the middle section, and near the end. It also has several long straight stretches. The summit is a rounded crest just past the Old Post Office Road turnoff. Once you've recovered, buckle up for the rapid descent back the way you came. It's easy to eclipse the 50-mile-per-hour mark.

Back at Boulder Canyon Drive, turn left, then take an immediate right onto Magnolia

Road, which is marked by a yellow street sign that reads simply, "Steep Mountain Road." Indeed, the Magnolia climb gains 2135 feet in just 4.5 miles, with an average gradient of 9 percent. But it's the first 2 miles that are the real killer. Even if you're fit, this climb will *not* make you feel good about yourself. It's difficult to find a rhythm, and you'll be out of the saddle a lot.

The only good news is that after a brutal opening salvo, the climb backs off slightly. There's even a short downhill section around mile 17. But then the road pitches up again, not as steep as before, but still not easy. If you need a break, aim for the pull-off at mile 18.1. On a clear day, it offers an amazing view of the distant Indian Peaks.

At mile 19.0, you'll reach the end of the climb and of the pavement. Catch your breath, and enjoy another ripping descent back to Boulder Canyon Drive. Just make sure to check your speed. It's easy to overshoot the lower switchbacks. Back at Boulder Canyon, turn right and return to town, picking up the bike path on your right at mile 25.8, and arriving at the start point at mile 28.1. Now decide which climb you think is the hardest.

The road sign says it all: Magnolia Road is a beast with numerous pitches above 14 percent. Compact cranks are strongly recommended.

MILEAGE LOG

0.0	Ride starts from Eben G. Fine Park at 101 Arapahoe Ave. in Boulder
0.1	Head west (toward mountains) on Boulder Creek Path
1.0	Bike path turns into crushed gravel
2.3	Exit bike path, and turn left onto Boulder Canyon Dr. continuing west
3.5	Pass through short tunnel
4.7	Right onto Sugarloaf Rd.
9.5	Reach Sugarloaf Rd. summit. Turn around and return to Boulder Canyon Dr.
14.2	Left onto Boulder Canyon Dr.
14.5	Right onto Magnolia Rd.
19.0	Reach end of pavement and summit of Magnolia Rd. Turn around and return to Boulder Canyon Dr.
23.7	Right onto Boulder Canyon Dr.
25.8	Right off Boulder Canyon Dr. back onto Boulder Creek Path
28.1	Return to Eben G. Fine Park

19 FLAGSTAFF ROAD

Difficulty:	Moderate
Time:	1–2 hours
Distance:	12 miles out-and-back
Elevation gain:	2173 feet
Best seasons:	Spring to fall
Road conditions:	Shoulder comes and goes, but traffic typically light. Be wary of loose gravel in the turns.

GETTING THERE: From downtown Boulder, head 1.4 miles south on Broadway St., then turn right onto Baseline Rd. Chautauqua Park is 1.1 miles up Baseline on left on Kinnikinnick Rd. Free parking, water, and restrooms.

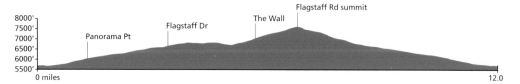

In a town where Lycra is considered casual wear and it's a badge of honor to own a bike that's more expensive than your car, the ride up Flagstaff Mountain is the quintessential Boulder area climb.

Back in the 1980s, Flagstaff often played host to the opening prologue of the famed Coors Classic bike race. In 2012, it was the site of the dramatic stage 6 finish of the USA Pro Challenge, where some of the world's top professionals duked it out in front of mammoth roadside crowds.

But don't be scared off by all this major league history. Outside of a few steep pitches, the ascent of Flagstaff is relatively gentle compared to some of Boulder County's other climbs. The average gradient for the entire ascent, which locals call "Super Flag," is 8.2 percent. But if you opt for just "Flagstaff," which means turning around about two-thirds of the way up, that percentage drops to a reasonable 6.7 percent, just a touch above the standard highway grade.

Climbing begins in earnest about a half mile in, just past the turnoff for the Gregory Canyon Hiking Trail, where Baseline Road changes names to Flagstaff Road. Here you'll find the steepest pitch in the first half of the climb (briefly approaching 10 percent). But that only lasts about a third of a mile, and the sprawling, scenic view of Boulder to your east will help distract your mind from the pain in your legs.

At mile 1.1, you'll bend around another hairpin turn, passing Panorama Point on the right and then the swanky Flagstaff House Restaurant, also on your right. By now the grade has eased off to the 6 percent range, and it won't go above that again unless you opt to take on the climb's tough final 1.7 miles.

If you're just out for a casual spin, sit back and enjoy the scenery. With each turn of your cranks, the view to the east grows broader and wider, taking in the University of Colorado campus, Boulder Reservoir, and on a clear day, the cluster of skyscrapers in distant

The Flagstaff "Wall" has great views of Boulder, but on the way up you'll be too busy suffering to notice.

Denver. Alongside the road expect to see rock climbers on the grippy sandstone boulders that line much of the route, as well as hikers making their way up Flagstaff Mountain Trail, which crosses the road several times.

You're also likely to get buzzed by at least a couple rapidly moving cyclists. Flagstaff is the area's preeminent proving ground for local pros and hammerhead amateurs, who head there looking to hone or test their fitness. The fastest of the fast can spin from the Gregory Canyon turnoff to the Flagstaff Mountain summit in less than thirty minutes. Don't be surprised if it takes you twice that.

At mile 3.4, you'll reach the intersection of Flagstaff Drive, which Ts in from the right. This seasonal road heads 0.7 mile to the northeast before reaching its looped terminus. There you'll find several scenic overlooks, plus picnic tables, shelters, restrooms, and the outdoor Sunrise Circle Amphitheater, which is indeed a great place to watch the sun rise. In fact it's such a spectacular spot that three of my good friends have gotten married there.

Many riders opt to conclude their climb-

ing here and head back down to Boulder. But if you decide to tackle Super Flag, prepare for some pain. After you spin back down to Flagstaff Road, it's another 1.7 miles to the summit, including a one city-block long stretch known (un)affectionately as "The Wall." Here the gradient kicks as high as 16 percent before receding back to a more manageable pitch for the final half mile.

If you need a rest at the top of "The Wall," stop at the Lost Gulch overlook on the right. It has a few benches and affords breathtaking views of the far-off Indian Peaks Wilderness with its multiple snowcapped peaks. (Try Ride 13 to Brainard Lake to get a closer look.)

From here the road bends hard left, and soon after makes its way up a final set of steep switchbacks before reaching the top of the climb, elevation 7697 feet. The long line of mailboxes on the right side of the road marks the unofficial finish line for anyone racing up Super Flag.

Now catch your breath, take a drink, and get ready for a fast, fun descent back to Boulder.

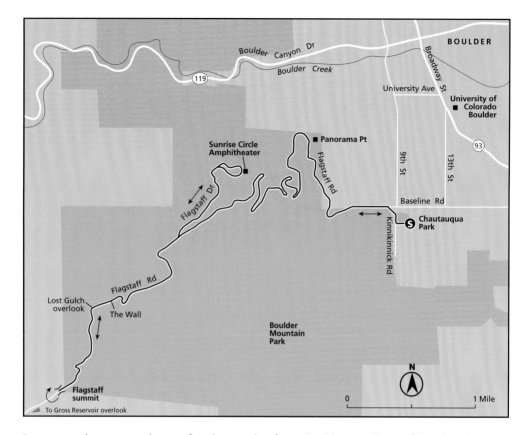

Just remember to watch out for deer and check your speed coming into the tight switchbacks. Occasionally there's loose gravel on the road.

Route variation: To extend your ride and get in some more climbing, continue away from Boulder on Flagstaff Road. After gently rolling for about a mile, the road drops steeply past Walker Ranch, and then climbs to the Gross Reservoir overlook. Follow the pavement to its end at around mile 10.3, then turn around and head back.

MILEAGE LOG

0.0 Exit Chautauqua Park, and turn left on Baseline Rd.
0.4 Stay straight, continuing on Flagstaff Rd.
3.4 Right on Flagstaff Dr.
5.1 Return to Flagstaff Rd. and turn right
6.8 Arrive at summit and turnaround point
     Gross Reservoir extension:
    6.8   **Continue on Flagstaff Rd. to Gross Reservoir overlook**
  10.3   **Turn around where pavement ends**
  20.6   **Finish at Chautauqua Park**
12.0 Finish at Chautauqua Park

20 GROSS DAM LOOP

Difficulty:	Challenging
Time:	4–6 hours
Distance:	53.3 miles
Elevation gain:	6342 feet
Best seasons:	Spring to fall
Road conditions:	Shoulder varies from wide to nonexistent, but majority of ride on secondary highways or county roads. Route includes 6.4-mile gravel section, including 2.5-mile descent. Use caution. Short tunnel at mile 48.4 on Boulder Canyon Dr. Use full lane.

GETTING THERE: From downtown Boulder, head 1.4 miles south on Broadway St., then turn right onto Baseline Rd. Chautauqua Park is 1.1 miles uphill on left on Kinnikinnick Rd. Free parking, water, and restrooms.

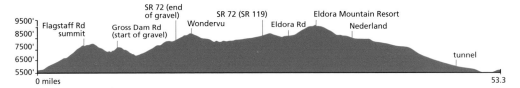

Another of Boulder County's classic multi-surface rides, the Gross Dam Loop has everything from steep climbs (paved and dirt), to winding fast descents (also paved and dirt), to a boatload of spectacular high mountain scenery, especially with the out-and-back on Shelf Road.

Like it does for the Flagstaff Road route (Ride 19), your day starts at Boulder's Chautauqua Park at the base of the Flatirons. Turn left out of the parking area and up you go, grinding to the Flagstaff Road summit 5 miles ahead. The bad news is that you get almost no warm-up. The good news: you'll immediately bang out 2000 feet of climbing. Or maybe that's bad news too.

Regroup and recoup, then continue away from Boulder. The road rolls gently for a mile or so, then just as the view opens up, drops rapidly past Walker Ranch, before rolling on

to the Gross Reservoir overlook. Be careful through here; turns are tight and sometimes sandy.

At mile 9, just past the crest of a short, steep climb, turn left onto the dirt of Gross Dam Road (look for the sign with a blue arrow). You'll continue climbing for a few hundred feet, then commence the twisty, sometimes choppy 2.5-mile descent to the base of Gross Dam. I've ridden this road dozens of times on a road bike without issue, but it definitely commands your full attention. Stay focused and loose.

Around mile 11.5 the road levels out just as you cross South Boulder Creek. Stay left here to remain on Gross Dam Road, following the sign toward Denver and State Route 72. Here climbing renews for 3 miles (average gradient 7 percent, elevation gain 1100 feet). Views of Gross Dam and Denver's

Getting off the beaten (and paved) path is one of the great joys of riding road bikes in Colorado. Pictured here is Gross Dam Road, which traces the eastern edge of Gross Reservoir. (Lisa Sumner)

urban sprawl occasionally peek through the forest wall, but you'll likely be too busy suffering to notice.

Mile 14.7 brings a brief respite. But less than a mile ahead, you'll turn right off Gross Dam Road, returning to pavement—and climbing—on Coal Creek Canyon Road (SR 72). It's a steady 2-mile push to the tiny town of Wondervu, elevation 8632 feet (which has food and drinks).

Once you are rehydrated, commence the mostly downhill run to the intersection of SR 119. Then head north toward Nederland on what's better known as the Peak to Peak Highway, an ever-rolling ribbon of road that traces the eastern edge of the Rockies between Black Hawk and Estes Park.

Yet another punchy climb sets you up for the descent into Nederland. But just before you arrive in this rough-around-the-edges mountain town, turn left on Eldora Road and then left again on aptly named Shelf Road. This 7.8-mile out-and-back bumps up your climbing by 950 feet and offers stunning views of the Indian Peaks on the way to Eldora Mountain Resort, base elevation 9200 feet. Now spin back to SR 119, turn left, and continue into Nederland, which has food and drinks.

At the traffic circle in downtown Nederland, take the second right toward Boulder and Boulder Canyon Drive (SR 119). This road can get fairly busy, especially on the weekend. But you'll be going downhill the whole time, so it's not hard to keep pace with the cars. Fifteen rapid miles later you'll be back in Boulder. Turn right on 6th Street, and follow it to Baseline Road and on to Chautauqua Park.

Route variation: For roughly the same amount of climbing but less time on sometimes busy SR 72, turn left onto Crescent Park Drive at mile 14.7 and follow it to SR 72.

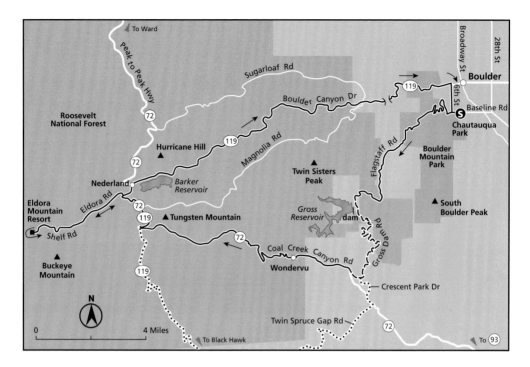

Go left here, then a half mile later turn right onto Twin Spruce Gap Road. Three miles ahead, stay left to continue on Gap Road. Two miles ahead begin another gravel road section, which continues to the intersection with SR 119. Turn right here, and 6.5 miles later, you'll rejoin the main route, heading north toward Nederland.

MILEAGE LOG

0.0   Exit Chautauqua Park, and turn left on Baseline Rd.
0.4   Stay straight, continuing on Flagstaff Rd.
5.1   Reach top of Flagstaff Rd. climb
9.0   Left onto Gross Dam Rd. (start of gravel road section)
11.5   Finish gravel road descent
12.0   Left, continuing on Gross Dam Rd.
13.2   Reach railroad crossing
14.7   Stay straight on Gross Dam Rd.

Twin Spruce Gap Rd. option:
14.7   **Left onto Crescent Park Dr.**
15.7   **Left onto SR 72**
16.2   **Right onto Twin Spruce Rd.**
19.2   **Left onto Gap Rd.**
25.6   **Right onto SR 119, rejoining main route**

15.4   Right onto SR 72 (Coal Creek Canyon Rd.), and reach end of gravel road section
17.5   Reach Coal Creek Canyon Rd. summit and Wondervu
25.4   Right onto the combination SR 72, SR 119, and Peak to Peak Highway

27.8	Left onto Eldora Rd. (County Road 130) toward Eldora
29.2	Left onto Shelf Rd.
31.7	Reach Shelf Rd. summit and turnaround point
35.6	Left onto SR 72 (also SR 119 and Peak to Peak Highway)
35.9	Arrive in Nederland
36.4	Take second right in traffic circle, continuing on SR 119 (Boulder Canyon Dr.)
48.4	Pass through tunnel
51.6	Return to Boulder
52.1	Right onto 6th St.
52.6	Quick left and then a right continuing on 6th St.
53.1	Left onto Baseline Rd.
53.3	Return to start at Chautauqua Park

21 BOULDER BIKE PATHS

Difficulty:	Easy
Time:	1–2 hours
Distance:	14.2 miles
Elevation gain:	281 feet
Best seasons:	Early spring to late fall (possible in winter)
Road conditions:	Majority of route on multiuse path, with remainder on residential roads or roads with designated bike lanes.

GETTING THERE: Ride starts from Eben G. Fine Park at 101 Arapahoe Ave. in Boulder. From intersection of Broadway and Pearl streets in downtown Boulder, head 0.3 mile south on Broadway, then turn right onto Arapahoe Ave., heading west for 0.8 mile. Park is on the right. Free parking, restrooms, and water.

Every year the US cycling media puts together lists of the country's most cycling-friendly cities, and every year Boulder ranks at or near the top of those lists. The primary reason? This city of nearly 100,000 has more than 300 miles of dedicated bike paths and bike lanes, making it possible to get almost anywhere in town without riding in the main flow of traffic. It's little wonder that Boulder has the country's second-highest percentage of bike commuters.

My suggestion for exploring my home-town by bike is simply that—go explore. The mountains (always to your west) make a nifty

navigation tool. In lieu of this less structured approach, try this family-friendly route that takes you from the city's western edge to its eastern border and back, while passing a host of landmarks, playgrounds, and parks.

The ride starts at Eben G. Fine Park, which is just a handful of blocks west of downtown on the southern bank of Boulder Creek. From here, head east (away from the mountains) on the Boulder Creek Path.

Follow this path for 4.2 miles, as it jogs through downtown, past Boulder High, and along the northern border of the University of Colorado campus. If you're ever in doubt

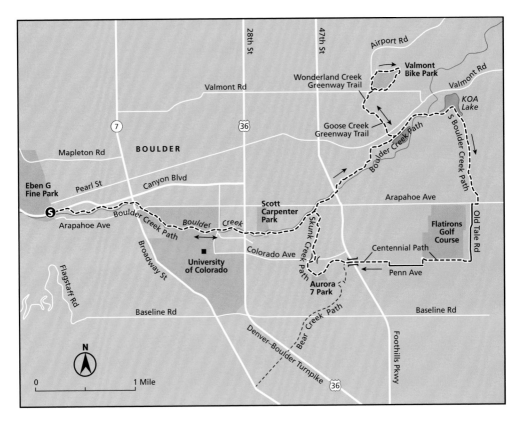

about which direction to go, choose the path that keeps you closest to the creek. Along the way, check out the Boulder Creek underwater stream observatory on the left at mile 2.1, just before the path crosses from the creek's left to right bank for the first time.

At mile 3.3, go left and then immediately right to stay on Boulder Creek Path. At mile 3.9, go right again, and at mile 4.2, turn left onto the Goose Creek Greenway Trail, then stay right at the next intersection, which puts you on the Wonderland Creek Greenway Trail. A few hundred feet up this path, turn right off the Wonderland Creek Path, and head due north toward the intersection of Valmont and Airport roads.

Now cross the street and spin through one of the city's true crowning achievements, the 40-acre Valmont Bike Park, a two-wheeler's playground that includes pump tracks, sin-

gletrack trails, dirt jumps, a slopestyle course, and dedicated cyclocross circuit, which played host to the 2014 US National Championships. Follow the bike path on a counterclockwise loop around the park, exiting on the west side near the playground and restrooms (where there is water).

Now turn left onto Airport Road, cross the intersection at Valmont Road, and rejoin the Wonderland Creek Greenway Trail, heading back toward the Boulder Creek Path. At mile 6.3, turn left onto the Boulder Creek Path heading east. At mile 6.8, stay right, taking the south fork and the South Boulder Creek Path, keeping KOA Lake on your left as you begin winding south along Boulder's eastern edge. Look right for splendid views of the Flatirons and Rocky Mountains.

At mile 8.0, cross under Arapahoe Avenue, then continue south on the South Boulder

The Boulder Creek Path runs east–west through the heart of the city, passing numerous parks and playgrounds along the way.

Creek Path (Old Tale Road). Follow this designated bike lane for a half mile to the road's end, then pick up the bike path and immediately turn right onto the Centennial Path. It points you back to the west, as you pedal alongside the Flatirons Golf Course.

At mile 9.1, exit the bike path, and turn left on 55th Street, following the sign for the Pennsylvania Avenue Route, which will be your next right. Continue a half mile west on Pennsylvania Avenue, then turn left at mile 9.7, rejoining the Centennial Path. Just up the way, take the overpass over Foothills Parkway, then continue west following signs toward the University of Colorado campus.

At mile 10.4, turn right onto the Skunk Creek Path. A tenth of a mile later, go right at the fork, following the path under Colorado Avenue. Less than a mile later you'll intersect the Boulder Creek Path. Turn left and head back to Eben G. Fine Park.

Route variations: Other options are nearly limitless. Check out the south side of Boulder via the Bear Creek Path, which is on your left just after you cross the Foothills Parkway overpass and then a short bridge. Shorten the ride by taking the Goose Creek Greenway Trail back into downtown.

Or pass through the University of Colorado campus by taking Colorado Avenue west to the 28th Street Frontage Road, then going left and immediately right into the 28th Street underpass. Continue west, then go left on Regent Avenue, which will bring you to the Broadway Path. Go right and you'll parallel campus on the way back to the Boulder Creek Path.

MILEAGE LOG

0.0	From Eben G. Fine Park, head east on Boulder Creek Path
1.0	Stay right, continuing on Boulder Creek Path
2.4	Stay right, continuing on Boulder Creek Path

3.3	Left across bridge and then immediate right, continuing on Boulder Creek Path
3.9	Right, continuing on Boulder Creek Path
4.2	Left onto the Goose Creek Greenway Trail
4.5	Right onto Wonderland Creek Greenway Trail
4.6	Right off Wonderland Creek Greenway Trail toward Valmont Bike Park
4.8	Cross intersection of Valmont and Airport roads, then pick up bike path in northeast corner of intersection heading east
5.0	Stay left, entering Valmont Bike Park
5.4	Circle counterclockwise through center of park on wide dirt path, exiting on west side just past playground and restrooms
5.6	Left on Airport Rd.
5.7	Cross Valmont Rd., then rejoin Wonderland Creek Greenway Trail, heading back toward Boulder Creek Path
6.3	Left, rejoining Boulder Creek Path heading east
6.8	Right, taking south fork of S. Boulder Creek Path
8.0	Cross below Arapahoe Ave., continuing on S. Boulder Creek Path (Old Tale Rd.)
8.5	Where Old Tale Rd. dead-ends, rejoin bike path
8.6	Right onto Centennial Path, heading west
9.1	Exit bike path, then left on 55th St., following sign for Pennsylvania Ave.
9.2	Right on Pennsylvania Ave.
9.7	Left back onto Centennial Path
9.9	Straight over Foothills Pkwy. overpass
10.0	Straight, following signs to University of Colorado campus
10.4	Right onto Skunk Creek Path
10.5	Right at fork, following path under Colorado Ave.
11.2	Left, rejoining Boulder Creek Path heading west
14.2	Return to start point at Eben G. Fine Park

22 MORGUL-BISMARK LOOP

- - - - - - - - - - -

Difficulty:	Moderate
Time:	1–2 hours
Distance:	20.5 miles
Elevation gain:	1276 feet
Best seasons:	Spring through fall
Road conditions:	Majority of route travels smooth road with wide shoulder, no shoulder and light traffic on S. 76th St., and shoulder and sometimes heavy traffic on SR 93.

GETTING THERE: From downtown Boulder, head south on Broadway St., and then east on Baseline Rd. to its intersection with Gapter Rd. Park your car at the Bobolink trailhead parking area.

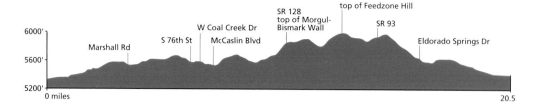

If you asked a group of Colorado bike racers to name the most famous race route in the state, it's a safe bet the Morgul-Bismark Loop would garner the majority vote. While not the most scenic or challenging ride in the state, its place in Colorado cycling lore is secure thanks to starring roles in both the famed Coors Classic bike race and the movie *American Flyers,* a campy 1985 Kevin Costner flick about bike racing.

In real life, the Morgul-Bismark is a scenic and rolling 13.3-mile loop that's punctuated by three short but punchy climbs. During the days of the Coors Classic (once dubbed the world's fourth-biggest stage race behind the grand tours of France, Italy, and Spain) the Morgul-Bismark was the site for an always challenging affair, where the likes of Greg LeMond and Bernard Hinault spun furiously fast laps on this shadeless circuit situated at the south end of Boulder County.

The Coors Classic closed up shop in 1988, but racing on the famed loop lives on, most recently as part of the Superior Morgul Classic, a multiday event geared primarily toward amateur racers. But the majority of the two-wheeled traffic you'll encounter on the Morgul loop is simply local riders out on a lunch ride.

There are numerous ways to get onto the main circuit (check the map), but for the sake of free parking and a nice warm-up spin, this ride starts at the Bobolink trailhead at the intersection of Gapter and Baseline roads. From this small dirt parking lot on the east side of Boulder, pedal right onto Baseline Road, then take an immediate right onto Cherryvale Road.

From here it's a 3.5-mile straight shot south to Marshall Road, which marks your official entry point onto the Morgul-Bismark circuit proper. Along the way you'll spin past Baseline Reservoir, pass through the intersection at South Boulder Road, and cross the bridge over US Highway 36. And though you're only a few miles from bustling downtown Boulder, the scenery here is dominated by open grassland, grazing cattle, and sprawling views of the nearby Flatirons.

When you reach Marshall Road, go left and start channeling your inner bike racer. The shoulder remains wide and smooth as you trend gently uphill for 2 miles, before heading downhill while paralleling US 36. At mile 6.3, turn right onto South 76th Street. There's no shoulder here, but it's a quiet street behind a large shopping plaza, so traffic is usually minimal.

Next go left at West Coal Creek Drive, spinning past the shoppers on your left and a residential neighborhood on the right. At mile 7.3, reach McCaslin Boulevard. Turn right onto McCaslin, and immediately start climbing up what local cyclists call "The Hump," a half-mile grind that averages about 5 percent. Once you're over the top, there's a rapid downhill punctuated by a trip through a small traffic circle at the intersection of Coalton Road. Be careful.

Once you're safely through the circle, take a swig from your water bottle, breathe deep, and get ready to tackle the famed Morgul-Bismark Wall. The summit of this 1.4-mile climb was the finish line during the Coors Classic days, and it is usually the spot where friendly group rides devolve into battles of attrition.

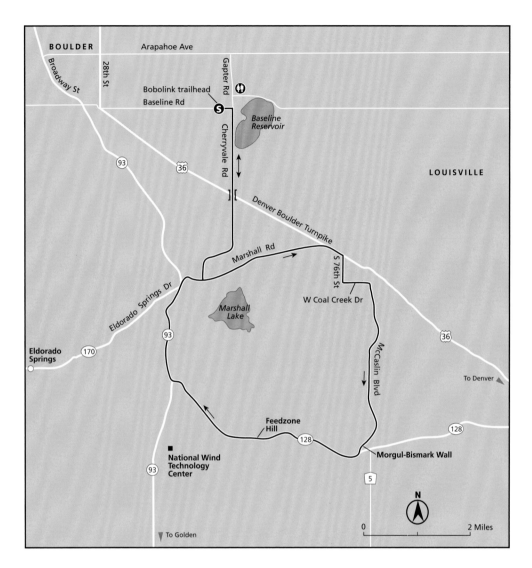

The average grade for the whole climb is just 4.1 percent. But after a gradual beginning, it gets increasingly steeper, finishing with a nasty kick that has pitches steeper than 12 percent.

Once you're over the top, turn right onto State Route 128 (also known as West 120th Avenue), and soak in the wide westerly views of the Front Range foothills and the looming Rocky Mountains. At about eleven o'clock is the mouth of Eldorado Canyon. Over at two

thirty you'll spot the towering figure of Longs Peak, one of fifty-three peaks in the state that exceed 14,000 feet in elevation.

Here you'll also catch your first glance of the white wind turbines that are part of the National Wind Technology Center, which is considered one of the nation's premier wind energy research facilities from its advantageous (read: often very windy) perch on Boulder County's southern periphery. The largest of these wind turbines stands 262 feet

The famed Morgul-Bismark circuit remains a staple of the local amateur racing scene—and is a great lunchtime loop.

tall and has blades that are 164 feet long, creating a rotating diameter of 331 feet. It's an impressive sight.

The road rolls gently downhill for about a mile, increasing in grade the farther you go. Try to maintain your speed if you can, as the day's last challenge looms: the brief, but punchy Feedzone Hill, which is about 0.75 mile with an average grade of 4.7 percent. As you may have guessed, you won't find the "Feedzone" reference on any official road maps. Instead the name comes from the days of the Coors Classic, when team helpers passed midrace lunch bags to competing pro riders.

Once you're over the top, it's another gradual drop before the road pitches up ever so slightly as you roll up to the intersection

of SR 93. Turn right here, and head back to Boulder.

At the bottom of the descent, take a right at the traffic light, which puts you on Eldorado Springs Drive. (A left here would send you to the springs themselves, which are 3 miles to the west at the mouth of Eldorado Canyon. The public pool out there is a great place to take a swim on a hot day.)

After a few hundred feet, turn right at the stop sign, rejoining Marshall Road. A quarter mile later, turn left back onto Cherryvale Road, and head back to your car at the Bobolink trailhead just off Baseline Road.

Oh, and in case you're wondering about this route's name, legend has it that Morgul (a cat) and Bismark (a dog) belonged to one of the Coors Classic race directors. Go figure . . .

0.0   From Bobolink trailhead parking lot, right onto Baseline Rd.

0.1   Right on Cherryvale Rd.

1.7   Cross over US 36, continuing on Cherryvale Rd.

3.6   Left on Marshall Rd.

6.3   Right on S. 76th St.

6.8   Left on W. Coal Creek Dr.

7.3   Right on McCaslin Blvd.

9.0   Use caution in traffic circle

10.6   Right on SR 128

14.5   Right on SR 93

16.5   Right on Eldorado Springs Dr.

16.6   Right on Marshall Rd.

16.9   Left on Cherryvale Rd.

20.4   Left on Baseline Rd.

20.5   Left into Bobolink trailhead parking lot

FRONT RANGE SOUTH

Scale 14,115-foot Pikes Peak—by bike! Roll around the Air Force Academy campus. Spin past stunning red sandstone shapes in Garden of the Gods. Cross above the bottomless expanse of the Royal Gorge. Cruise along the world's largest outdoor art mural. These are just some of the cycling adventures to be found along the southern edge of Colorado's Front Range.

23 AIR FORCE ACADEMY LOOP

Difficulty:	Moderate
Time:	¾–1½ hours
Distance:	14 miles
Elevation gain:	1130 feet
Best seasons:	Year-round
Road conditions:	Shoulder width varies, but wide, smooth roads and low speed limit.

GETTING THERE: From I-25, drive to exit 156B, 14 miles north of downtown Colorado Springs. Merge onto North Gate Blvd. and head west. This road turns into Academy Dr. In 1 mile, enter the US Air Force Academy through North Gate entrance. Visitor hours are from 8:00 AM to 6:00 PM daily, and you need to show valid ID. Continue on Academy Dr. for another 4 miles to visitor center on left. Free parking, water, and restrooms.

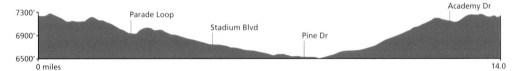

In September 1986, six weeks after Greg LeMond became the first American to win the Tour de France, cycling history was made again when the road cycling world championships were held on US soil for the first time. The site of this historic happening was the campus of the US Air Force Academy. On that day, LeMond crossed the line seventh among eighty-seven finishers of the 162.5-mile circuit race. Afterward he complained to the press that the seventeen-lap affair's lack of punch had made the race too easy.

Easy or not, a spin around the perimeter of the academy's gleaming campus is an iconic cycling experience. The roads are baby-bottom smooth and there's an array of impressive scenery, including long-distance views of the vast Eastern Plains, the tree-covered

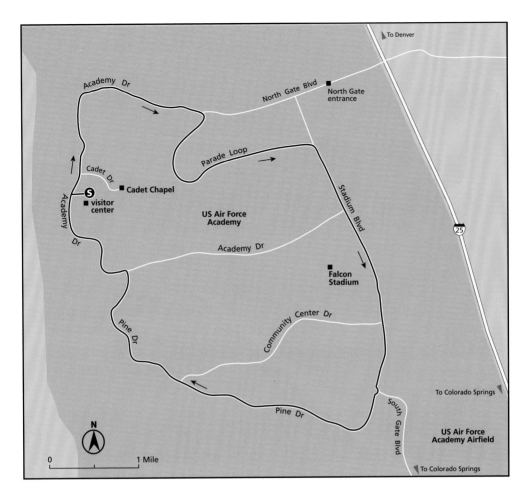

Rampart Range, and the campus itself, which is highlighted by the famed Cadet Chapel with its seventeen 150-foot-tall, fighter jet–inspired spires.

This mellow 14-mile spin starts at the visitor center (which is just west of the chapel), then heads north on Academy Drive. After turning right out of the parking lot, there's a brief climb, followed by a straight, fast descent. On your right spot various athletic fields, including the practice grounds for the Air Force Academy football team.

As the road bends right, there's a short, gradual climb. If you're feeling winded when you get to the summit (or simply want to learn more about your surroundings), turn

right into the pull-out. It has a nice overlook, plus a series of plaques detailing various campus landmarks.

Otherwise keep spinning as the road heads downhill again. Beware of the cement drainage area that runs adjacent to Academy Drive. It drops off quickly and has several hazardous metal grates.

Just as the road flattens out, turn right on Parade Loop. It's a quieter road—and this is the route used for the Front Range Cycling Classic, an annual springtime amateur road race. Here you'll face the ride's steepest climb, the Parade Loop Popper. But it's only a third of a mile, and once you're over the top, you'll be trending downhill for most of the next 5 miles.

The final leg of the Air Force Academy Loop propels you to the base of the Rampart Range, which lines the western edge of this military academy campus.

At mile 5.2, Parade Loop Ts into Stadium Boulevard. Glance left and spot the impressive B-52 Bomber display, then turn right, heading south. There's another guardhouse along this stretch of road and sometimes they ask for ID, so make sure to carry your driver's license in your jersey pocket just in case.

At mile 6.3, you'll see Falcon Stadium on your right. This 46,692-seat facility is home to the academy's Division I football team, as well as the site of annual graduation ceremonies. At mile 8, stay right, merging onto Pine Drive, which quickly bends around to the west. This marks the point where you officially start climbing back to the starting

point. But the pitch is almost always gradual, rarely kicking above 6 percent; the entire Pine Drive climb is 3.5 miles long and gains about 750 feet.

At mile 12.3, Pine Ts into Academy Drive. Turn left here, pushing your way up one more short climb. At the top, glance right, taking in what's considered the best overlook view of Cadet Chapel and its magnificent spires. One mile later, you're back at your car. Now go change and take a tour of the chapel—or head out for another lap. Remember that LeMond and company did seventeen on a slightly shorter loop during that "too easy" race back in 1986.

0.0   Exit visitor center parking lot, turning right on Academy Dr.
1.3   Right on Academy Dr., ascending North Gate climb
2.7   Right on Parade Loop
5.2   Right on Stadium Blvd.
8.0   Stay right, merging onto Pine Dr.
12.3   Left onto Academy Dr.
14.0   Finish ride at visitor center

24   PIKES PEAK GREENWAY TRAIL

Difficulty:	Easy to Moderate
Time:	3–4 hours
Distance:	41 miles out-and-back (shorter options)
Elevation gain:	909 feet
Best seasons:	Early spring to late fall (possible in winter)
Road conditions:	Entire route is on multiuse path. Some unpaved sections, including final 10 miles of approach to Fountain Creek Regional Park.

GETTING THERE: Ride starts from Woodmen Rd. Park-n-Ride on north end of Colorado Springs. From I-25, take exit 149 for Woodmen Rd., then turn west (toward mountains) at end of exit ramp. Small park-and-ride lot is on west side of highway about a quarter mile ahead on your right.

Someday, if all proceeds as planned, you'll be able to ride north to south nonstop across Colorado on multiuse paths. The Colorado Front Range Trail, as the ambitious project is known, will stretch 876 miles from Wyoming to New Mexico, connecting fifteen cities, fourteen counties, and numerous smaller communities along Colorado's Front Range, including Fort Collins, Boulder, Denver, Colorado Springs, and Pueblo. The estimated completion date is sometime around 2050 according to the state's top recreation trails officer.

To date, roughly 300 miles are done, including the Pikes Peak Greenway Trail, a mostly flat, 14-mile multiuse path that bisects the heart of Colorado Springs from the Air Force Academy in the north to the El Pomar Youth Sports Complex in the south. This 41-mile out-and-back ride includes the entirety of that trail, plus portions of the unpaved Fountain Creek Regional Trail, the next southern link in this growing cross-state chain.

Along the way, you'll be treated to a relaxing spin along the banks of Monument and Fountain creeks, plus great long-distance views of Pikes Peak to the west, and access to about a dozen trail spurs that lead into various parts of Colorado's second-largest city. Total climbing is just a shade under 1000 feet, and the only hills of even modest significance come about 3 miles from the turnaround point.

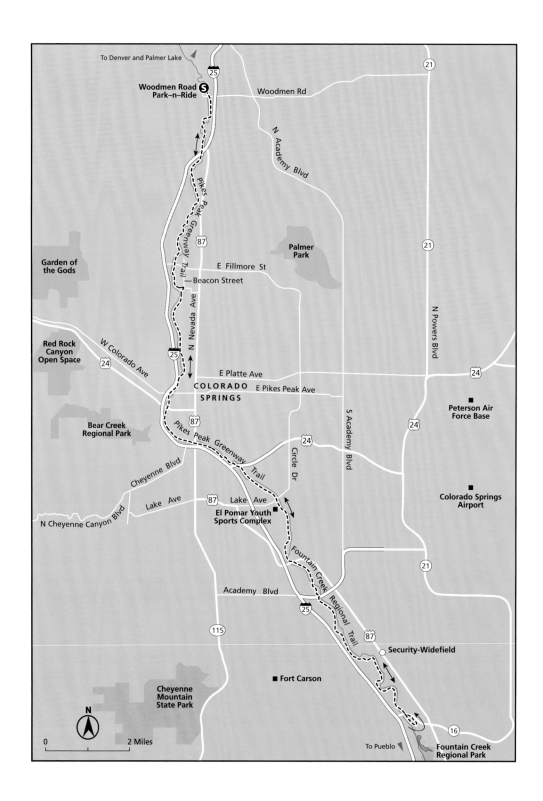

To Denver and Palmer Lake

Woodmen Road **S**
Park–n–Ride

Woodmen Rd

25

21

21

N Academy Blvd

Pikes Peak Greenway Trail

87

Palmer Park

E Fillmore St

Beacon Street

Garden of the Gods

N Nevada Ave

N Powers Blvd

Red Rock Canyon Open Space

24

W Colorado Ave

25

E Platte Ave

24

COLORADO SPRINGS

E Pikes Peak Ave

Peterson Air Force Base

S Academy Blvd

Bear Creek Regional Park

87

Pikes Peak Greenway Trail

Cheyenne Blvd

24

Circle Dr

24

Lake Ave

87

Lake Ave

Colorado Springs Airport

N Cheyenne Canyon Blvd

El Pomar Youth Sports Complex

Fountain Creek Regional Trail

21

Academy Blvd

25

115

87

Security-Widefield

Cheyenne Mountain State Park

Fort Carson

N

16

0   2 Miles

To Pueblo

Fountain Creek Regional Park

The scenic mixed-surface Pikes Peak Greenway Trail runs the length of Colorado Springs, offering a bounty of picturesque views along the way.

Start the ride at the Woodmen Road Park-n-Ride, just west of Interstate 25 on the north end of Colorado Springs. From the parking lot, head downhill on the connector path, then turn right onto the Pikes Peak Greenway Trail. You'll be pedaling on pulverized granite for a few minutes, then transition onto pavement for the majority of the trip through the city. Routefinding is fairly straightforward. Follow the signs for the main trail; if in doubt, hug the creek bank. Also keep your eyes open for Pikes Peak Greenway Trail mileage markers. These two-foot-tall stone pillars count down as you head south.

During the first 5 miles, you'll cross Monument Creek a handful of times. At mile 5.8, you briefly leave the path, turning right onto Beacon Street, and almost immediately turn right again back onto path. Fifty feet

ahead, turn left (before the bridge) and start the route's first extended unpaved section, a smooth 2.3-mile stretch of crushed granite that skirts the west side of downtown Colorado Springs before ending around mile 8.2.

There's another half-mile unpaved stretch starting at mile 8.8, then 2 more miles of pavement before unpaved trail returns for the remainder of the trek to the turnaround point at Fountain Creek Regional Park. All of these dirt sections are easily rideable on a road bike. But less confident riders may be more comfortable on a cyclocross or hybrid bike, especially for the southern section, where the trail is occasionally sandy and loose in spots.

The upside of this off-road adventure is that it gets you out of the city and into nature. Portions of the trail run through lush life-supporting riparian zones that are home to a variety of birds, beaver, deer, and fox. Other stretches wind through open grassland dotted with grazing cattle.

At mile 13.1, the trail changes to the Fountain Creek Regional Trail, as it traces the eastern edge of the El Pomar Youth Sports Complex, a great place to use the restroom, refill your bottles, or to stop and let the kids play. The ensuing 7 miles brings more natural habitat before you reach the turnaround point at Fountain Creek Regional Park, a popular fishing and picnicking spot. The park restrooms are open from April to October.

From here, either head back the way you came on the prescribed route, or keep exploring. The Fountain Creek Regional Trail continues for another few miles, and someday, if all goes according to plan, will reach all the way to New Mexico.

Route variation: From the start point, turn left (north) onto the Pikes Peak Greenway Trail, which soon becomes the Santa Fe Regional Trail. This mostly unpaved 14.5-mile multiuse path connects Colorado Springs to the town of Palmer Lake, passing the east side of the Air Force Academy along the way. From Palmer Lake, you can continue another 5 miles on the Greenland Trail to the Greenland Open Space. Like the main route, these two trails can be ridden on a road bike, but less confident riders may be more comfortable on a cyclocross or hybrid bike.

MILEAGE LOG

0.0	From park-n-ride, head down connector path, then right on Pikes Peak Greenway Trail
1.5	Cross creek, continuing on Pikes Peak Greenway Trail
1.7	Stay left, continuing on Pikes Peak Greenway Trail
2.3	Cross creek, continuing on Pikes Peak Greenway Trail
2.8	Cross creek, continuing on Pikes Peak Greenway Trail
3.4	Stay left, continuing on Pikes Peak Greenway Trail
5.3	Cross Polk St. and continue on Pikes Peak Greenway Trail
5.8	Right onto Beacon St., and then immediately right back onto Pikes Peak Greenway Trail
5.9	Left before bridge, continuing on Pikes Peak Greenway Trail (start of unpaved section)
8.2	End of unpaved section
8.3	Cross creek, continuing on Pikes Peak Greenway Trail
8.8	Start of crushed granite section
9.4	Cross creek, continuing on Pikes Peak Greenway Trail (end of unpaved section)
10.6	Cross creek, continuing on Pikes Peak Greenway Trail
10.7	Start of crushed granite section, which continues to turnaround point
11.1	Cross creek, continuing on Pikes Peak Greenway Trail
12.0	Cross Fountain Creek, continuing on Pikes Peak Greenway Trail
13.1	Stay left at trail fork, merging onto the Fountain Creek Regional Trail
13.4	Straight, continuing on Fountain Creek Regional Trail
14.4	Left at trail fork, continuing on Fountain Creek Regional Trail
19.9	Cross creek, continuing on Fountain Creek Regional Trail
20.3	Arrive in Fountain Creek Regional Park, circle lake, then head back to start
41.0	Return to start at Woodmen Road Park-n-Ride

Difficulty:	Easy
Time:	½–1 hour
Distance:	5.8 miles (longer options)
Elevation gain:	729 feet
Best seasons:	Year-round
Road conditions:	Wide shoulder and smooth pavement. Be wary of inattentive drivers.

GETTING THERE: From I-25 in Colorado Springs, take exit 146 for Garden of the Gods Rd. In 2.3 miles, turn left on N. 30th St. In 1.5 miles, turn right entering the free park via Gateway Rd. In a half mile, turn right on Juniper Way Loop. Follow this road a third of a mile to main north parking lot on left. Free parking, restrooms, and water.

First, a little history. Way back in August 1859, a couple of surveyors were out doing their thing when they happened upon a beautiful swath of monolithic red sandstone formations just west of what would become modern-day Colorado Springs. Upon gazing at this natural splendor, surveyor no. 1 said to surveyor no. 2, "This would be a capital place for a beer garden." (He must have been Bavarian.)

Surveyor no. 2, who is labeled "a young and poetic man" in various historical accounts, was taken aback by the thought of planting

Red sandstone spires and smooth, wide-shouldered roads make a spin around Garden of the Gods a truly magical cycling experience.

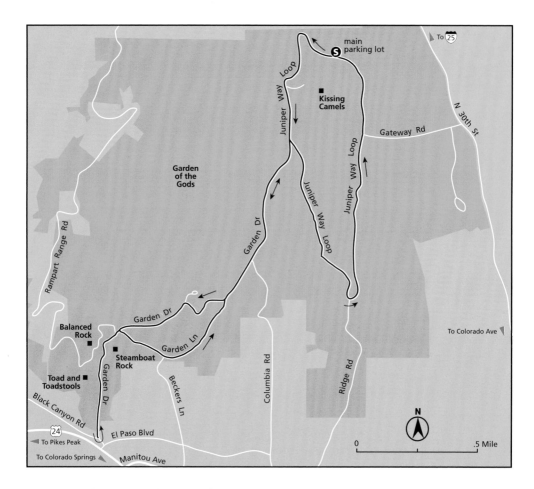

a pub in such a magical place, and fired back, "Beer garden? Why this is a place fit for the gods. We will call it Garden of the Gods." And so it was.

Ironically, the last private owner of this land, a chap named Charles Elliott Perkins, turned the land over to his children, who, knowing how much their dad had revered the place, donated the land to the city of Colorado Springs in 1909 on the condition that it, "Shall remain free to the public, where no intoxicating liquors shall be manufactured, sold, or dispensed, and where no building or structure shall be erected except those necessary to properly care for, protect, and maintain the area as a public park." Indeed, the *biergarten* never had a chance, which is

just as well considering that Garden of the Gods is one of those truly magical natural wonders that ought to remain unspoiled.

As for cycling there, the smooth, wide-shouldered roads that crisscross the park are perfect for a mellow family outing or an add-on to a longer Colorado Springs–area ride. And if you're feeling particularly masochistic, link a spin around the park with a ride up 14,115-foot Pikes Peak (Ride 27), which looms high in the sky to the southwest of the park.

Starting from the main north parking lot, turn left onto the one-way Juniper Way Loop. There's a brief climb before the road swings around to the south and trends downhill to the intersection of Garden Drive at mile 0.7. If you're riding with children or just looking to keep things short, turn left to stay on the Juniper Way Loop, and you'll be back at your car in no time.

Otherwise, stay right on Garden Drive, and continue a mostly downhill spin to the park's most famous landmark, Balanced Rock, at mile 2. You won't have any trouble spotting this marvelous site, where a 700-ton house-sized boulder seems miraculously perched just above the right side of the road. On weekends in the summer, this is typically the most crowded area of the park, as gawkers take turns posing for photos in front of the famous rock.

Just across the way is Steamboat Rock, which looks a little bit like the bow of a steamship, and provides a convenient median for the road to loop around. You can also head a little farther down Garden Drive, spying the Toad and Toadstools formation on your right, before turning around at the intersection with Black Canyon Road and heading back the way you came. This short up-and-down section is included to extend the ride and add some climbing. But feel free to turn around whenever you want.

Once you pass Balanced Rock again, bear right onto Garden Lane, which returns you to Garden Drive, and then the intersection with Juniper Way Loop at mile 4. From there it's less than 2 miles back to your car. Along the way, keep your eyes peeled for other famous rock formations, including the Keyhole Window, Sleeping Giant, Cathedral Rock, and Kissing Camels, which comes into sight just before you get back to the starting point. And if you feel like riding more, head out for another lap. The Garden of the Gods is certainly worth a second look—as long as you're not looking for a beer.

MILEAGE LOG

0.0	Left out of main north parking lot onto Juniper Way Loop
0.7	Right, merging onto Garden Dr.
2.0	Pass Balanced Rock
2.3	Make a U-turn at intersection with Black Canyon Rd.
2.6	Pass Balanced Rock again
2.7	Right onto Garden Ln.
3.3	Merge back onto Garden Dr.
4.0	Right onto Juniper Way Loop
5.8	Return to start

26 CHEYENNE CAÑON

Difficulty:	Moderate
Time:	1–2 hours
Distance:	11 miles out-and-back
Elevation gain:	1697 feet
Best seasons:	Early spring to late fall
Road conditions:	Majority of route on narrow mountain road with minimal shoulder. Sightseeing traffic can be heavy during summer weekends.

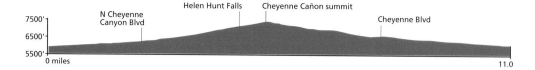

GETTING THERE: Ride starts at intersection of S. Tejon St. and Cheyenne Blvd. From downtown Colorado Springs, go south on S. Tejon St. for 1.6 miles to the point where road turns into Cheyenne Blvd. There is free on-street parking.

The short but tough grind up Cheyenne Cañon is *the* proving ground climb for nearly every cyclist living in or around Colorado Springs. In 3.2 miles this winding mountain road gains a lung-busting 1216 feet with an average gradient of 7 percent. Stop the clock in less than twenty minutes, and you're at the upper end of the amateur racer class. Sub-seventeen puts you among the local elite, which includes pros and athletes training at the nearby US Olympic Training Center. The record as of this book's publication is a jaw-dropping thirteen minutes, thirty-four seconds set by Colorado-based pro rider Tom Danielson.

Start the ride at the intersection of South Tejon Street and Cheyenne Boulevard. This provides about 2.5 miles of easy warm-up spinning before you reach the North Cheyenne Cañon Park entrance gate and the beginning of the climb. From here the narrow, creek-lined road rises abruptly to the west through a canyon that's cut 1000 feet deep into towering granite rock walls.

The first few miles are relatively mellow, then comes a nasty 15 percent pitch about halfway up. From here the climb backs off again for a mile or so before kicking hard for the final push through a quartet of forest-lined switchbacks to the end of the pavement at the Gold Camp Road parking lot, elevation 7444 feet.

If you run out of gas before reaching the top, stop at the Helen Hunt Falls overlook (mile 5), which has bathrooms, a concession stand, and a few picnic tables where you can watch the roadside creek tumble out of the forest. On the way back down, take extra caution. There are numerous blind corners and a high concentration of rubbernecking drivers often distracted by the superb scenery.

Route variation: No conversation about Cheyenne Cañon would be complete without mentioning the Gold Camp Road climb, which traverses the east and south flanks of Mays Peak, before dumping into the same dirt parking lot where the Cheyenne Cañon climb ends. The standard route (used in the area's weekly time-trial series) starts adjacent to Bott Park at the intersection of South 26th Street and Howbert Street. From there, head west on South 26th, which turns into Bear Creek Road. At mile 1.1, turn right on Gold Camp Road, which sees little traffic. A mile later, stay straight, continuing on Gold Camp Road to the end of the pavement at Point Sublime, which has fantastic views of Colorado Springs and the distant plains. This section is 4.4 miles with an average grade of 4 percent and a total elevation gain of 867 feet.

Most people turn around here, but if you're not afraid of a little dirt, you can ascend another 2.4 miles on 3 percent grade to the intersection with the Cheyenne Cañon climb. This stretch of road can be a little rough in spots and includes a pair of short stone tunnels.

Another option is to climb Cheyenne Cañon, then descend Gold Camp Road. This variation requires extra caution going downhill on dirt, but you have fewer worries about

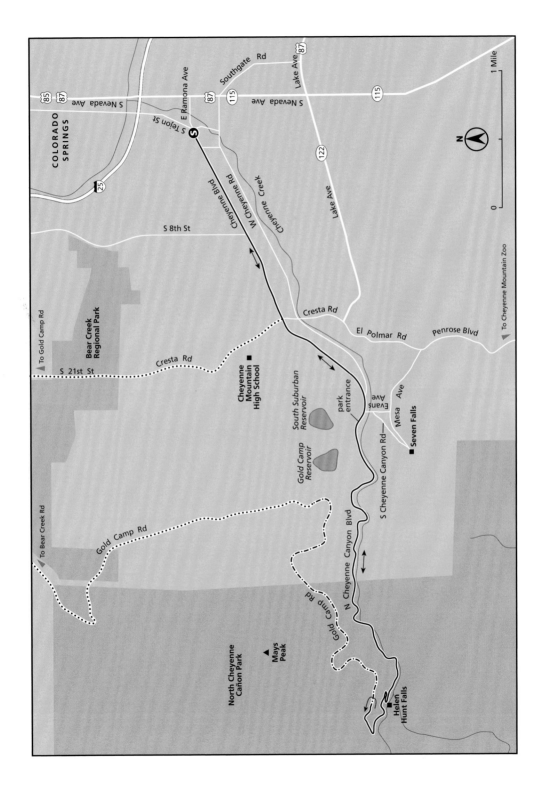

COLORADO SPRINGS

To Gold Camp Rd

Bear Creek Regional Park

S 8th St

S 21st St

Cresta Rd

Cheyenne Mountain High School

South Suburban Reservoir

Gold Camp Reservoir

To Bear Creek Rd

Gold Camp Rd

Gold Camp Rd

North Cheyenne Cañon Park

Mays Peak

N Cheyenne Canyon Blvd

Helen Hunt Falls

S Cheyenne Canyon Rd

Evans Ave

Mesa Ave

Seven Falls

park entrance

El Polmar Rd

Penrose Blvd

Cresta Rd

To Cheyenne Mountain Zoo

Cheyenne Blvd

W Cheyenne Rd

Cheyenne Creek

S Tejon St

E Ramona Ave

Southgate Rd

Lake Ave

Lake Ave

S Nevada Ave

S Nevada Ave

85

87

87

115

115

122

25

N

0

1 Mile

It's just 3.2 miles long, but the steep winding road up Cheyenne Cañon packs plenty of punch.

wayward drivers, and you get to do a loop instead of an out-and-back. To get back to the main route, take Gold Camp Road to Lower Gold Camp Road, then turn right on South 21st Street, and proceed 2.1 miles to the intersection of Cheyenne Boulevard. Turn left and the starting point is just a few blocks ahead.

Finally, if you're looking for a little more gradual climbing, add the spin up to the Cheyenne Mountain Zoo, which is 2 miles from the bottom of the Cheyenne Cañon climb. From the Cheyenne Cañon entrance gate, go east on Cheyenne Boulevard, take a quick right onto Evans Avenue, and then go left on Mesa Avenue, which becomes Penrose Boulevard. Continue on Penrose, which becomes Cheyenne Mountain Zoo Road about a half mile before you reach the zoo.

0.0	Head west on Cheyenne Blvd.
2.5	Right at fork, continuing on North Cheyenne Canyon Blvd.
5.0	Pass Helen Hunt Falls overlook
5.5	Reach turnaround point at summit of North Cheyenne Canyon Blvd.
8.5	Left at fork, continuing on Cheyenne Blvd.
11.0	Return to start

27 PIKES PEAK

Difficulty:	Epic
Time:	3–6 hours
Distance:	38.8 miles
Elevation gain:	7175 feet
Best seasons:	Late spring to early fall
Road conditions:	Shoulder comes and goes, but traffic is typically slow-moving. Second half of ride includes extended steep descent. Make sure your brakes are in good working order. Traffic is heavy during summer weekends. Pikes Peak Hwy. charges $12 per person entry fee between May 1 and November 30; $2 less the rest of the year.

GETTING THERE: Ride starts from dirt parking lot adjacent to intersection of US 24 and Fountain Ave. in Cascade. From downtown Colorado Springs, head west on W. Cimarron St., which becomes US 24 (Midland Expressway). After 10 miles, exit onto Fountain Ave., and parking area will be on your right.

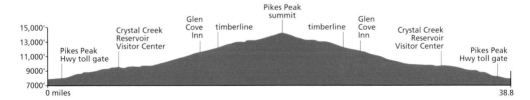

How steep is the road to the summit of Pikes Peak, elevation 14,115 feet? Steep enough that visitors arriving by automobile are asked to save all picture-taking stops for the descent, thus reducing the chance of overheating brakes. So steep that it's recommended you don't use air conditioning on the way up to help avoid engine failure. Steep enough that

about a third of the way down all cars are stopped to have their brake temperature measured; anything hotter than three hundred degrees, and drivers are directed to a nearby parking lot for a thirty-minute cooldown.

Needless to say, if you're planning to tackle Pikes Peak by bike, leave the carbon wheels at home (unless you have disc brakes). No need

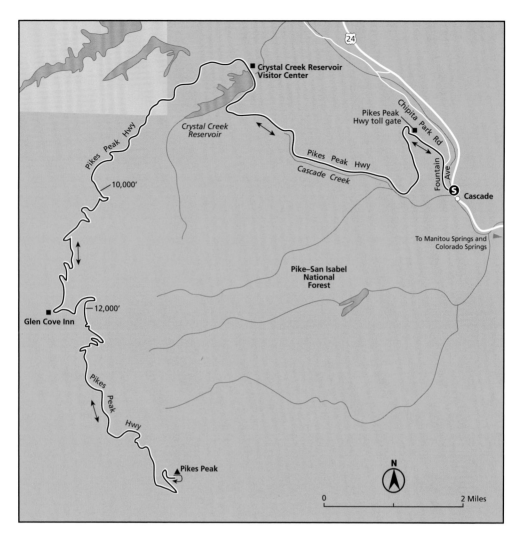

to risk braking-induced wheel failure during what's an already exceptionally difficult task. The climb from Cascade to the summit of Pikes Peak is one of Colorado's toughest rides, gaining 7175 feet in 19.4 miles with roughly 10 of those miles above 10,000 feet. The average gradient for the entire climb is a stiff 6 percent, with numerous sections exceeding 10 percent, including several nasty pitches above tree line where oxygen is sparse.

By comparison, the ride up 14,130-foot Mount Evans (Ride 35) is 27.6 miles with a nearly identical elevation gain but much lower average gradient (4.5 percent). The Pikes Peak Highway, which has been fully paved only since 2011 and open full-time to cyclists only since 2013, is also in far better shape, lacking the teeth-rattling freeze-thaw-cycle-induced seams that plague many high mountain roads.

Before you roll out, make sure to pack plenty of just-in-case gear (rain jacket, gloves, hat, leg warmers, etc.). Though it may be a warm sunny day at the start, it could be thirty to forty degrees cooler at the summit. Also make sure to start early. (The road opens at

Around mile 14 of the trip up Pikes Peak, you'll pass the 12,000-foot mark—and tree line. From here it's just another 5.4 miles and 2115 feet of climbing to the summit. (Lisa Sumner)

7:30 AM during peak season.) Otherwise, you risk exposure to the afternoon thunderstorms that are so common during summertime in the Rockies. Lightning on Pikes Peak can be very dangerous.

So why expose yourself to so much suffering and potential peril? Because this is "America's Mountain," the most visited peak in North America, and the inspiration for the song "America the Beautiful," written by Katherine Lee Bates while she was taking in the summit's spectacular panoramic scenery. It's also one hell of a cycling challenge, requiring equal parts fitness and fortitude. Unless you're an aspiring Tour de France pro, expect to be pedaling uphill for at least three hours.

The most common starting point, and the one referenced here, is just off US Highway 24 at the intersection with Fountain Avenue in Cascade. At mile 0.3, stay left, rolling underneath the Pikes Peak Highway sign. Less than a mile later, reach the Pikes Peak Highway toll gate, and pay the entry fee. The remainder of the ride is painfully straightforward: Pedal to the skyscraping summit, passing through three distinct ecosystems.

At mile 3, you get your first view of Pikes Peak hovering in the distance. At mile 7, you pass the official start line for the Pikes Peak International Hill Climb car and motorcycle race. The record ascent time as of spring 2014 was an astounding eight minutes, thirteen seconds. Figure you have at least two hours to go. Around mile 7.5 the peak returns to view dead ahead. You'll eventually be climbing up the northern flank of what's part of the Continental Divide.

At mile 10, you cross from the montane zone into the subalpine zone (less vegetation, typically higher winds). Four miles farther is the 12,000-foot mark, a.k.a. the alpine zone. Look for the "Timberline" sign planted in the barren landscape on the right side of the road, and know that there's now 40 percent less oxygen available in the air you're breathing than at sea level. Don't be surprised if you start feeling a little punch-drunk. Elevation can do strange things to the mind and body. Even one hard turn of the cranks can push you into the red.

Also know that some of the ride's steepest pitches remain, with sections of 10, 12, and even 14 percent separating you from the summit. Look around at the amazing long-distance views. When you reach the top, snap a picture in front of the official summit sign, take in the amazing 360-degree panorama, check out the monument to Bates's famous song, and then head into the Summit House where you can top off your bottles and grab a well-earned snack. The kitchen is famous for its donuts, and there's also an oxygen bar if you need to recharge or stem the effects of hypoxia.

Finally, don't overlook the significance of the trip down. The road's in great shape and full of the sweeping turns cyclists dream about. Just remember that bikes must obey the same rules, including the speed limit, as cars. Take your time and take in the sights. It's a lot easier to look around when your heart's not beating out of your chest.

MILEAGE LOG

0.0	Start from parking lot near the US 24 and Fountain Ave. intersection in Cascade
0.1	Head north on Fountain Ave. away from highway
0.3	Stay left onto Pikes Peak Highway
1.0	Pass Pikes Peak Highway toll gate
6.0	Pass Crystal Creek Reservoir Visitor Center
9.7	Pass the 10,000-foot elevation mark
13.0	Pass Glen Cove Inn
14.0	Pass 12,000-foot mark and timberline
19.4	Reach Pikes Peak summit
26.8	Pass Glen Cove Inn
38.8	Return to start point in Cascade

28 ARKANSAS RIVER TRAIL

Difficulty:	Easy
Time:	2–3 hours
Distance:	28.2 miles
Elevation gain:	912 feet
Best seasons:	Early spring to late fall (possible in winter)
Road conditions:	Majority of ride is on well-maintained multiuse path. Minimal shoulder on road inside Lake Pueblo State Park, but traffic is typically light and slow-moving. Portions of bike path in state park are in poor shape with many cracks and seams.

GETTING THERE: Ride starts from large parking lot along Locust St. across from Runyan Field and adjacent to Runyan Lake. From downtown Pueblo at the intersection of Main St. and Grand Ave., head east on Grand, then turn right (south) onto Santa Fe Ave. In a half mile turn left onto Locust, and parking area is a half mile ahead on the right.

At 3 miles in length, the Pueblo Levee Mural is recognized by the Guinness Book of World Records *as the world's largest continuous painting. The adjacent Arkansas River Trail is a great way to check it out.*

Urban bike paths are a metaphorical look inside the soul of a city. If a path is underutilized, full of litter, or otherwise neglected, it probably says something (arguably negative) about the place. Conversely, if a path is well maintained, clean, and bustling with activity, it's likely that the surrounding community has embraced the importance of things such as healthy living and environmental stewardship.

In the case of Pueblo's Arkansas River Trail, the message is distinctly positive. This well-used path is clean, nicely maintained, and home to one of Colorado's most unique outdoor art exhibits, the Pueblo Levee Mural. Indeed, the giant walls of the adjacent river levee that were once a mess of unsightly graffiti have been transformed into a 3-mile-long piece of artwork that's been recognized by the *Guinness Book of World Records* as the world's largest continuous painting.

Your "gallery" tour starts at Runyan Lake, just a few blocks east of downtown Pueblo's lovely Historic Arkansas Riverwalk (a great place for a post-ride meal and libation). From the parking area, turn right onto the bike path that circles the lake, heading west toward the distant Sangre de Cristo Mountains. Turn right at the first fork, then make a quick left, crossing to the Arkansas River's south bank.

Now hug the south shore for the ensuing 4 miles, with the massive mural your constant companion above the far bank. The giant painting is actually a series of pieces depicting everything from surreal fantasy scenes to Bob Marley to the mascots of the city's various educational institutions. It's a fabulous display of creativity and talent.

At mile 4.2, cross the river again, leaving the mural behind and heading into a forested area that brings you to the city's Nature and Raptor Center at mile 5.3 (brief mandatory dismount; food and drink are available). From here it's another mile and a half of tranquil spinning to the eastern border of Lake Pueblo State Park.

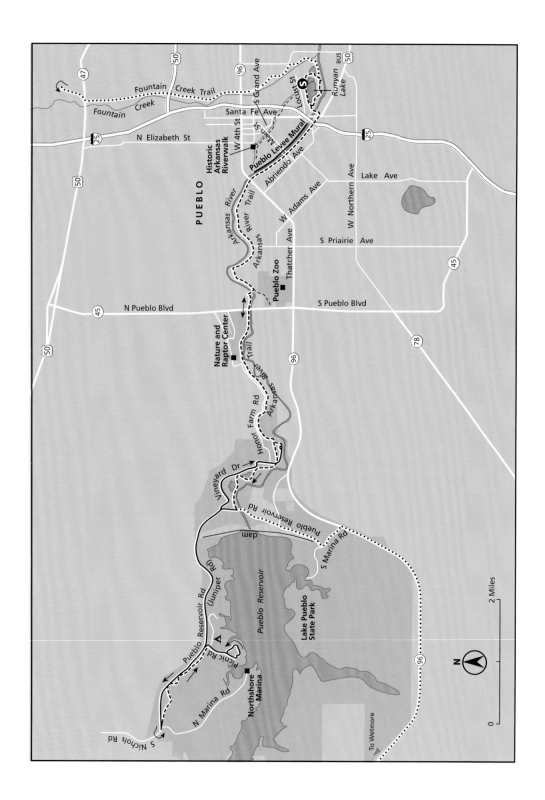

Fountain Creek Trail

Fountain Creek

47

50

96

S Grand Ave

Locust St

Runyan Lake

BUS 50

S

Santa Fe Ave

S Union

N Elizabeth St

25

25

W 4th St

Historic Arkansas Riverwalk

Pueblo Levee Mural

Abriendo Ave

Lake Ave

PUEBLO

Arkansas River

Arkansas River Trail

W Adams Ave

W Northern Ave

S Priairie Ave

45

50

50

45

N Pueblo Blvd

Arkansas

Thatcher Ave

Pueblo Zoo

S Pueblo Blvd

78

Nature and Raptor Center

River Trail

96

Arkansas River

Honor Farm Rd

Vineyard Dr

Pueblo Reservoir Rd

dam

Pueblo Reservoir Rd

S Marina Rd

S Marina Rd

Pueblo Reservoir Rd (Juniper Rd)

Lake Pueblo State Park

Pueblo Reservoir

Picnic Rd

Pueblo Reservoir Rd

N Marina Rd

S Nichols Rd

Northshore Marina

96

To Wetmore

N

0   2 Miles

You can't ride around the lake, but there are some great overlooks and a few stiff climbs on the north side. To get there, proceed to the end of the bike path, then with the large reservoir dam directly in front of you, turn right onto Pueblo Reservoir Road. It's a stiff mile-long climb to the top of the dam, and another 3.2 miles to this ride's turnaround point at the park's north gate (which has restrooms).

On the way out, you'll notice a bike path running alongside the road. It's worth using if traffic is heavy, but the path is littered with annoying cracks, bumps, and seams that I prefer to avoid. On the way back, take the short right-turn detour onto Juniper Breaks Campground Road, which loops past Northshore Marina and some more great overlooks. Then return to Pueblo Reservoir Road, turn right, and drop back down toward the river. At the bottom of the hill, turn left onto Vineyard Drive toward the Rock Canyon area. This beautiful little stretch of limestone cliff–lined road avails a different perspective than what you got along the bike path.

At mile 19.6, turn left onto Honor Farm Road where you're faced with a short, sharp climb, and then a quick descent back to the bike path. Turn left onto the path, and it's a mellow 8-mile spin back to Runyan Lake with the chance to see the mural art from a fresh angle along the way.

Route variations: For a little extra bike path time, add a 10-mile (or less) out-and-back on the Fountain Creek Trail, which wanders through vegetation along the banks of the creek for the entire length of its northeast run to the Colorado State University, Pueblo campus. Pick up the trail on the east side of Runyan Lake by either turning left onto the path out of the parking lot and then staying left at the ensuing fork, or going right at the last two trail forks on your way back from Lake Pueblo State Park.

Or if you're looking for a bigger ride with more climbing, add the out-and-back to the small town of Wetmore via lightly traveled State Route 96, which is part of the Frontier Pathway Scenic and Historic Byway. Pick up the highway by exiting the south end of Lake Pueblo State Park via Pueblo Reservoir Road to a left on South Marina Road. Then turn right (west) on SR 96. From there it's 23 miles to Wetmore on a road that trends uphill, gaining about 2300 feet. The toughest climb is a nasty half-miler about 2 miles outside town.

MILEAGE LOG

0.0	From Runyan Lake parking lot, go right (west) on bike path along lake
0.3	Right at intersection, turning onto Arkansas River Trail
0.4	Left across Arkansas River via bridge, then right on Arkansas River Trail
2.7	Continue straight on Arkansas River Trail
4.2	Right across bridge, continuing on Arkansas River Trail
5.3	Mandatory dismount to pass Nature and Raptor Center
5.4	End of mandatory dismount area
6.9	Right at trail fork, continuing on main bike path
7.2	Stay straight across road, continuing on bike path
8.7	Right onto Pueblo Reservoir Rd.

Wetmore out-and-back option:

8.7	**Left onto Pueblo Reservoir Rd.**
10.2	**Left on South Marina Road**
10.7	**Right onto SR 96**
33.7	**Arrive in Wetmore, turn around, and head back to main route**

13.0	Reach turnaround point at park's north entrance gate
13.0	Head back toward Pueblo on Pueblo Reservoir Rd.
14.8	Right onto Juniper Breaks Campground Rd.
15.2	Left, continuing on Juniper Breaks Campground Rd.
15.8	Right, continuing on Juniper Breaks Campground Rd.
16.2	Right onto Pueblo Reservoir Rd.
18.6	Left onto Vineyard Dr. toward Rock Canyon
19.6	Left on Honor Farm Rd.
20.2	Left onto main bike path, heading back toward Pueblo
22.2	Mandatory dismount to pass Nature and Raptor Center
22.3	End of mandatory dismount area
23.5	Cross bridge, then left continuing on Arkansas River Trail
27.2	Cross bridge, then right continuing on Arkansas River Trail
27.3	Stay straight to do counterclockwise lap of Runyan Lake back to start point
27.9	Stay left, continuing on lap of Runyan Lake
28.2	Return to starting point at Runyan Lake parking area

Fountain Creek Trail add-on:

28.2	**Continue east past Runyan Lake on bike path**
28.4	**Cross Fountain Creek bridge**
28.5	**Left on Fountain Creek Trail**
33.5	**Reach end of Fountain Creek Trail and turn around**

29 HARDSCRABBLE CENTURY

Difficulty:	Epic
Time:	5–8 hours
Distance:	105.1 miles
Elevation gain:	7672 feet
Best seasons:	Spring to fall
Road conditions:	Shoulder comes and goes, but majority of route is on lightly traveled state highway. Route includes 14.5-mile and 4.5-mile stretches on US 50, which has ample shoulder but can be busy, especially during summer. Some sections of rough road on approach to Royal Gorge south entrance gate, which is closed during off-season, typically from mid-November to Memorial Day. Royal Gorge Park charges all entrants a $20 entrance fee. Skyline Dr. near Cañon City is single-lane, one-way road with steep downhill section. Use caution.

GETTING THERE: Ride starts in Pioneer Park at the intersection of Pikes Peak Ave. (SR 67) and 3rd St. in Florence, 30 miles west of I-25 near Pueblo. From intersection of Main St. (SR 115) and SR 67 in Florence, go west on Main St. for three blocks, then turn right on Pikes Peak Ave. Pioneer Park is three blocks ahead on right. Free parking, restrooms, and water.

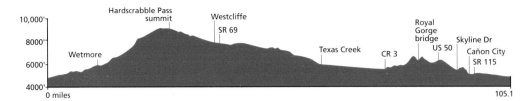

The Hardscrabble Century came and went before my cycling time. But the event's legend lives on thanks in large part to its course. While there are plenty of harder 100-milers, few can match this route's high quality of roads and sheer diversity of sights and scenery.

During this loop ride that starts and finishes at Pioneer Park in Florence, you'll climb above 9000 feet, plummet into the massive Wet Mountain Valley, slice through the narrow Arkansas River Canyon, cross the famed Royal Gorge suspension bridge, and roll along one of Colorado's most remarkable little roads.

Your pedaling—and climbing—starts in Florence, a small city in south central Colorado best known as the site of a federal supermax prison, which houses such renowned bad guys as Ramsi Yousef, Ted Kaczynski, and Terry Nichols. You get to ride right by the place about 2.5 miles into the route. It's good to be on this side of the barbed wire.

When you pass the prison, you'll have already gained a few hundred feet, and the road continues to climb for most of the next

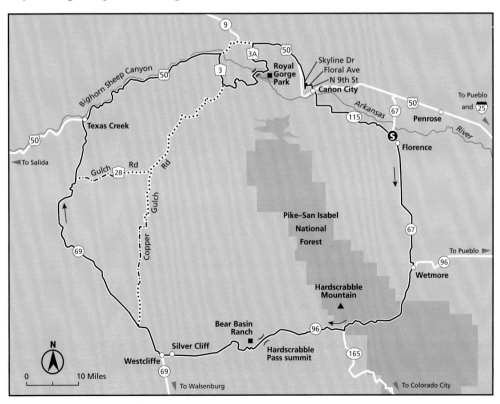

The towering Sangre de Cristo Range provides a stunning backdrop for much of this 100-plus-mile loop in south central Colorado.

24 miles. The toughest stretch is from Wetmore to the summit of Hardscrabble Pass, a 15.1-mile grind that gains nearly 3000 feet and averages 4 percent. Don't be fooled by the low gradient. This is one of those stair-step climbs that kicks, backs off, then kicks again. It's also incredibly deceptive. My first time up, I thought I was approaching the summit multiple times, only to come around a corner and see more climbing ahead. For the record, the summit is at mile 26.7. Peak elevation is 9085 feet.

You'll know you're close to the top when you hit a steep and straight mile-long stretch where the road ahead appears to drop off the edge of the earth. Then without warning, a massive wall of gray granite rises abruptly into the western skyline. This is the Sangre de Cristo Range, your constant companion for the next 25 miles.

The road flattens out for the ensuing 3 miles, as you roll across Bear Basin Ranch. Enjoy this respite—and the massive mountain views.

At mile 28, you'll begin to lose much of the altitude you just gained. It's nearly all downhill for the next 8 miles, as you drop into the vast Wet Mountain Valley. Up ahead are the side-by-side towns of Silver Cliff and Westcliffe; both have several options for food and water.

On the far side of Westcliffe, turn right onto State Route 69, the beginning of the route's rolling northbound leg. You'll continue trending downhill for the next 24 miles, but it won't always feel that way—especially if the wind is in your face. This is definitely not a ride I'd choose to do alone. Drafting becomes essential as your legs tire.

Initially the surrounding landscape is wide open (look for Pikes Peak sticking out to the north), but piney forest and walls of rock slowly close in as you descend toward the Arkansas River. By mile 54 your mountain views are gone, replaced by towering granite cliffs.

Mile 61.7 brings you to the town of Texas Creek, where you'll turn right onto US Highway 50 for the easterly run along the Arkansas River through Bighorn Sheep Canyon. The scenery here is tremendous, but make sure to keep your eyes on the road. US 50 is among the state's busiest east–west arteries, and its shoulder width ebbs and flows. Single-file riding is strongly advised during this 14.5-mile stretch.

At mile 76.2, turn right onto County Road 3, which leads to a stunning Royal Gorge overlook where a 1200-foot-long suspension bridge crosses nearly 1000 feet above the Arkansas River. The road up to the south entrance is narrow, lumpy, and steep in spots. But don't expect to see too much traffic. Most visitors enter the park from the more developed north side. Also know that this detour wasn't part of the original event's route.

This stretch of the ride provides an up-close look at the damage caused by the wildfire that swept through the area in June 2013, claiming thousands of acres and forty-eight of Royal Gorge Park's fifty-two buildings. The bridge itself suffered only minimal damage, but the park was closed for nearly a year, only fully reopening in September 2014. Pay the park entrance fee, ride across the bridge, snap some photos, and then climb the occasionally steep 5 miles back to highway. Be careful. The road in the park is narrow and usually busy. If the south entrance is closed (typically from mid-November to Memorial Day) and you still want to see the bridge, you can enter the park through the north gate.

At mile 88.2, turn right onto US 50. Four and half miles later, turn left onto Skyline Drive, a designated bike route leading into Cañon City, and begin the aforementioned "remarkable little road" stretch. For the next 2.5 miles, you'll be rolling up and down a car-wide strip of pavement hanging atop a narrow ridgeline high above the highway. It's honestly one of the scariest roads I've ever driven. But on a bike, it's blissful. Just be careful on the way down.

At the bottom of the hill enter Cañon City. Wiggle your way through town, then hook up with southbound SR 115 (another great stretch of road), which encompasses the final 9 miles back to the start in Florence. Now revel in the fact that you just completed one of the best century rides in Colorado—or anywhere else as far as I'm concerned.

Route variations: If you opt to skip the Royal Gorge and stay on US 50 all the way into Cañon City, you'll reduce mileage to 96.3 and climbing to 6114 feet.

If you prefer gravel grinding to rolling on a busy US highway, there are two options that cut off the 14.5-mile stretch on US 50 between Texas Creek and the Royal Gorge south gate turnoff. Just make sure you're adequately prepared for off-road riding, as the condition of these roads can vary greatly.

Option one is to turn right onto Copper Gulch Road 3.3 miles after you pass through Westcliffe. The first 3.3 miles of this small rural byway are paved. That's followed by 8 miles of gravel before pavement returns for the ensuing 13 miles to the intersection of CR 3 where you turn right, rejoining the main route on the way to Royal Gorge's south entrance. This variation reduces your total mileage to 91.5.

If you want to avoid US 50 but still complete a century, option two only subtracts about 5 miles. To do it, turn right on CR 28 (Gulch Road), which is 19 miles past Westcliffe. The first 3.2 miles of CR 28 are dirt, then it's paved for the next 3.4 miles to the intersection with Copper Gulch Road. Turn left here, and it's 10.8 paved miles to the intersection of CR 3, where you turn right to rejoin the main route.

MILEAGE LOG

0.0	From Pioneer Park, head south on SR 67 (Pikes Peak Ave.)
0.2	Left onto SR 115 (Main St.)
0.5	Right onto SR 67 (Robinson Ave.)
11.6	Arrive in Wetmore, and turn right onto SR 96
26.7	Arrive at summit of Hardscrabble Pass
36.3	Arrive in Silver Cliff
37.3	Arrive in Westcliffe
37.9	Right on SR 69

Copper Gulch Rd. option:

40.6	**Right onto Copper Gulch Rd.**
64.9	**Right onto CR 3, rejoining main route**

Gulch Rd. option:

56.3	**Right onto CR 28 (Gulch Rd.)**
62.9	**Left onto Copper Gulch Rd.**
73.7	**Right onto CR 3, rejoining main route**

61.7	Arrive in Texas Creek, and turn right onto US 50
76.2	Right on CR 3 toward Royal Gorge Park's south entrance

Skip Royal Gorge option:

76.2	**Straight on US 50**
79.1	**Rejoin main route, continuing on east US 50**

78.9	Left at fork, continuing on CR 3
80.0	Stay left, merging onto CR 3A
82.2	Arrive at Royal Gorge Park's south gate
83.5	Cross Royal Gorge bridge, and continue on CR 3A
84.8	Left at fork, continuing on CR 3A
88.2	Right onto US 50
92.7	Left onto Skyline Dr.
95.3	Arrive in Cañon City and stay straight, merging onto Floral Ave.
95.6	Right onto N. 9th St.
96.4	Stay straight, merging onto SR 115
97.3	Left, continuing on SR 115
98.4	Right, continuing on SR 115
99.0	Left, continuing on SR 115
101.6	Straight, continuing on SR 115
104.4	Arrive in Florence and turn left onto Main St. (SR 115)
105.0	Left on SR 67 (Pikes Peak Ave.)
105.1	Return to start at Pioneer Park

30 HIGHWAY OF THE LEGENDS

Difficulty:	Challenging
Time:	3½–5 hours
Distance:	44.2 miles
Elevation gain:	5260 feet
Best seasons:	Spring to fall
Road conditions:	Minimal shoulder on majority of route, but pavement is in good shape. Traffic is typically fairly light, except on weekends during the summer tourist season.

GETTING THERE: Ride starts at the town park in Cuchara, 28 miles southwest of Walsenburg and the intersection of US 160 and I-25. From I-25, take exit 52 (from the north) or exit 49 (from the south), and then follow the I-25 business route into Walsenburg where you pick up US 160. Go 11 miles west on US 160, then turn left onto SR 12. Follow SR 12 through the small town of La Veta and on to Cuchara. Turn left on Oak St., and you'll see the park directly ahead. Free parking, restrooms, and water.

Officially, Highway of the Legends (a.k.a. State Route 12) is a historical reference to a number of landmark events from this area's colorful past. But the Colorado Scenic and Historic Byway's name is equally applicable in a cycling context. Nearly all of the 82 miles that connect Walsenburg to the north with Trinidad to the south are two-wheeled nirvana. Traffic is light, scenery is stunning, and the ascent of Cucharas Pass is one of those great climbs that's both challenging and interesting.

To keep mileage and difficulty manageable, I've started this route in the small town of Cuchara, 28 miles southwest of Walsenburg and Interstate 25. This approach puts the total out-and-back mileage at 44.2 and total climbing around 5260 feet. If you're looking for something longer, check out the two route variations below. If 44 miles is too much, turn around sooner.

From the start point in Cuchara's town park, turn left (west) onto SR 12. You're finished routefinding; you're just getting started climbing, however. Immediately you'll be heading uphill toward the summit of Cucharas Pass, elevation 9995 feet. The north-side ascent is the steadier of the two. Over the next 6.1 miles you'll gain about 1500 feet, spinning up a tree-lined road that averages a near constant 5 percent. Along the way spot the Cuchara Mountain Resort, a ski area that's been in and (more recently) out of business over the last decade. You'll also be treated to fantastic views of the Spanish Peaks, a pair of conical summits that dominate the eastern skyline.

The first 3.7 miles of the climb are fairly

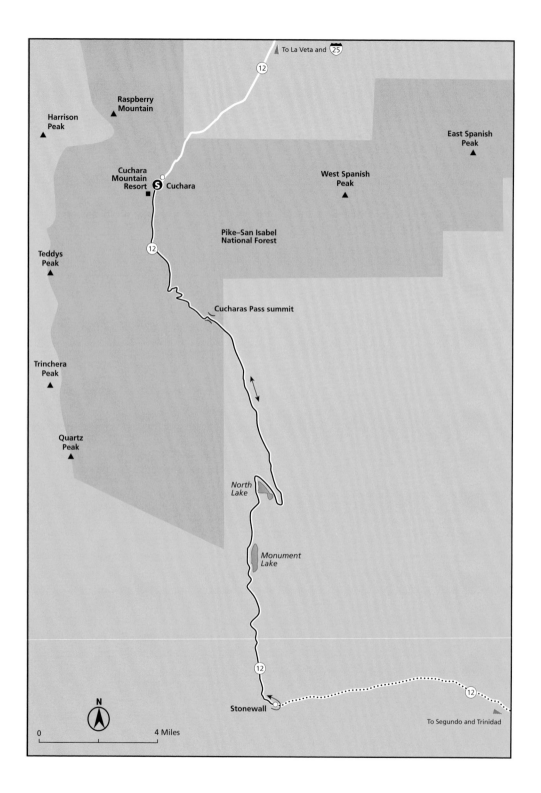

To La Veta and 25

12

Raspberry
Mountain

Harrison
Peak
▲

East Spanish
Peak
▲

Cuchara
Mountain
Resort
■ **S** ○ Cuchara

West Spanish
Peak
▲

Pike–San Isabel
National Forest

12

Teddys
Peak
▲

Cucharas Pass summit

Trinchera
Peak
▲

Quartz
Peak
▲

*North
Lake*

*Monument
Lake*

12

Stonewall ○ ·········· 12
To Segundo and Trinidad

N

0   4 Miles

The south side of Cucharas Pass is the toughest climb along the Highway of the Legends, especially the final mile, which hovers around 10 percent gradient and is known locally as Soul Crusher Hill.

straight. Look ahead at around eleven o'clock, and you can see the saddle where the summit is. There's a series of switchbacks during the middle portion of the climb, then the road straightens out again for the tough final 1.3 miles. You'll know you're close to the top when you see roadside mile marker 22 on your right.

The summit views of the vast southern skyline are stunning. On a clear day you can spot 12,584-foot Little Costilla Peak, the tallest mountain in northeast New Mexico. Once you catch your breath, drop down the south side of Cucharas Pass. The first mile and a half are fairly steep, then the pitch backs off as you roll through a beautiful little valley, then trace the shores of North Lake around mile 13.5. You'll be trending downhill the whole time, but there are numerous short uphill pops to keep things interesting in both directions.

Around mile 16.5 you'll skirt the western shore of Monument Lake. Soon after, the road drops away again, as you begin the gradual descent into Stonewall. Look straight ahead and you'll spot the back side of the small town's namesake, a 250-foot-tall stone wall that's part of the Dakota Sandstone Formation. This section is about a mile long and fifteen feet thick. It's a truly impressive and unique sight, especially up close.

Top off your bottles and fuel reserves at the general store in Stonewall, then head back the way you came. The return trip to the Cucharas Pass summit is 16.3 miles and gains about 2000 feet. The good news is that the first 15 are fairly gentle, averaging about 2 percent. The bad news is that the final mile (known locally as Soul Crusher Hill) hovers around 10 percent and gains almost 500 feet. Thankfully when you get to the top, you're done climbing.

You'll barely turn a crank during the final 6.1 miles back to the start in Cuchara.

Route variation: Instead of driving to Cuchara, start and finish in La Veta, which bumps your total mileage to 66 and increases your climbing by about 1500 feet. The stretch of SR 12 between the two towns is a beautiful rolling road through grassy countryside, with great views of the Dakota Wall (part of the same formation as seen in Stonewall), Devils Stairsteps (another giant rock formation), Goemmers Butte (a small volcano that never erupted), and Profile Rock (sort of looks like George Washington). Or go even longer, and mimic the Stonewall Century, an event that's been held on and off since the early 2000s. It starts in La Veta and follows SR 12 to Segundo before turning around. This pushes round-trip mileage to 104 and total climbing to around 7500 feet.

MILEAGE LOG

0.0	From town park in Cuchara, head west on SR 12
6.1	Arrive at summit of Cucharas Pass
13.5	Pass North Lake
16.5	Pass Monument Lake
22.1	Arrive at turnaround point in Stonewall
27.7	Pass Monument Lake
30.7	Pass North Lake
38.4	Return to summit of Cucharas Pass
44.2	Return to start point in Cuchara

NORTHERN ROCKIES

Like to climb? Then head to Colorado's Northern Rockies. From the steady ramps of Rabbit Ears Pass to crossing the Continental Divide on Independence Pass to tackling North America's highest paved road, which ascends the skyscraping summit of Mount Evans, you'll find hundreds of miles of scenic suffering here. Nonclimbers, don't fret. The bike paths around Lake Dillon and through Glenwood Canyon are fun for the whole family. Want something in between? Try one of the bucolic rural road loops near Steamboat Springs. There are fantastic paved and unpaved options.

31 RABBIT EARS PASS

Difficulty:	Challenging
Time:	2½–3½ hours
Distance:	32 miles out-and-back
Elevation gain:	2967 feet
Best seasons:	Spring to fall
Road conditions:	Ample shoulder on this sometimes busy highway.

GETTING THERE: From downtown Steamboat Springs, drive to city's transit center parking lot, adjacent to community center at 1605 Lincoln Ave. Free parking, restrooms, and water.

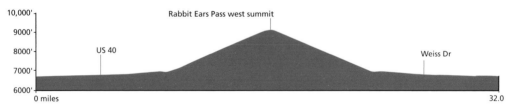

Almost every Colorado cycling community has its proving ground, that one climb where all the local riders know their best time to the top. In Steamboat Springs, that one climb is the west side of Rabbit Ears Pass. It's not the area's most scenic ride, and the majority of the route (which is along US Highway 40) is busy with fast-moving traffic. But what Rabbit Ears lacks in traditional cycling allure it makes up for in pure punch.

Following a mellow, 8.8-mile easterly spin out of Steamboat Springs to the base of the pass, it's a 7.2-mile grunt to the west summit at 9400 feet. The average gradient is 6.2 percent with 2354 feet of elevation gain. Pro-level riders can complete the climb in about thirty-five minutes. For the rest of us, breaking an hour is a respectable effort.

This ride starts from the large parking lot adjacent to the Steamboat Springs transit center. From here you can either roll east out of town on Lincoln Avenue, which doubles

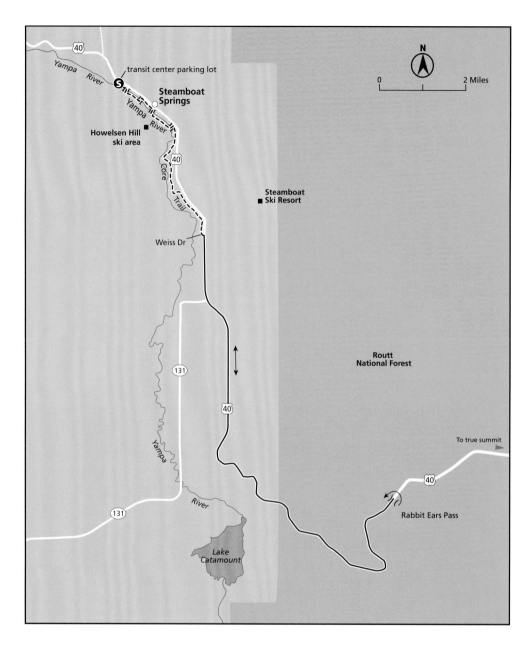

as US 40, or for a more tranquil beginning, jump on the Yampa River Core Trail, which is situated behind the transit center along the banks of the Yampa River.

Unless you're in a big hurry or are riding with a large group, take the trail, which parallels the Yampa through town as it winds past groves of cottonwood trees, prime fishing holes, and numerous scenic overlook benches and picnicking spots. Along the way, you'll cross back and forth over the river twice, and get a prime view of the Howelsen Hill Ski Area, the oldest continuously operating ski area in Colorado, running since 1915.

Midway up Rabbit Ears Pass you're treated to superb long-distance views of Lake Catamount and the sprawling valley below.

Yes, that giant ramp you see gets used by Nordic ski jumpers who are training for the Olympics.

Follow the river trail for about 4.5 miles until it intersects with Weiss Drive. Here, make a left onto Weiss and then an immediate right onto US 40. That's it for routefinding. The rest of the ride follows the highway through the Yampa River valley and then up Rabbit Ears Pass.

The next 4 miles are basically flat, as you make your way out of town and then roll past open ranchland. Finally, around the 9-mile mark, the work of the day comes into view, as the highway begins to climb in front of you in a long straight line. This first pitch is arguably the toughest, with the gradient hovering around 7 percent for a half mile. After that,

it backs off slightly, but this is definitely one of those climbs where you can find a rhythm and stay there, as there is little change in pitch on the way to the top.

The best views come into sight around the 11-mile mark. Look right and you'll spot the shimmering waters of Lake Catamount in the valley below. In the fall, the distant hillsides light up with the colors of changing aspen leaves. It's truly a sight. There are a couple pull-offs along this stretch of the climb if you want to get a better look—or just stop to catch your breath.

At the 14-mile mark, as the road bends 180 degrees to the left, the views disappear for good, obscured by pine trees lining both sides of the highway. Two miles later you reach the west side summit, which doesn't amount to much more than a large pull-off area on the north side of the road. From here it's another 7.5 miles to the true summit of Rabbit Ears Pass and the Continental Divide (elevation 9426 feet). But the road is narrower in that section, and all the climbing is essentially done, so I prefer to turn around at the west summit and head back down. However, if you want to see the famed Rabbit Ears rock formation, you need to pedal those extra miles.

Whatever you decide, the descent back to Steamboat is fantastic. The road is in good shape, the shoulder is wide, and with very few sharp turns and a steady 7 percent grade, you can go as fast as gravity (and your nerve) will allow.

MILEAGE LOG

0.0	From Steamboat Springs transit parking lot, turn left onto Yampa River Core Trail
4.5	Turn left off trail and onto Weiss Dr.
4.6	Turn right onto US 40
8.8	Begin Rabbit Ears Pass climb
16.0	Reach west summit of Rabbit Ears Pass
32.0	Return to start point

32 DEEP CREEK STEAMBOAT SPRINGS

Difficulty:	Moderate
Time:	2–3 hours
Distance:	39 miles
Elevation gain:	1970 feet
Best seasons:	Spring to fall
Road conditions:	Narrow shoulder in spots, but route is on very quiet country roads. Includes a 23-mile gravel road section. Avoid it after recent rain.

GETTING THERE: From downtown Steamboat Springs, drive to city's transit center parking lot, east of community center at 1605 Lincoln Ave. Free parking, restrooms, and water.

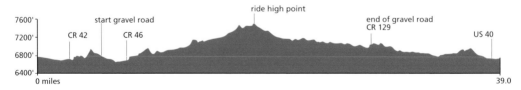

Spring in Europe is a special time. For ten days in early April, the attention of the bike racing world centers on the brutally rough, cobbled farm roads that crisscross the countryside of northern France and Belgium's Flanders region. These two famed locales are host sites for Paris–Roubaix and Ronde van Vlaanderen, arguably the two toughest single-day bike races in the world. Besides being amazing spectacles of suffering and determination,

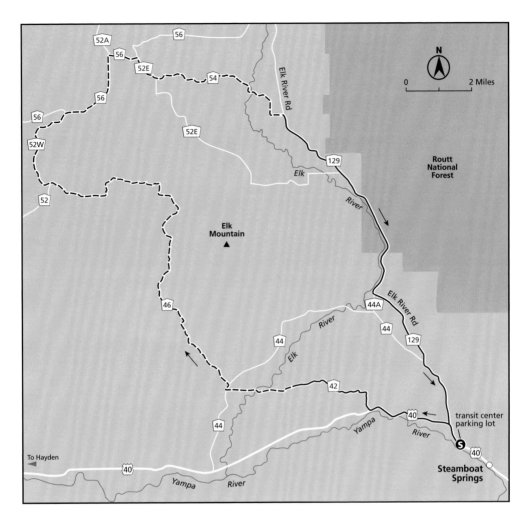

these cobbled classics have helped expand the boundaries of what is considered acceptable terrain for road bikes. The Deep Creek ride out of Steamboat Springs is the perfect example of these broadened horizons. This rolling, 39-mile loop with nearly 2000 feet of climbing includes about 23 miles of gravel road—Colorado cycling's version of cobblestones.

If you're brand new to road cycling, this shouldn't be the first ride you attempt. But anyone with a decent comfort level on a bike—and a little sense of adventure—will fare just fine, as the majority of the unpaved sections are on well-maintained gravel roads.

Just remember that as on any mixed-surface ride, some basic caveats apply. Wider tires and/or lower tire pressure will help smooth out the ride. Always pack at least one spare tube and a pump or CO_2 inflator device just in case you suffer a puncture. And don't head out on this route if it's rained or snowed recently. Wait at least a few days for things to dry out.

Like the other Steamboat Springs area rides, the Deep Creek ride starts at the city's transit center parking lot, at 1605 Lincoln Avenue. From here, take a left onto Lincoln, which doubles as US Highway 40, and then

Dirt-road riding is a quintessential part of the cycling experience in and around Steamboat Springs. (Moots/Jamie Kripke)

head west out of town. This road is usually pretty busy, but there's a sizable shoulder and motorists around here are generally friendly to cyclists. Steamboat Springs is nicknamed Bike Town USA, after all.

Continue west 3 miles, then take a right onto County Road 42—exhale and rejoice. The next 35 miles of this route are on blissfully quiet, rolling rural roads. The first of several short climbs comes at around the 4-mile mark. A mile and a half later, the road turns to dirt just before you make the first of two crossings over the tranquil Elk River. Look to the right and spot Elk Mountain, a.k.a. the Sleeping Giant, because from certain vantage points that's what it looks like. Closer in, the road is lined with open grassland interspersed with the occasional grove of cottonwood trees or herd of grazing cattle. It's Rocky Mountain pastoral beauty at its finest.

At mile 7.4, take a right onto CR 44 and then a nearly immediate left onto CR 46. For the next 11 miles, the route trends gently uphill, taking you to the ride's high point at around 7400 feet. The climbing is never terribly steep, but you certainly can make it hard if you want to. This section also includes a nearly 2-mile stretch (from mile 16 to mile 17.8) that's effectively two-track because the center of the road is soft and loose. Ride where the road looks packed down and firm, which invariably will be the left- or right-side tracks.

Just before you reach the high point, merge onto CR 52 at mile 17.8, then continue ahead onto CR 52W as the road bends around to the right. At mile 20.4, turn right on CR 56, which runs past the old Deep Creek Cemetery. At mile 22.7, stay right on CR 56, then go right onto CR 52E about a half mile later. Then at mile 24.2, go left onto CR 54, as you continue looping back east toward Steamboat. Off to the north is a great long-distance view of 12,182-foot Mount Zirkel, the highest summit in Colorado's Park Range. Just remember to remain cautious as you soak in the scenery. You're still on gravel road for another 4 miles.

After another Elk River crossing (at mile 27), the route returns to pavement as you make a right onto CR 129, which takes you all the way back to Steamboat. The shoulder is narrow through here, but traffic is light. Keep an eye out for a final glance at the Elk River, which runs parallel to the road for a few miles before bending west for its eventual meeting with the Yampa. At mile 38.4, turn left back onto US 40, and head back to the start point at the transit center.

MILEAGE LOG

0.0	From Steamboat Springs transit center, turn left onto Lincoln Ave. (US 40)
3.0	Right onto CR 42
5.5	Begin gravel road section
7.4	Right onto CR 44
7.5	Left onto CR 46
17.8	Merge onto CR 52
17.9	Right onto CR 52W
20.4	Right onto CR 56
22.7	Right on CR 56
23.4	Right onto CR 52E
24.2	Left onto CR 54
28.4	Right onto CR 129 (end of gravel section)
38.4	Left onto US 40 (Lincoln Ave.)
39.0	Return to start

33 COAL MINE–OAK CREEK LOOP

Difficulty:	Challenging
Time:	3½–5 hours
Distance:	51.2 miles
Elevation gain:	3655 feet
Best seasons:	Spring to fall
Road conditions:	Shoulder comes and goes, but nearly entire ride is on quiet country roads in good condition.

GETTING THERE: From downtown Steamboat Springs, drive or ride to city's transit center parking lot, east of community center at 1605 Lincoln Ave. Free parking, restrooms, and water.

Each year, the League of American Bicyclists puts together a list of the most bicycle-friendly communities in the country. And each year, Steamboat Springs is on that list. The small city in northern Colorado has earned gold status multiple times, being recognized for its ample bike lanes, local cycling advocacy programs, scenic multiuse trail system, and, of course, a lot of great cycling routes (both mountain and road). No wonder Steamboat bills itself as Bike Town USA (they've even copyrighted the phrase).

If you can do just one road ride while you're there, choose the Coal Mine–Oak Creek Loop. The scenery is sublime, the roads are smooth and quiet, and the distance and difficulty toe that fine line between tough and over the top.

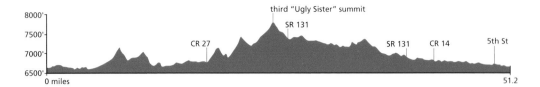

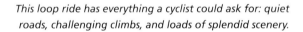

Like the other Steamboat Springs area rides in this book, this loop begins at the city's transit center parking lot, at 1605 Lincoln Avenue. From here, roll west away from downtown on the Yampa River Core Trail. In a half mile, turn left off the trail onto 13th Street, and follow it across the river, continuing on what becomes County Road 33. Locals (especially cyclists) often refer to CR 33 as Twenty Mile Road because from Steamboat Springs it's roughly 20 miles to the Peabody Energy Twentymile Mine.

In between, you'll roll through peaceful countryside dotted with grassy meadows, hay fields, cattle ranches, and cottonwood groves. Off to the northwest is Sleeping Giant Mountain; flat-topped Emerald Mountain stands sentinel on your left. The first 10 miles of this ride are identical to the Emerald Loop (Ride 34). Six miles in is the first of a half

dozen punchy climbs that together bring this ride's total elevation gain to 3655 feet. Here you rise about 530 feet over 3.5 miles before a rapid mile-long descent brings you to the foot of the next ascent, which is shorter and more gradual. By mile 12 you're back on the flats, pedaling through a quintessential Colorado landscape: high plains in the foreground, snowcapped mountains in the distance. And the road? It's in great shape and often completely lacking any vehicle traffic whatsoever. It's little wonder that my friend Jon, who works for Steamboat-based bike maker Moots, deems this ride one of his all-time favorites.

At the 18-mile mark, just after a wall of sandstone has begun to encroach on the right side of the road, you arrive at the intersection with CR 27. Straight ahead is the coal mine, which influenced the name of this ride. Turn left here and begin climbing the first of three

This loop ride has everything a cyclist could ask for: quiet roads, challenging climbs, and loads of splendid scenery.

successive ascents known locally as the "Ugly Sisters." Together, they amount to 1000 feet of elevation gain over the span of 7.2 miles. The good news is that besides a little suffering on these gentle climbs, there is nothing ugly about this scenic stretch of road.

Two miles past the summit of the third "Sister," you'll reach the intersection of State Route 131. Go right here, and head into the small town of Oak Creek, where you can grab a snack and top off your bottles. Then continue south on SR 131 for about 2 miles until you reach the intersection with CR 14. Go left here, heading toward Stagecoach State Park and Reservoir. The road trends downhill for the next 4 miles as you roll up to and then along the left side of the reservoir. Here begins the day's final climb, a gentle riser that's less than 2 miles.

Continue on CR 14 until you run back

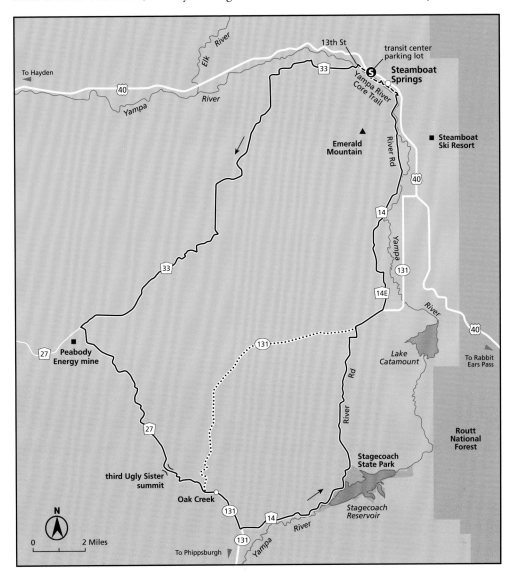

into SR 131, take a right, go about a half mile, and then go left onto CR 14E, which soon becomes CR 14 again. Better known locally as River Road, it takes you back into town, while serving up great views of the river and the Steamboat Ski Resort.

You'll also pass through the old Brooklyn neighborhood, which was built as a separate town in the early 1900s. Back then, Steamboat was a dry community, while Brooklyn served as the locale for the saloons, pool houses, and red light district. At mile 49.7,

turn right on 5th Street, then take a quick left onto the Yampa River Core Trail, and head back to the starting point at the transit center. Now ditch the bike, grab some swim trunks, and head out to Strawberry Park Hot Springs—bar none, the best in the state.

Route variation: Instead of going into Oak Creek, you can turn left at SR 131 and pick up the main route at the intersection of SR 131 and CR 14. This option eliminates the Stagecoach State Park section and knocks 2.8 miles off the total distance.

MILEAGE LOG

0.0	Start at Steamboat Springs transit center at 1605 Lincoln Ave.
0.1	Right onto Yampa River Core Trail
0.5	Left off bike path and onto 13th St.
0.6	Cross Yampa River, and continue on what is now CR 33
18.0	Left onto CR 27
26.9	Right on SR 131
	SR 131 option:
	26.9 Left onto SR 131
	36.9 Rejoin main route
28.9	Left onto CR 14
39.7	Right on SR 131
40.9	Left on CR 14E
42.6	Merge onto CR 14
45.6	Left, continuing on CR 14 (River Rd.)
49.7	Right on 5th St.
49.8	Left onto Yampa River Core Trail
51.2	Return to start

34 EMERALD LOOP

Difficulty:	Moderate
Time:	1½–2½ hours
Distance:	28 miles
Elevation gain:	1883 feet
Best season:	Spring through fall
Road conditions:	Narrow shoulder in spots, but route on very quiet country roads. Includes well-maintained, 6-mile gravel road section.

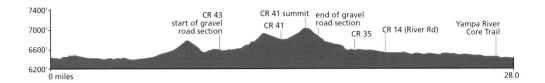

7400'
7000'
6600'
6200'

CR 43
start of gravel
road section

CR 41 summit
CR 41

end of gravel
road section

CR 35

CR 14 (River Rd)

Yampa River
Core Trail

0 miles   28.0

GETTING THERE: From downtown Steamboat Springs, drive to city's transit center parking lot, east of community center at 1605 Lincoln Ave. Free parking, restrooms, and water.

Like the Deep Creek Steamboat Springs route (Ride 32), the Emerald Loop is a fantastic mixed-surface ride out of Steamboat Springs. This rolling, 28-mile trek around Emerald Mountain, a local lunch ride staple, has a delightful mix of baby-butt-smooth paved country roads and 6 miles of well-maintained gravel roads. At a steady pace, it takes about one and a half hours.

Like all the Steamboat Springs–area rides in this book, the Emerald Loop starts at the city's transit center parking lot, at 1605 Lincoln Avenue. From here, jump on the Yampa River Core Trail, and turn right, heading west. In about a half mile, turn left off the trail and onto 13th Street. Follow this south across the Yampa River, and continue on what becomes County Road 33. Within minutes you leave

The mixed-surface Emerald Loop ride is a favorite lunchtime excursion for employees of Steamboat Springs–based bike maker Moots. Stop by their small factory and take the tour if you have a little extra time. (Moots/Jamie Kripke)

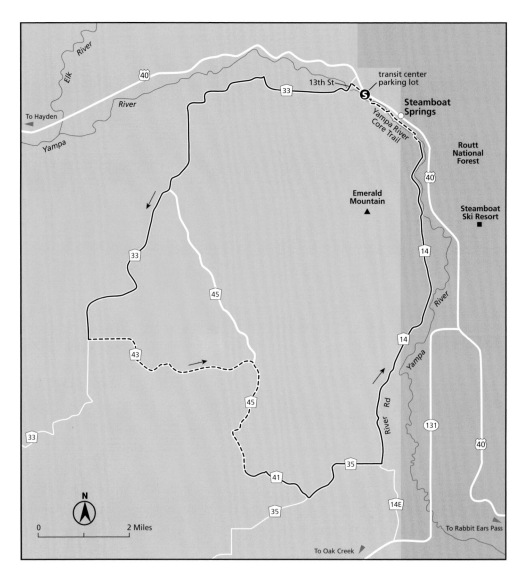

Steamboat behind, cruising into countryside that's marked by open meadows, fields of hay, groves of cottonwood trees, and grazing cows. Glance off to the northwest and spy Sleeping Giant Mountain. For reference, its head is on the left and its toes are on the right.

After 6 miles of easy spinning, the road pitches up for the first of three sustained climbs. You'll gain about 530 feet over 3.5 miles before a rapid mile-long descent pro-

pels you toward your next turn at the 10-mile mark. Here go left onto CR 43, which marks the beginning of the ride's gravel section. This stretch of road is usually in great shape, but as always, make sure to bring along a spare tube and pump just in case you get a puncture.

About a mile into the gravel section, you begin another gentle climb, this one lasting about 2 miles. That's followed by a quick descent, then a right turn onto CR 41, and another even easier, mile-long ascent. Next comes the crux of the ride, a steep downhill that runs past the old one-room Hilton Gulch schoolhouse. I call this the crux simply because if you're a nervous descender or don't spend much time riding off-pavement, you may get a little sketched out. But if you remember to keep your speed in check and relax your upper body, you'll be fine. (Or ride this route in reverse and climb the Hilton Gulch section if you prefer.)

Just as the road flattens out around the 16-mile mark, you reach the end of the gravel section, turning left onto the pavement. About 2 miles later, merge left onto CR 35. And 2 miles after that, turn left onto CR 14, better known locally as River Road. It takes you all the way back into Steamboat Springs—and offers up great views of the Yampa River along the way.

At the 26.5-mile mark, right after you pass the local ice arena, turn right on 5th Street. Then take a quick left onto the Yampa River Core Trail, and head back to the starting point at the transit center.

MILEAGE LOG

0.0	Start at Steamboat Springs transit center at 1605 Lincoln Ave.
0.1	Right onto Yampa River Core Trail
0.5	Left off bike path and onto 13th St.
0.6	Cross Yampa River, and continue on what is now CR 33
10.0	Left onto CR 43 (start of gravel road section)
13.8	Right onto CR 41
16.0	Left onto paved road
18.0	Left onto CR 35
19.6	Left on CR 14 (River Rd.)
26.5	Right on 5th St.
26.6	Left onto Yampa River Core Trail
28.0	Return to start

35 MOUNT EVANS

Difficulty:	Epic
Time:	4–6 hours
Distance:	55.2 miles out-and-back
Elevation gain:	7132 feet
Best seasons:	Late spring to early fall
Road conditions:	Shoulder is narrow or nonexistent. Many seams, cracks, and large potholes above tree line.

GETTING THERE: Ride begins just south of I-70 at the Clear Creek Ranger District office at 101 SR 103 in Idaho Springs. Parking, restrooms, and water.

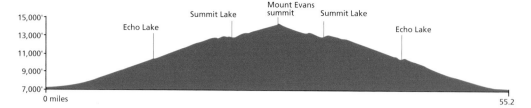

It's hard to pick a single superlative that fully encapsulates the ride to the summit of Mount Evans, at 14,130 feet the highest paved road in North America. Magical. Masochistic. High. Hard. Historic. Epic. Otherworldly. Collectively, they all apply. Individually, each falls short.

Yes, Mount Evans is one of those special rides that belongs on the bucket list of every self-respecting cyclist. It's a Colorado classic in the purest sense of the word. In 28 miles, nearly all of it uphill, the road ascends a shade over 7100 feet. Above tree line, which comes around the 16-mile mark, there is 40 percent

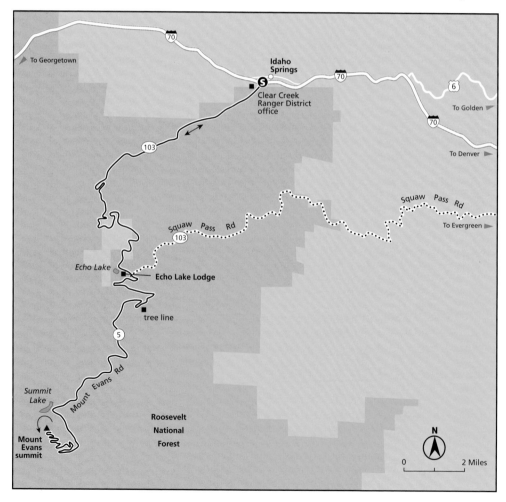

The bad news: You'll likely be pedaling uphill for three hours or more on your way to the Mount Evans summit. The good news: The scenery gets better and better the higher you go.

less oxygen in the air than at sea level. Up there, it can snow any day of the year.

But on a clear day, when the sun is shining bright and the sky is deep Colorado cobalt blue, it's one of the most magical places you'll ever pedal a bicycle. From the parking lot at the summit, you can spy nearly all of Colorado's Continental Divide, spot wandering mountain goats, and peer down on distant Denver. Indeed, up there, the Mile High City is more than a vertical mile below your feet.

Of course, getting to the summit by bicycle is not a simple task. Acclimation, fitness, and fortitude are all paramount to success. If you're popping through Denver on a quick business trip and looking to sneak in a ride, I'd suggest you look elsewhere. Most people who travel above 10,000 feet experience mild symptoms of altitude sickness. Shortness of breath, fatigue, mild headaches, dizziness,

and nausea are all common side effects. Add in the fact that you'll likely be spending at least three hours pedaling uphill, and it's clear that this is not a ride for the undertrained or unprepared.

The right gear is also critical. I've been to the summit by bike a half dozen times. I've been rained on (and sometimes hailed on) during all but one of those rides. Even if it's seventy-five degrees and sunny at the start in Idaho Springs, it could be freezing at the top. On average, the temperature drops 3.5–5 degrees for every 1000 feet of elevation gained. That means you must always pack at least a light rain jacket. Personally, I won't go up there up without gloves and a beanie. I usually stuff arm and knee warmers in my jersey pockets too.

Finally, don't forget your common sense. The weather can change quickly high in the Rockies, and the top of a fourteener is a bad place to be during a thunderstorm. If you hear a siren emanating from the summit, it means lightning is in the area and it's time to turn around.

The ride starts just south of Interstate 70 on State Route 103 in Idaho Springs. You can also reach the summit road via Squaw Pass (Ride 5). The first 6.5 miles are reasonably easy, as you gently roll along smooth pavement up a grade that averages no more than 4 percent. Then, as the road makes a sweeping 180-degree left-hand turn, the real work begins. Here the grade increases to 5–6 percent and stays that way until mile 13.1 when you reach your first and only refueling point, at Echo Lake Park and the Echo Lake Lodge.

There's a gift shop, restrooms, and a cafeteria inside the lodge. It's also worth taking a long look around. Echo Lake (with the mountains you're about to climb looming in the background) makes for a truly spectacular setting. Now get back on your bike, and take a right onto SR 5. There's a toll station a few hundred feet up the road, but as of 2012, bikes enter free. The road to the top of Mount Evans was originally part of an early 1900s-era plan to link Longs Peak to the north with Pikes Peak to the south. Connecting this trifecta of 14,000-foot peaks proved too much for the technology of the time, though, and that project was abandoned.

But construction of the Mount Evans road continued as part of a new plan to create a sprawling Denver Mountain Parks system, and the primitive road to the summit was finally completed in 1930. At the time, it was hailed as the highest automobile road in the world. These days, SR 5 closes after Labor Day weekend and reopens in mid-June, weather permitting. Some years, the transportation department opens the road a few days early for cyclists only. Check CoTrip.org for information.

Around the 16-mile mark, the shelter of tree line recedes, as you rise above 11,500 feet. Now the sheer enormity of the task becomes clear. Look up and spot the thin line of a road carved into the side of this craggy mountain. Scan higher and find the white observatory dome perched near the summit. This alpine tundra zone is one of the harshest landscapes on the planet, a place where only the heartiest plants and animals survive. For me, this is also where the mental games begin. Long, straight stretches of wind-whipped pavement promise progress, only to reveal more of the same around each ensuing corner. At the same time, the impact of each pedal stroke is magnified. Just a few hard turns on the cranks leave you winded, even dizzy.

If you're a true masochist, sign up for the annual Bob Cook Memorial Mount Evans Hill Climb race, which started in 1962 and was renamed in 1981 to honor five-time winner Bob Cook, who died of cancer at age twenty-three. At the time of his death, Cook held the route record at 1:54:27. As of 2014, the top mark belongs to pro rider Tom Danielson (1:41:20).

Whatever your pace, you'll be happy to reach the 20-mile mark. Here the road actually tips downhill on the way to the inappropriately named Summit Lake. Be cautious during this section. The freeze-thaw cycle has created seams, cracks, potholes, and heaves in the pavement. Hold your bars tight. Once you're past Summit Lake, the most grueling test begins: 5 miles spread over fifteen switchbacks that climb the final 1330 feet. Thankfully, the pitch is never more than 6 percent, and if the wind is blowing hard, it'll be at your back at least some of the time. You're also likely to encounter mountain goats grazing on the side of the road.

The final turn is a tight right-hander that spits you into a small parking lot, which has bathrooms but not water. The actual summit (at 14,264 feet) is a short walk up a rocky path. But honestly, I've never been up there. Pedaling nearly 28 miles uphill has always seemed like enough. And who likes to hike in cycling shoes anyway? Instead, take in the sights. To the south and west are Pikes Peak, the Sangre de Cristo Mountains, South Park, and Mount Holy Cross. To the east sit Longs Peak, Chief Mountain, and the entire Denver metro area. Now clip in and head back to your car. There's a 28-mile descent waiting for you—and you earned every inch of it.

Route variation: You can also reach the summit of Mount Evans via Squaw Pass Road. From Bergen Park in Evergreen, it's 18.7 miles up Squaw Pass Road to the Echo Lake Lodge, and another 14.5 miles to the summit of Mount Evans. See Ride 5 for further details.

MILEAGE LOG

0.0	Start in Idaho Springs on SR 103
13.1	Right on SR 5
22.2	Pass Summit Lake
27.6	Reach Mount Evans summit and turnaround point
33.0	Pass Summit Lake
42.1	Left on SR 103
55.2	Finish in Idaho Springs on SR 103

36 GUANELLA PASS

Difficulty:	Challenging
Time:	3–5 hours
Distance:	50 miles out-and-back
Elevation gain:	7185 feet
Best seasons:	Spring through fall (road closed in winter)
Road conditions:	Shoulder is narrow or nonexistent, but traffic is minimal. Portions of rough, broken pavement and a 3.7-mile dirt road section on south side of summit. Guanella Pass Rd. is typically closed from mid-October to Memorial Day, but dates vary based on snowpack. Check CoTrip.org for current status.

GETTING THERE: Ride starts just off I-70 at the Gateway Visitor Center at 1491 Argentine St. in Georgetown, about 50 miles west of downtown Denver. Take I-70 to exit 228, go under highway, and then turn right onto Argentine St. Visitor center will be on your right. Free parking, water, and bathrooms.

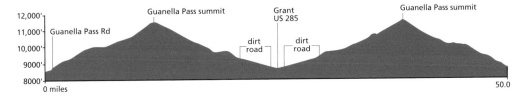

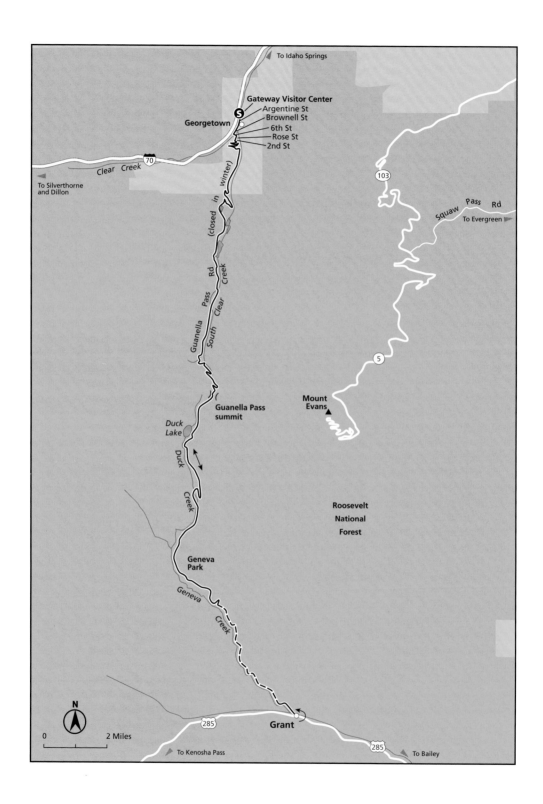

To Idaho Springs

Gateway Visitor Center
Argentine St
Brownell St
6th St
Rose St
2nd St

Georgetown

S

Clear Creek

70

To Silverthorne
and Dillon

103

Squaw Pass Rd

To Evergreen

Guanella Pass Rd (closed in winter)

South Clear Creek

5

Mount Evans

Guanella Pass summit

Duck Lake

Duck Creek

Roosevelt National Forest

Geneva Park

Geneva Creek

N

0   2 Miles

Grant

285

To Kenosha Pass

285

To Bailey

Not so long ago, Guanella Pass Road was reserved for only the most adventurous road cyclists. The north-side approach to this 11,669-foot summit was paved only partway up. And even this "good" section was a mess of broken pavement and potholes. The south side? Just as bad.

Back in the early 2000s, a professional-level road race traveled from Boulder to Breckenridge via Guanella Pass, and some riders (including 2000 winner Scott Moninger) actually switched to *mountain bikes* for the descent from the summit. Fortunately, those rough-road-riding days are gone—mostly. In 2010, work on a protracted paving project was completed, turning the 12-mile ride from Georgetown to the Guanella Pass summit into one of Colorado's premier alpine climbs.

Alas, the news about the road south of the summit is not quite as good. While the scenery is equally tremendous, only 9 of its 13 miles are paved. And even the paved sections are rough in spots. Bottom line: If you decide to tackle this entire 50-mile out-and-back, bring a pump and extra tubes, and be on high alert on the south side. The reward for your bravery and caution is a ride on church-quiet roads that are surrounded by spectacular Rocky Mountain vistas. But if you'd rather tackle only one tough climb and skip the dirt road riding, turn around at the summit instead of descending the south side.

Whatever you decide, the ride starts at the Gateway Visitor Center at 1491 Argentine Street in Georgetown. Turn right out of the parking lot, heading into the heart of this old Victorian town. At the 0.6-mile mark, take a left on 6th Street, then a quick right onto Rose Street. Four blocks later, take a left onto 2nd Street, and you're essentially done with routefinding. A block later you're on Guanella Pass Road and the climbing begins.

The first 4.5 miles are the toughest, with the gradient hovering between 6 and 8 percent. The road then levels out for a few miles as you pass three small lakes and a hydroelectric plant, then tips upward again for the final push to the summit (total elevation gain 3250 feet). The good news is that the higher you go, the better the scenery gets. After starting among thick, green stands of pine, fir, spruce, and aspen, you'll roll past wide mountain meadows, parallel a gurgling creek, spin by a trio of shimmering lakes, and finally rise above tree line where you're surrounded by rugged alpine tundra flanked by high mountain peaks. At the summit there are several pull-offs and a primitive bathroom, but no water.

Now it's decision time. Either descend back to Georgetown, or push southward to tackle the full out-and-back. If you go all in, the first 3 miles of the descent are fairly gradual and in the open. But after a pair of tight switchback turns, you duck below tree line, and the pavement starts to deteriorate. Take extra care through this section. Tree shadows can make it tough to spot road hazards.

At the 18-mile mark, the road flattens as you emerge from the trees and roll into picturesque Geneva Park. This is another potential turnaround point that gets you two climbs but no dirt-road riding. If you continue, you will begin descending again a half mile later where the pavement gives way to a short dirt-road section. It lasts only a few hundred yards. Then you return to pavement for another half mile, before starting the main 3.7-mile dirt-road section, which runs from mile 20.7 to 24.4.

Depending on when the road was last graded, this section can be a little rough. The key is to relax and take it slow, especially during the first 1.5 miles, which is the steepest section on dirt. After that, the road flattens out before returning to pavement. It's another half mile to the turnaround point at the intersection with US Highway 285 and the tiny town of Grant, where you can fill your bottles and grab a snack at the old Grant Country Store. Just be careful crossing the highway.

This remote stretch of road that cuts through the central Rockies once featured in an epic road-cycling race between Boulder and Breckenridge.

Now flip around and head back to Georgetown. The south side Guanella Pass climb is about a mile longer than the north, but not quite as steep. When heading up the dirt-road section, find a gear that lets you stay in the saddle, which maintains better rear-wheel traction. Also, be cautious when descending the north side; it doesn't get a lot of sun, which can lead to occasional patches of ice or snow, especially during early spring and late fall. Back in Georgetown, take a little time to walk around. A federally designated National Historic Landmark, the town is full of old buildings and mining structures that date back to the Colorado silver boom of the late 1800s.

MILEAGE LOG

0.0	From Gateway Visitor Center, turn right onto Argentine St.
0.5	Left, merging onto Brownell St.
0.6	Left onto 6th St.
0.7	Right onto Rose St.
0.8	Left onto 2nd St.
0.9	Straight, merging onto Guanella Pass Rd.
12.0	Summit of Guanella Pass
20.7	Start of dirt road section
24.4	End of dirt road section
25.0	Turn around where you intersect US 285 in Grant
25.6	Start of dirt road section
29.3	End of dirt road section
38.4	Summit of Guanella Pass
50.0	Return to start

37 LAKE DILLON LOOP

Difficulty:	Easy to Moderate
Time:	1½–3 hours
Distance:	32 miles
Elevation gain:	1537 feet
Best seasons:	Late spring to early fall
Road conditions:	Majority of ride on paved multiuse path. Two short road sections have good pavement and ample shoulder.

GETTING THERE: Ride starts in large parking lot adjacent to SR 9 just west of downtown Breckenridge. To get there from intersection of Main St. and Ski Hill Rd., head one block west on Ski Hill Rd., then go right on SR 9. Gondola South parking lot will be on your right; parking is free except during ski season.

Breckenridge is best known as a winter sports destination. Its sprawling ski resort is one of North America's largest, with trails cut into five of the peaks that make up the majestic Ten Mile Range. But the town and surrounding Summit County offer fantastic cycling opportunities too. As of this writing, the League of American Bicyclists had bestowed prestigious bicycle-friendly community status upon Breckenridge five years running.

The area's cycling centerpiece is the Summit County Recreational Pathway System, a paved, 55-mile multiuse trail network that connects Breckenridge, Frisco, Silverthorne, Dillon, Keystone, and Copper Mountain. It's possible to roll out from any of these spots and put together a scenic, leisurely spin. Or you can link up with one of several high mountain roads, such as Loveland Pass, Hosier Pass, or Vail Pass (see Copper Triangle, Ride 38).

But the Lake Dillon Loop is all about smelling the proverbial roses. Or in this case, the columbine, since it's the Colorado state flower. The ride starts just west of downtown Breckenridge at the large Gondola South parking lot. (There are restrooms adjacent to the gondola loading station.) From the parking lot, head north, crossing Watson Avenue

and merging onto the Blue River section of the rec path, which is to the right of the station. For the next 6 miles, you'll trend gently downhill, rolling toward Lake Dillon.

On your left, spot the Ten Mile Range, a wall of towering peaks that reach above 12,000 feet. On your right is State Route 9, a main north–south artery in this mountainous central section of the state. The path itself jumps back and forth across the Blue River, a great cooldown spot on hot days. At mile 5.8, near the intersection of SR 9 and Swan Mountain Road, turn left, staying on the rec path as it bends around the west side of Summit High School. Just past the high school, go straight at the fork, continuing north toward Lake Dillon, which is now just ahead on the right.

After catching a glimpse of the lake (it's actually a reservoir that provides water for the Denver metro area), the path bends left, funneling you into the woods, where lodgepole pines line the trail. This short section is one of this route's highlights; it's as though you're on a scenic hiking trail, but instead of walking you're riding your bike on a paved path. (The path also changes names here. You're now on the Frisco–Farmer's Korner section.)

Around mile 8, you'll pop out of the woods on the southern edge of Frisco. At mile 8.1, turn right and parallel Miners Creek Road to its intersection with SR 9. Cross the highway, then rejoin the rec path and head left on what will be a clockwise spin around the lake. This takes you toward Frisco Lakefront Park and Marina. Routefinding can get a little tricky through here, as there are a number of spurs. But if you follow the signs for Dillon and hug the lakeshore, you'll stay on course.

At mile 12.2, just after passing through

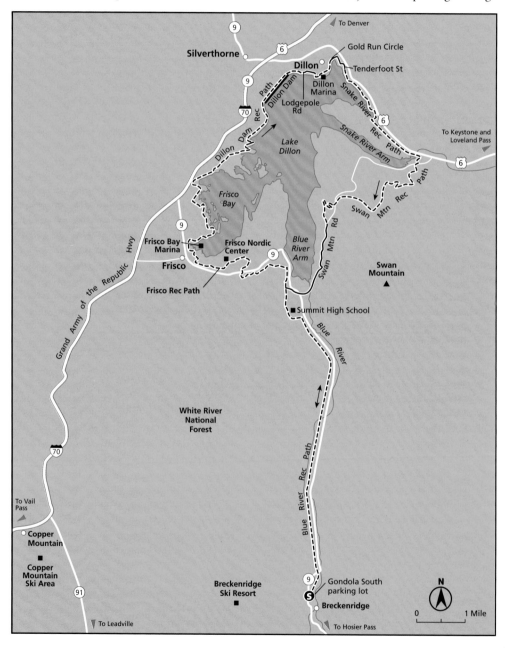

The 55-mile Summit County Recreational Pathway System loops around Lake Dillon and connects the communities of Breckenridge, Frisco, Silverthorne, Dillon, Keystone, and Copper Mountain.

a lovely section of wetlands, the path (now called the Dillon Dam Rec Path) heads east, paralleling Dillon Dam Road. It takes you to the dam, which provides an impressive view of just how much water these artificial shores capture.

Just after exiting the dam, at mile 16.3, the path ends momentarily, dropping you onto Lodgepole Road. Continue to hug the shoreline, rejoining the path above the Dillon Marina. Then briefly leave it again, turning right on Gold Run Circle and then right onto Tenderfoot Street. Finally rejoin the path at mile 17, where Tenderfoot Street runs into US Highway 6. Now you're on the Snake River section of the trail, which runs along the lake's northeast shore toward Keystone.

At mile 19.5, just after crossing the Snake River pedestrian bridge, turn right onto the Swan Mountain Rec Path to commence the ride's lone climb of significance, as you roll away from the lake and head up Swan Mountain. The next 2 miles gain about 400 feet at an average grade of 4 percent. But the pain is diminished by the fact that you'll again be enjoying the bliss of a bike path cut through the woods like a hiking trail.

Just as you crest this climb, cross Swan Mountain Road to rejoin the path. You briefly descend and then tackle one more gradual ascent. At mile 23.5, you reach the Swan Montain Road summit and a small parking lot with access to the hiking-only Sapphire Point Trail (where my sister got married). Catch your breath, then turn right, merging onto Swan Mountain Road for the quick descent to the intersection with SR 9, which completes your loop of the lake.

The rec path is across the road. Roll ahead a few hundred feet, then take a left at the fork, and retrace the route's first 6 miles back to Breckenridge.

0.0	From Gondola South parking lot, head north, cross Watson Ave., and merge onto Blue River Rec Path
5.8	Left, staying on rec path as it wraps around west side of Summit High School
8.1	Right at rec path intersection, cross SR 9, then rejoin path
16.3	Merge onto Lodgepole Rd., then quickly rejoin rec path above Dillon Marina
16.7	Exit rec path, turning right onto Gold Run Circle
16.8	Right onto Tenderfoot St.
17.0	Straight, rejoining rec path as it parallels US 6
19.5	Right at fork of rec path just after crossing Snake River pedestrian bridge
19.7	Cross Swan Mountain Rd., and rejoin rec path
22.5	Cross Swan Mountain Rd., and rejoin rec path
23.5	Reach rec path summit, merge onto Swan Mountain Rd., go right, and descend
25.2	Cross SR 9 intersection, and rejoin rec path
25.5	Left at rec path fork, heading back to Breckenridge
32.0	Return to start

38 COPPER TRIANGLE

Difficulty:	Challenging to Epic
Time:	4½–6½ hours
Distance:	79.3 miles
Elevation gain:	6952 feet
Best seasons:	Spring through fall
Road conditions:	Ample shoulder or bike path on majority of ride. Shaded sections of Vail Pass bike path can be snowpacked or icy in spring and fall.

GETTING THERE: You can start from anywhere along this loop, but traditional roll-out point is adjacent to Copper Mountain ski area, just south of I-70 and SR 91 intersection. From I-70, take exit 195 toward Copper Mountain and Leadville. Parking, bathrooms, and water at the combination gas station and coffee shop on the east side of SR 91, across the street from the main entrance to Copper Mountain.

Each August, several thousand cyclists roll away from the Copper Mountain ski area and take on the 79.3-mile Copper Triangle loop, which includes four tough, high-alpine ascents and enough amazing Rocky Mountain scenery to fill a trilogy of coffee table books. If the timing is right, sign up. This charity ride raises money for the Davis Phinney Foundation for Parkinson's disease and is an exceptionally well-run affair. Even if you don't participate in the fund-raiser, this route still belongs on any cyclist's bucket list. It's a true Colorado classic that's both grueling and gratifying.

It's possible to start from numerous points along the "triangle" and ride in either direction. However, I prefer to mirror the event and

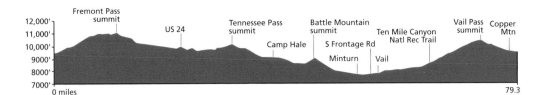

spin a clockwise course starting from Copper Mountain. This approach saves the Vail Pass bike path section for last, meaning you'll be away from traffic when you're likely to be most fatigued.

From Copper Mountain, head south on State Route 91. It's single-file shoulder for the first few miles along this tree-lined road. But soon the views and the shoulder open up, and the climbing begins. Ascent no. 1 is the gradual push to the summit of Fremont Pass, the route's high point at 11,318 feet. The

entire climb is about 7.5 miles with a grade just under 3 percent. There's even a few short downhill sections.

Make sure to look over your shoulder to take in the snowcapped peaks of the Ten Mile Range behind you. This opening climb also allows an up-close look at the area's primary industry, molybdenum mining. There's a huge tailing pond on the right side of the road about a third of the way up, and the main mine is on your left just as you reach the summit.

The climb up Vail Pass ends with a spin past the shimmering waters of Black Lake.
Just ahead is the summit—and then the rollicking descent back to Copper Mountain.

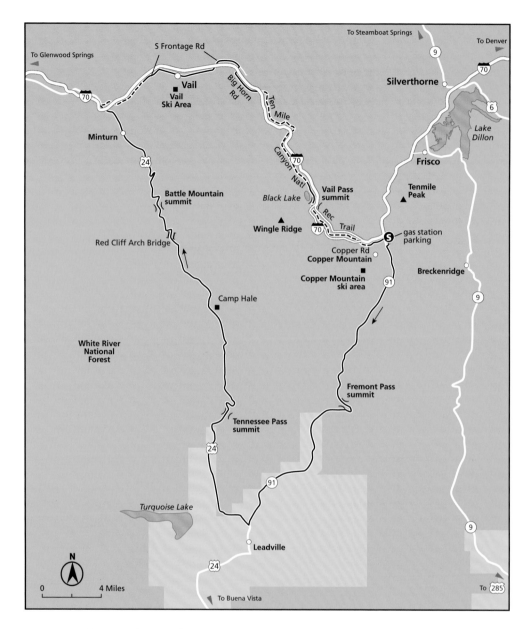

To Steamboat Springs

To Denver

To Glenwood Springs

S Frontage Rd

Vail

Vail Ski Area

70

Big Horn Rd

Ten Mile

Canyon Natl

9

70

Silverthorne

6

Lake Dillon

Minturn

24

70

Frisco

Battle Mountain summit

Black Lake

Vail Pass summit

Rec Trail

70

Tenmile Peak

Red Cliff Arch Bridge

Wingle Ridge

gas station parking

S

Copper Rd
Copper Mountain

Breckenridge

Copper Mountain ski area

91

9

Camp Hale

White River National Forest

Fremont Pass summit

Tennessee Pass summit

24

91

9

Turquoise Lake

Leadville

24

9

N

0   4 Miles

To 285

24

To Buena Vista

Once you're over the top, the route trends downhill for 11 miles as you roll along the East Fork Arkansas River. Off in the distance are the towering Collegiate Peaks. Up ahead is Leadville, the highest incorporated city in the United States, elevation 10,152 feet. The Copper Triangle route turns right onto US Highway 24 just before Leadville city limits.

But if you need to top off your bottles or grab a snack, there's a gas station and grocery store just a few blocks up the road. US 24 marks the second leg of the triangle, and begins with some easy pedaling through a flat, wide-open valley. Look left to see Mount Elbert, the highest peak in Colorado (14,440 feet).

Around mile 27, the road turns gently

uphill again, this time for the 3-mile Tennessee Pass climb, average gradient 2.7 percent. At the top is the Continental Divide and a memorial to the famed 10th Mountain Division of the US Army, which trained in the area and then fought in Italy during World War II. From this summit, another long, smooth descent awaits, as you head to the base of Battle Mountain. Along the way you pass the remnants of the 10th's main training base at Camp Hale (near mile 37). Look for the concrete ruins of the old field house on the right (east) side of the road. There's a pull-off with interpretive signs if you want to learn more.

The Battle Mountain climb (2 miles, 4.5 percent) starts at mile 43, just after you cross the majestic Red Cliff Arch Bridge, which carries US 24 over the Eagle River. This section is one of the most scenic of the ride, especially in the fall when the aspen leaves are changing. If you need to refuel, look for the turnoff to the small town of Red Cliff on the west side of the road just before you cross the bridge.

Once you reach the Battle Mountain summit, it's a fast, twisting descent to Minturn and the lowest point of the ride. There are numerous food and drink options, including the historic Minturn Saloon, which has been serving burgers and beers since the early 1900s. Just on the other side of Minturn, you pass underneath Interstate 70, and then merge onto a bike path that takes you into Vail at mile 55. It's possible to stay on the bike path all the way through this chi-chi resort town, but it's arguably easier to pedal the frontage road, which has an ample shoulder.

Either way, continue east through Vail, and you wind up on Big Horn Road, which takes you to the base of Vail Pass and the Ten Mile Canyon National Recreation Trail, the route's final climb. Just after you pass the Gore Creek Campground on your left, there's a gate. From here it's 8.7 car-free miles to the summit with a net elevation gain of 1751 feet.

The climb starts on an old frontage road that parallels I-70 for the first few miles. Look for the names of famous professional cyclists painted on the road. This section of the route is a staple of the Colorado bike racing scene, and has been featured in the USA Pro Challenge race numerous times in recent years. At the 68-mile mark, turn right off the road and onto the bike path, which immediately passes underneath the highway, and then continues climbing on the other side. At the path's terminus, merge onto the service road, passing the sparkling cobalt blue waters of Black Lake no. 2 and then Black Lake itself. Follow the road straight ahead to the summit. There's a rest stop with bathrooms here, and this is where you return to bike path for the route's final leg.

Now buckle up for the winding, scenic descent back to Copper Mountain via the east side of Vail Pass. The highway is split here with the path running down the middle. But the lanes are far enough apart that you'll forget how close you are to Colorado's busiest thoroughfare; simply enjoy this wonderful alpine cycling experience. Stay on the bike path all the way to its end at Ten Mile Circle in Copper Mountain Village. Then continue east, as the road merges with Copper Road and intersects with SR 91. The gas station where you started from is just across the street.

MILEAGE LOG

0.0	From gas station parking lot, turn left, heading south on SR 91
22.0	Right onto US 24
53.3	Cross under I-70, and right onto bike path toward Vail
54.6	Merge onto S. Frontage Rd.
55.8	At traffic circle, continue straight on S. Frontage Rd.

58.5	At traffic circle, continue straight on S. Frontage Rd.
61.4	Continue onto Aspen Ln. (Frontage Rd. East)
62.4	Right under highway, and merge onto Big Horn Rd. heading east
64.8	Continue past gate on Ten Mile Canyon National Recreation Trail
68.3	Right onto path to stay on Ten Mile Canyon National Recreation Trail
73.5	Right onto CR 16 (Shrine Pass Rd.)
73.6	Slight left on CR 16 (Shrine Pass Rd.)
73.9	Right to rejoin Ten Mile Canyon National Recreation Trail
78.3	Left off path onto Ten Mile Circle in Copper Mountain Village
78.4	Right onto Copper Road (Ten Mile Circle)
79.3	Cross SR 91 and return to start

39 GLENWOOD CANYON

Difficulty:	Easy
Time:	2–3 hours with shorter options
Distance:	32.7 miles out-and-back
Elevation gain:	896 feet
Best seasons:	Spring through fall
Road conditions:	Majority of route on well-maintained bike path.

GETTING THERE: Ride starts at Two Rivers Park. From downtown Glenwood Springs, head north on Grand Ave., crossing over Colorado River and I-70, then turn left onto 6th St. In a half mile, turn left onto Devereux Rd. Park is two blocks ahead on your left. Free parking and restrooms.

On the east end of the Glenwood Canyon Recreation Trail, there's a tourist sign with the headline "A Grand Boulevard." The accompanying description explains that the 15-mile stretch of Interstate 70 immediately to the west is considered the "most celebrated stretch of interstate highway in the United States," an engineering marvel whose construction took thirteen years and cost nearly a half billion dollars.

What it fails to mention is that the best way to see this amazing feat of human engineering (not to mention a spectacular stretch of the Colorado River and the towering canyon itself) is from the multiuse path that parallels the highway. Only then can you slow down

and truly appreciate this surreal juxtaposition of natural beauty and a massive construction project that required 300 workers, 30,000 tons of steel, and 810,000 tons of concrete. The result: two 4,000-foot-long tunnels, four full-service rest areas (all accessible from the bike path), 15 miles of retaining walls, 40 bridges, and, of course, the roadway itself.

The ride starts on the opposite end of the canyon in the busy tourist town of Glenwood Springs, which has a full range of services, including several soothing hot springs—perfect for when you're done pedaling.

From Two Rivers Park, head east on the River Trail as it parallels this flat-water section of the Colorado River. About a quarter mile

The section of path near the Hanging Lake trailhead splits away from the highway, making it a supremely tranquil way to explore majestic Glenwood Canyon.

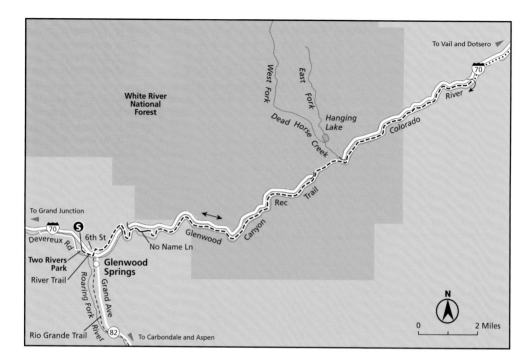

in, you come to its confluence with the Roaring Fork River and the intersection with the Rio Grande Trail, another fabulous multiuse path that links Glenwood Springs and Aspen.

Stay left, continuing on the River Trail as it crosses underneath I-70, then takes an immediate right onto North River Street. At the 1-mile mark, the road dead-ends and the Glenwood Canyon Recreation Trail begins. That's essentially it for routefinding, as you'll spend most of the next 15 miles on a bike path.

The lone exception is at mile 3.1, where the path dumps you onto No Name Lane and you face the ride's only true climb, a half-mile riser that averages 6 percent. Just after you crest the summit and pass through an inter-

section, look for the continuation of the trail on your right. It's all bike path the rest of the way to the turnaround point at mile 16.3.

Along the way keep your eyes peeled for bighorn sheep, check out the pulsing whitewater, and revel in the peaceful quiet you'll encounter during the stretch from mile 10.5 to 11.5, when the trail peels away from the highway, which temporarily disappears into the Hanging Lakes tunnels. Pack a picnic, bring the kids, and enjoy.

Route variation: Extend the ride by about 3 miles each way by continuing east to the small town of Dotsero after you reach the east end of the Glenwood Canyon Recreation Trail. This section is on a quiet frontage road with a minimal shoulder.

MILEAGE LOG

0.0   From Two Rivers Park, head east on River Trail
0.4   Left, crossing under I-70
0.5   Right onto N. River St.
0.9   Merge onto Glenwood Canyon Recreation Trail

2.0	Follow path over I-70
3.1	Exit path onto No Name Ln.
3.4	Crest small hill, and turn right onto Glenwood Canyon Recreation Trail
11.2	Pass Hanging Lake trailhead
16.3	Pass under I-70, and reach trail end and turnaround point

Extension to Dotsero:

16.3	**Take Frontage Rd. to Dotsero**
19.6	**Turnaround point**
39.3	**Return to start**

| 21.4 | Pass Hanging Lake trailhead |
| 32.7 | Return to start |

40   TURQUOISE LAKE LOOP

Difficulty:	Moderate
Time:	1½–2½ hours
Distance:	23.3 miles
Elevation gain:	2341 feet
Best seasons:	Spring through fall
Road conditions:	Occasional rough pavement and minimal shoulder, but entire ride on lightly traveled roads.

GETTING THERE: Ride starts at intersection of Harrison Ave. and 6th St. in downtown Leadville, which is 100 miles west of Denver. Take I-70 west 65 miles to exit 195, then follow US 24 south for 35 miles to Leadville. US 24 becomes Harrison Ave. Free on-street parking and services in the area.

Unless you're the most casual of cyclists, you've likely heard of Leadville, Colorado. Not only is it the highest incorporated city in the United States (elevation 10,152 feet), it's also home to the famed Leadville Trail 100 mountain bike race; the list of past winners includes the likes of Floyd Landis, Levi Leipheimer, and Lance Armstrong.

Whether any of those infamous former pro racers should retain their spot in the Leadville record book is a long argument for another day. But more than a race for stars (fallen or otherwise), Leadville is a massive amateur-participation affair, US cycling's version of the New York City Marathon.

The start of this ride, at the intersection of Harrison Avenue and 6th Street, is the precise location where that race starts. It's something

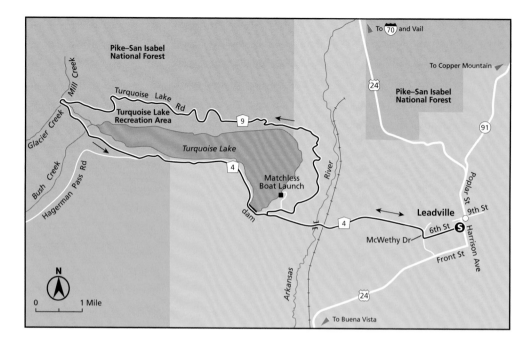

to ponder as you pedal west on 6th Street, rolling along the same tarmac that so many thousands of other cyclists have before you.

The good news is that you don't have a grueling 100-mile mountain bike ride in front of you. Instead the loop around Turquoise Lake is less than 25 miles and typically only takes a couple hours. (It gets a moderate rating only because of the elevation, which is above 9600 feet the entire ride.)

At the end of 6th Street, 0.8 mile into the ride, turn right on McWethy Drive, then stay left at the fork, continuing on what's now County Road 4. You trend downhill for the next 2 miles, before reaching the ride's low point at 9663 feet just as you cross a set of railroad tracks and then the Arkansas River. Now prepare to be treated to an amazing array of Rocky Mountain views, not to mention a superb, rolling spin on quiet forest roads.

At the 3.9-mile mark, there's a pull-off on the side of the road with a large map that details the Turquoise Lake Recreation Area. It's a great visual to help you get your bear-

ings and see where you're headed, which is a counterclockwise loop around the lake. Four-tenths of a mile later, turn right onto Turquoise Lake Road to officially begin that loop. The next 4.5 miles bring a series of gentle rollers as you head north and then west. Along the way, you'll pass a number of spur roads that access the lake. Pick one and pedal down it; the views are fantastic. My favorite is the road to the Matchless Boat Launch at mile 4.6. At the end of it, the sky opens up, revealing mountains, the lake, and the dam that created it. This side excursion adds about a mile to the trip.

Back on the main route, the ride's lone serious climb begins at the 7.9-mile mark and gains 760 feet in 3 miles, as you grind your way to the ride's high point at 10,722 feet. The grade averages a reasonable 4 percent, but there are a few stiff kicks along the way. Up top there's occasional openings in the pine forest, unveiling the lake and the road on the other side. Three and a half quick miles later, you too will be on that other side, having rapidly surrendered all that elevation you gained

The road down to the Matchless Boat Launch has superb views of the towering Collegiate Peaks, which include nine mountains that reach above 14,000 feet.

during the descent to the route's westernmost point.

From here it's essentially a straight shot back to Leadville with a few small climbs along the way. At the 15.5-mile mark, you'll pass the turnoff for Hagerman Pass Road, which is the first major climb in the Leadville mountain bike race. Three miles later, cross over the dam. On the other side is the intersection where your 15-mile lap of the lake began.

Now simply retrace your path back to Leadville, taking caution as you cross the railroad tracks at mile 20.2. Finally, when you turn left back onto 6th Street and begin that final climb, think about all the cyclists who've traveled this path before you. This stretch of road is arguably the most revered site in American bike racing, the point where you can finally see the finish of the Leadville 100, which is also at the corner of 6th and Harrison.

MILEAGE LOG

0.0	From intersection of Harrison Ave. and 6th St., head west on 6th St.
0.8	Right onto McWethy Dr. (CR 4)
1.0	Left at fork, continuing on CR 4
3.1	Cross railroad tracks
3.4	Right at three-way fork, continuing on CR 4 toward Turquoise Lake
4.3	Right on Turquoise Lake Rd. (CR 9C)
6.3	Straight on Turquoise Lake Rd. (CR 9)
15.5	Straight on Turquoise Lake Rd. (CR 4)
19.0	Straight on Turquoise Lake Rd. (CR 4)
20.2	Cross railroad tracks
23.3	Return to start

41 INDEPENDENCE PASS

Difficulty:	Challenging
Time:	2–4 hours
Distance:	37.2 miles one-way
Elevation gain:	3120 feet
Best seasons:	Late spring to fall (road closed in winter)
Road conditions:	Minimal shoulder on majority of route. Several sections of narrow two-lane and single-lane road between mile 26.2 and 29.6. Use extreme caution. Watch for debris on road, especially during spring. Portion of road is closed seasonally, typically early November to late May. Check CoTrip.org for updates.

GETTING THERE: Ride starts at Twin Lakes Historic Center parking lot in the tiny town of Twin Lakes. To get there from Denver, go approximately 75 miles west on I-70, then take exit 195 to SR 91 south. Continue 23 miles on SR 91 toward Leadville, then merge onto US 24 eastbound. Follow US 24 for 14 miles, then go right on SR 82, reaching Twin Lakes in 6.5 miles. Parking lot will be on your left. Free parking and restrooms.

The best way to ride Independence Pass? That depends on where you're coming from. If the answer is Colorado's Front Range (Denver, Boulder, Fort Collins, etc.), you'll save yourself a large chunk of car time by heading to the tiny town of Twin Lakes, then heading up the pass's east side to the summit. But if

you're in Aspen (or somewhere farther west), the western approach is the way to go.

And if you're worried about the weather turning sour but still want to give it a go, consider starting from the summit and going downhill first. That way, if a squall rolls in (which can happen quickly in the Colorado

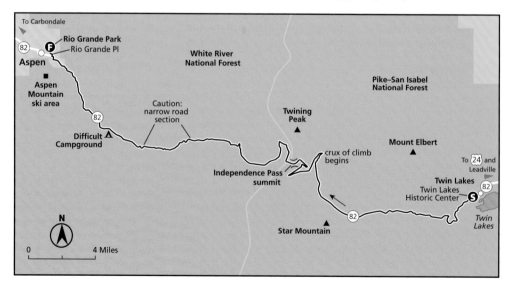

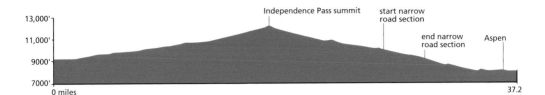

high country), simply turn around and pedal back to your car. You'll be a lot warmer—and safer—climbing rather than descending when it's cold and rainy.

As for difficulty, both sides of Independence Pass are legitimate *hors catégorie* ascents, but the western approach is definitely the tougher of the two. From Aspen to the summit is 18.2 miles with an average grade of 4 percent and an elevation gain of 4004 feet. From Twin Lakes to the top, it's a mile shorter with an average grade of 3 percent and an elevation gain of 3040 feet. In both cases, the average gradient is a bit deceiving because the road climbs so gently early on that it skews the number. Bottom line: Be prepared for some legitimate high-altitude suffering, especially if you take on both ascents in one day, which ends up being a 75-mile out-and-back with more than 7000 feet of climbing.

Either way, it's a breathtaking journey above tree line. With a summit elevation of 12,095 feet, Independence Pass is the second-highest paved through-road in the state (behind Trail Ridge Road, Ride 11) and the highest paved Continental Divide crossing in the United States. Views on the way up and on top are postcard-perfect, with snowcapped mountains, glimmering aspen groves, sprawling valleys, rugged alpine tundra, and meandering creeks and rivers all prominent parts of a stunning visual experience.

If you start in Twin Lakes, as is outlined here, the first 12.8 miles trend gradually uphill, gaining about 1600 feet. Then things get serious. Following a mile-long straight stretch through one of the aforementioned sprawling valleys, the road makes a 180-degree left and up you go. The next 4.5 miles are a grueling 5 percent, and the final 1.5 miles are above tree line, where available oxygen and shelter from the elements is low. Make sure to bring extra clothing no matter how warm it is at the start. Temperature swings of thirty degrees are not uncommon.

At the top, snap a photo in front of the Continental Divide sign and look east. On a clear day, you can see Mount Elbert, the state's highest peak (14,440 feet). Now buckle up for one of the more technical cycling descents in the state, where even professionals sometimes lose their nerve. Back in 2011, during a rainy stage of the USA Pro Challenge, then-race leader Levi Leipheimer was dropped by the leading group because he couldn't (or wouldn't) keep up on the descent. That cost Leipheimer his lead, though he eventually took it back and went on to win the overall title that year.

The primary reason for Leipheimer's trepidation was a 3.4-mile section (mile 26.2 to 29.6 on this route) where the road winds through several tight switchbacks and narrows to one lane. Whether you're going down or up, use extreme caution through here. The corners are tight, sightlines are short, and the pavement is bumpy.

Around the 31-mile mark, the road flattens out just as you pass Difficult Campground (aptly named when you're headed the other way). Five miles later, you roll into Aspen, home to some of Colorado's most expensive real estate, great people-watching, and four ski mountains (Aspen Mountain, Aspen Highlands, Buttermilk, and Snowmass). If you're riding back to Twin Lakes, it's 37.2 miles and 4004 feet of climbing away. If not, grab lunch and a beer. You earned it.

Finally, remember that due to wintertime snow accumulation, this stretch of State Route 82 closes seasonally (typically early November to late May). For this reason, it's also worth doing this climb right after the road opens in the spring. If it's been a big snow year, the banks along the side of the road may be well over your head.

MILEAGE LOG

0.0	From Twin Lakes Historic Center parking lot, turn left on SR 82
12.8	Crux of east side climb begins
17.3	Summit of Independence Pass
26.2	Start narrow road section
29.6	End narrow road section
36.0	Enter Aspen
36.7	Right, staying on SR 82
36.9	Right onto Rio Grande Place
37.2	Finish at Rio Grande Park

The 12,095-foot summit of Independence Pass rests along the Continental Divide, which separates water that will eventually flow into the Pacific and Atlantic oceans.

42 MAROON CREEK ROAD

Difficulty:	Moderate
Time:	1½–2½ hours
Distance:	22.2 miles out-and-back
Elevation gain:	2056 feet
Best seasons:	Spring to fall
Road conditions:	Minimal shoulder, but light traffic and great pavement.

GETTING THERE: From downtown Aspen, head west on SR 82, then turn right on Rio Grande Pl., and follow it a block and a half to Rio Grande Park on your right. There is on-street parking and bathrooms. The Aspen Visitor Center is across the street.

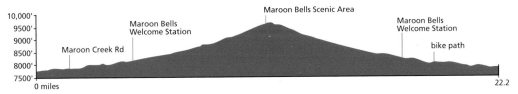

Butter-smooth pavement, restricted motorized vehicle traffic, and spectacular mountain views make the climb up Maroon Creek Road one of the best out-and-back rides in the state. This route starts at Rio Grande Park, a few blocks west of downtown Aspen near the Roaring Fork River. There is free two-hour parking around the park's perimeter and a parking garage across the street that charges $1.50 an hour. (Just make sure to take your bikes off the roof before you drive into the garage.)

Once you're on your bike, head west on Rio Grande Place, then make an immediate left onto North Mill Street, and then take your second right onto State Route 82, which doubles as Main Street through this section of Aspen.

Continue west on SR 82, as it takes a right (becoming North 7th Street), and then a left (joining West Hallam Street). At mile 1.5, enter a traffic circle, and take the second right onto Maroon Creek Road. That's essentially it for routefinding. You'll spend the next 9.5

miles heading gently uphill to the turnaround point at the Maroon Bells Scenic Area, which offers breathtaking views of arguably the most photographed peaks in all of North America.

The ascent gains a shade under 1700 feet with an average grade of 3.5 percent. The racer crowd can reach the turnaround point in less than forty minutes. But the scenery is so good, especially near the top, that it's better to take your time and take it all in. During the first few miles on this narrow, tree-lined road, you pass Aspen's elementary school, middle school, and then high school. A little farther up is the turnoff for the Aspen Highlands ski area. Soon after, signs of civilization begin to fade as the valley begins to narrow and you head deeper into the Elk Range.

At mile 4.7, you reach the Maroon Bells Welcome Station. Cyclists can continue beyond this point for free; motor vehicle access is restricted. During peak season (mid-June through September), private cars are not allowed past this point between 9:00 AM and 5:00 PM and must instead park at the Aspen

Highlands ski area and take a shuttle bus to the top. Outside that time frame, and in the off-season, drivers of motor vehicles have to pay a $10 entrance fee during daylight hours. The net effect is a blissfully quiet cycling experience.

Around mile 6, just as you pass the lovely Stein Meadow overlook, look dead ahead to spot your first glimpses of 14,025-foot Pyramid Peak. At the 11-mile mark, you reach the top of the climb, elevation 9643 feet. Look for the paved footpath on the right, and follow it up to the main overlook, situated at the edge of a yawning glacial valley that avails views of a vast wildflower field, the sparkling waters of Maroon Lake, and the famous Maroon Bells

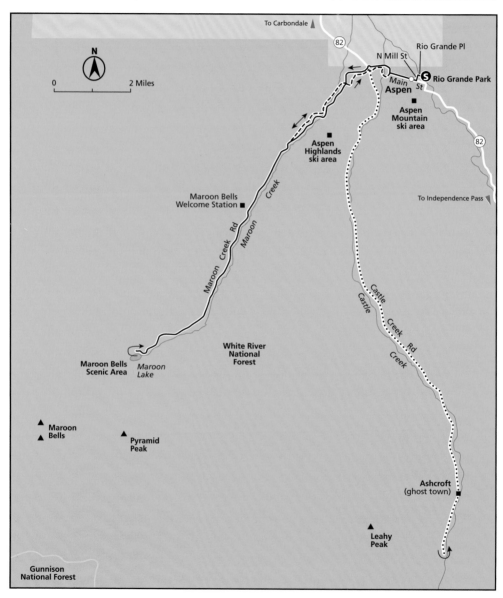

For obvious reasons, the Maroon Bells are likely the most photographed mountains in the state.

(Maroon Peak and North Maroon Peak), which both rise above 14,000 feet. There are bathrooms and water here.

Now flip around and head back down. The grade and turns are mellow enough that you'll barely have to touch your brakes until you return to the welcome station. Around the 19-mile mark, keep an eye out for the bike path on your left. It gets you away from traffic and provides some dramatic views of the deep gorge running alongside the road. Exit the path near the high school to get back on Maroon Creek Road, and retrace your tracks to Rio Grande Park. Or stay on the path as it cuts behind the high school and meanders toward downtown Aspen. (Just follow the signs.) The path eventually dumps you onto South 7th Street. Continue straight ahead for two blocks, and you'll run into SR 82 (Main Street). Take a right here and head back to Rio Grande Park.

Route variation: For a second helping of climbing on an equally scenic road, try the Aspen Double. Combine Maroon Creek Road with the out-and-back up nearby Castle Creek Road, which takes you past the Ashcroft ghost town. Castle Creek Road starts from the same roundabout as Maroon Creek Road, and climbs about 1600 feet during the 13-mile ride to the end of the pavement.

MILEAGE LOG

0.0	Start ride on Rio Grande Pl. adjacent to Rio Grande Park
0.1	Left on N. Mill St.
0.2	Right on SR 82 (Main St.)
0.8	Right on N. 7th St. (SR 82)
0.9	Left on W. Hallam St. (SR 82)
1.5	Second right out of traffic circle onto Maroon Creek Rd.
4.7	Pass Maroon Bells Welcome Station
11.0	Reach Maroon Bells Scenic Area, and turn around
19.3	Left onto bike path
19.9	Left to return to Maroon Creek Rd.
	Castle Creek side trip:
20.6	**Right onto Castle Creek Rd.**
33.6	**Turn around at end of pavement**
46.6	**Right onto bike path, and return to start**
22.2	Return to start

SOUTHERN ROCKIES

Old mining towns (Lake City), even older ghost towns (St. Elmo), and one of the all-time great mountain towns (Crested Butte) highlight the southern half of the Colorado Rockies. The area's cycling options run the gamut—with an emphasis on pedaling uphill. The routes over Slumgullion Pass and Cottonwood Pass cross the Continental Divide. When you're done riding, soak in the Mount Princeton Hot Springs near Salida.

43 SALIDA TO ST. ELMO

Difficulty:	Challenging
Time:	3½–5½ hours
Distance:	62.4 miles out-and-back
Elevation gain:	4100 feet
Best seasons:	Spring through fall
Road conditions:	Two gravel road sections totaling about 13 miles and two 4.4-mile sections on US 285 (with ample shoulder). Shoulder comes and goes on remainder of route.

GETTING THERE: Ride starts at Alpine Park in Salida. From downtown Salida, head south on F St., then turn left on E. 4th St. Park will be on your right. Free parking, bathrooms, and water.

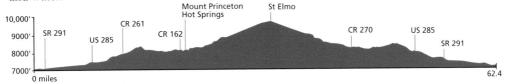

I didn't intend to go to St. Elmo the first time I did this ride. It started as a simple out-and-back from Salida to Mount Princeton Hot Springs. But as is often the case when rolling around Colorado, the road ahead was too tempting to turn around. I'm glad I didn't. The payoff was an up-close look at one of the state's most well-preserved ghost towns, not to mention extended time on a blissfully quiet and scenic old mining road. Just know that on top of 4100 feet of gradual climbing, this route includes about 13 miles of dirt road,

including the final 12 miles to and from St. Elmo, which can be a little bumpy and rough in spots. If you make the trek, heed the usual dirt road riding rules: Bring extra tubes, and consider pulling on a pair of bump-absorbing cycling gloves.

From Alpine Park near downtown Salida, wiggle north out of town to State Route 291, then continue northward, crossing the Arkansas River and taking in the distant Collegiate Peaks that dominate the western skyline. The entire range includes nine summits taller than

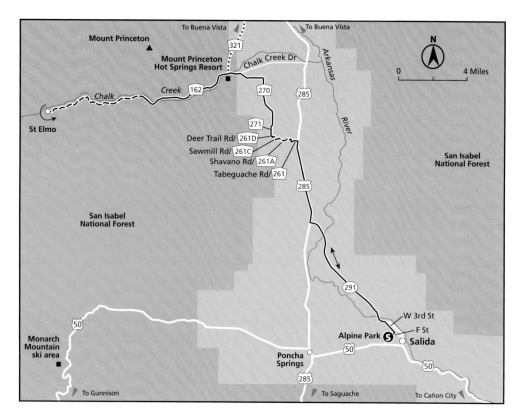

14,000 feet, including Mount Princeton, which you'll get a much better view of later in the ride.

After 8 gentle uphill miles on smooth pavement, turn right onto US Highway 285. This is the main north–south thoroughfare in the center of the state. But the shoulder is wide, and you're on it for just 4.4 miles. At mile 12.4, turn left onto County Road 261, which leads into the Mesa Antero neighborhood (look for the large stone sign). For the next 8-plus miles, you'll jog through this sparsely populated subdivision, trending northward and gradually uphill. You'll also encounter the first dirt road section, but this being a residential neighborhood, the mile-long stretch of Colorado *pavé* is usually smooth and well groomed.

At mile 19.1, you reach the main artery of this route, CR 162 (Chalk Creek Drive). Turn left and begin the long, gradual grind

to the old ghost town. Ahead on the right spy 14,204-foot Mount Princeton abruptly rising above the Arkansas River valley. Fortunately, you don't have to climb it; just ride along its southern flank as you penetrate this narrow valley dotted with meadows, aspen groves, and the occasional dude ranch. The road itself is in mostly good condition, save for the stray crack or pothole.

Around mile 19.6, after a brief downhill section, pass Mount Princeton Hot Springs Resort on your left. (Needless to say this is the perfect post-ride recovery locale, which also has a variety of lodging options and a small store if you need food or drink.) From here it's another 12 miles to St. Elmo, with the road continuing to trend uphill. At mile 25.4, just after a short but steep climb, you leave behind pavement for dirt for the final 6-mile push to the turnaround point. You can top off your bottles and buy a snack at the general

There are forty-three well-preserved structures in the St. Elmo ghost town, including the post office and the still-operational general store, where you can top off water bottles and grab a snack.

store. The town was originally founded in 1875 and has forty-three well-preserved structures. Take a few minutes to look around and get a feel for what life was like in an 1880s mining town. And in case you're wondering, according to the owner of the general store, the current full-time population of this once-bustling silver mining hub is three.

Now turn around and retrace your route back to Salida, remembering that your first 6 miles will be on gravel road—and this time you'll be headed primarily downhill. Use caution.

Route variation: You can also start in Buena Vista. From downtown, pedal 1 mile west on Main Street, then turn left on CR 321. Continue 8 miles south, picking up the main route at the intersection with Chalk Creek Drive.

MILEAGE LOG

0.0	From Alpine Park, head west on E. 4th St.
0.1	Right onto F St.
0.2	Left onto W. 3rd St.
0.8	Left onto SR 291
8.0	Right onto US 285
12.4	Left onto Tabeguache Rd. (CR 261)
12.8	Right on Shavano Rd. (CR 261A and start of gravel road section)
13.5	Right on Sawmill Rd. (CR 261C)
13.9	Right on Deer Trail Rd. (261D, end of gravel road section)
14.3	Right on CR 271

15.0	Straight as road becomes CR 270
19.1	Left on Chalk Creek Dr. (CR 162)
25.4	Start of gravel road section
31.2	Arrive in St. Elmo, the turnaround point
62.4	Return to start

44 SALIDA SPINNER

Difficulty:	Easy
Time:	1–2 hours
Distance:	17.6 miles
Elevation gain:	584 feet
Best seasons:	Spring to fall
Road conditions:	Includes 1.3 miles of gravel road and 2.8-mile stretch on busy highway with wide shoulder. Remainder is on rural roads with shoulder that comes and goes.

GETTING THERE: Ride starts at Alpine Park in Salida. From downtown, go south on F St., then turn left on E. 4th St. Park will be on your right. Free parking, bathrooms, and water.

Salida's not the first Colorado town that comes to mind when you think outdoor sports mecca. But it ought to be on the short list. Within a 30-mile radius is great skiing, world-class mountain biking, thrilling white-water boating, and plenty of excellent road

State Route 160 doesn't have much of a shoulder. But don't fret. You won't see many cars around here.

cycling routes, including this scenic 17.6-mile spin.

The ride starts at Alpine Park near downtown, then wiggles northwest through a residential neighborhood, before joining State Route 291 a half mile before it crosses the Arkansas River. The views here are classic Colorado, cattle-strewn ranchland in the foreground, the massive Collegiate Peaks filling the western skyline, deep blue sky (usually) hanging overhead. The weather is so consistently good around here that the area's known as Colorado's "banana belt."

After 7.2 miles of easy spinning, turn left onto County Road 191, a hard-packed gravel road. If you're uncomfortable on dirt, simply follow SR 291 for another half mile, then turn left onto US Highway 285. The two routes merge a few miles ahead. And while busy at times, US 285 has a wide shoulder in both directions. At mile 11.3, turn left off the highway onto CR 160, which is a designated bike route. This fabulous stretch of quiet country road has little traffic and great views of the northern tip of the mighty Sangre de Cristo Range.

Continue eastward on CR 160 as it winds past cottonwood groves and through swaying grassland, then turn left onto CR 154, which is also part of the signed bike route. Just ahead is man-made Franz Lake, which in the 1930s was one of the world's biggest commercial rainbow trout farms, shipping fish as far away as New York City. Its waters still teem with fish, while its shores are a haven for birds, deer, fox, and even the occasional bear.

At mile 16.1 the route runs back into SR 291. Go right here and retrace your route to Alpine Park. Or better yet, head downtown to grab a beer and a burger at one of the riverside restaurants. Salida does relaxation just as well as it does recreation.

Route variation: To ramp up the ride's difficulty, ride Poncha Pass by staying on US 285 at mile 11.3 instead of turning left onto CR 160. You'll climb gently for about a mile, then drop into Poncha Springs at the intersection of US 285 and US 50. Go left to continue south on US 285, and it's 7.4 miles and 1560 feet of climbing to the summit of Poncha Pass (elevation 9010 feet, average gradient 4 percent).

To return to Salida, head north on US 285 back through Poncha Springs, then turn right onto Airport Road (CR 140). Four miles later, turn left on Poncha Boulevard, and then right on 5th Street, which takes you to Alpine Park (35 miles, 2500 feet of climbing).

MILEAGE LOG

0.0	From Alpine Park in Salida, head west on E. 4th St.
0.1	Right onto F St.
0.2	Left onto W. 3rd St.
0.8	Left onto SR 291
7.2	Left onto CR 191 (start of gravel road section)
8.3	Right at fork, continuing on CR 191
8.5	Left onto US 285 (end of gravel road section)
11.3	Left onto CR 160

Poncha Pass option:

11.3	**Straight on US 285**
14.0	**Left, continuing on US 285**
21.4	**Reach Poncha Pass summit and turn around**
29.6	**Right onto CR 140 (Airport Rd.)**
33.6	**Left onto Poncha Blvd.**
34.3	**Right onto 5th St.**
35.0	**Return to Alpine Park**

13.5	Left at intersection, continuing on CR 160
15.0	Left at fork, continuing on CR 160
15.3	Left onto CR 154
15.5	Right, continuing on CR 154
16.1	Right onto SR 291
16.7	Right onto W. 3rd St.
17.4	Right onto F St.
17.6	Return to Alpine Park

Difficulty:	Moderate
Time:	3½–5 hours
Distance:	67.4 miles out-and-back (shorter options)
Elevation gain:	2872 feet
Best seasons:	Spring through fall
Road conditions:	Paved sections have ample shoulder and smooth pavement. There's a short dirt road section to connect to bike path if you add Prospect Rd. ascent.

GETTING THERE: Ride starts and finishes at the Crested Butte Chamber of Commerce at the corner of Elk Ave. and 6th St. Free parking, restrooms, and a visitor information center.

As grade-schoolers growing up in Crested Butte, my friends and I would spend countless summer hours walking the river, starting at the west edge of town and aimlessly wading downstream. Sometimes we'd ponder what would happen if we just kept walking. How far could we go? Where would we end up? Of course, the actual answer to how far was "Not very." For what was actually Coal Creek (not a river at all) was soon joined by the faster-moving Slate River. We'd need a boat if we wanted to press on. But none of us had one, so our adolescent attention turned elsewhere.

Fast-forward to adulthood, and this mostly mellow ride from Crested Butte to Gunnison and back always stirs up my memories of those lazy summer days following the water. For the ride does just that, tracing a southerly path from the higher climes of Crested Butte (elevation 8885 feet) gradually downward through the East River valley to Gunnison (elevation 7700 feet). Along the way, creeks, streams, and small rivers join forces, growing ever stronger as they collectively set out toward the Pacific Ocean.

From the start point at the Crested Butte Chamber of Commerce parking lot, soak in the views of the towering snowcapped Elk Mountains, where all that water comes from. Now head south on 6th Street, which becomes State Route 135 a few blocks later at the edge of town. There's a gentle rise here, but generally speaking, the road is flat or gradually downhill all the way to Gunnison. Your first significant water sighting comes at the 2-mile mark, when the Slate River ducks under the road.

Four miles later, the Slate joins the East River, adopting its name. Next, Cement Creek flows in, adding to the flow as the river wanders downvalley, slipping underneath the highway around mile 8.5. From there, the East River remains in sight on your right, flowing past the Roaring Judy Fish Hatchery before ducking under the road one final time in the small enclave of Almont at

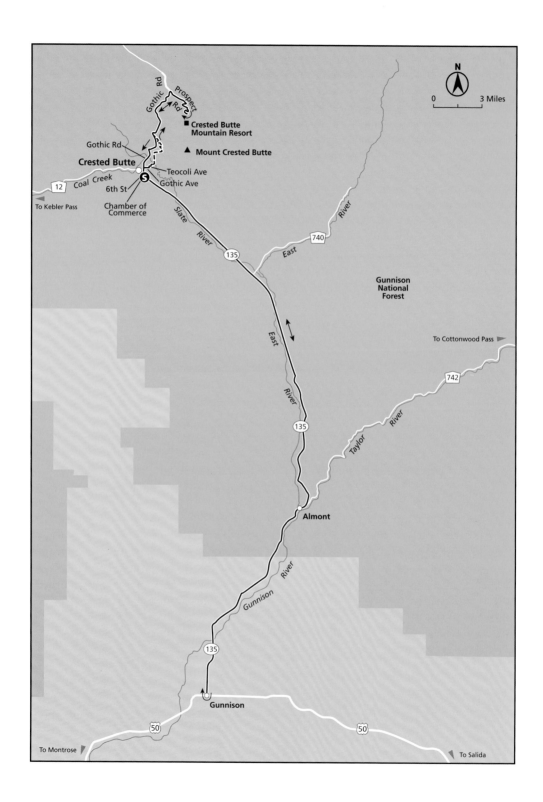

This bucolic stretch of quiet state highway between Crested Butte and Gunnison is lined with classic Old West scenes.

mile 17.4. Here the East River merges with the Taylor River, and the two tributaries become the Gunnison River.

You cross the Gunnison one more time at the 25-mile mark, then wave good-bye as it heads west on a journey that includes a pit stop in Blue Mesa Reservoir before carving through Black Canyon, and finally emptying into the Colorado River near Grand Junction. Keep spinning south on SR 135: roll into Gunnison at mile 26.3, then turn around at the intersection with US Highway 50. There's not much of a shoulder within Gunnison proper, but the speed limit is only 25 miles per hour. You can top off your bottles and grab a snack downtown, then make your way back to Crested Butte.

On the return leg, shift your attention from flowing water to the myriad mountain ranges. Cast a glance over your left shoulder, and spy the distant San Juans to the southwest. Scan the northwest for the majestic Anthracites. Farther along, at mile 40, the famed protruding peak of Mount Crested Butte returns to

your sight. And at mile 47 the Elk Range reappears.

Once you're back in town, you can either call it a day or add some climbing—and more great mountain scenery. If you opt to keep riding, continue north on 6th Street, then turn right on Gothic Avenue, left on 9th Street, and then right on Teocoli Avenue, which will lead you to the bike path. (Teocoli briefly turns to dirt road before hooking into the paved path on the left.) Follow the bike path, as it gradually winds uphill for the next 2.5 miles. Then merge onto Gothic Road, and keep climbing for another 2 miles.

The final kicker comes at the right turn onto Prospect Road. The pitch is never particularly steep, but by the time you reach the turnaround point, where pavement gives way to dirt, you're above 10,000 feet. From here it's an easy spin back to your car. And just to mix things up, skip the bike path and stay on Gothic Road all the way back to town. It's a gentle, winding descent that will have you flowing like water.

0.0	From Crested Butte Chamber of Commerce, head south on 6th St.
0.1	Continue south on SR 135
17.4	Arrive in Almont
26.3	Arrive in Gunnison
27.3	Turn around at US 50 intersection
54.5	Arrive in Crested Butte
54.8	Right on Gothic Ave.
55.1	Left on 9th St., then immediate right on Teocoli Ave.
55.2	Follow dirt road 0.25 mile to bike path
58.0	Exit bike path, and continue up Gothic Rd.
59.6	Right on Prospect Rd.
61.4	Arrive at Prospect Rd. summit and turn around
63.3	Left on Gothic Rd.
67.4	Return to start

46 COTTONWOOD PASS

Difficulty:	Challenging to Epic
Time:	4–6 hours
Distance:	68.2 miles point-to-point
Elevation gain:	4452 feet
Best seasons:	Late spring to early fall (road closed seasonally)
Road conditions:	Has 16.8 miles of dirt road, including final 13.7 miles to summit of Cottonwood Pass. Avoid these sections after recent rain. Cottonwood Pass closed in winter (typically early November to late May). Check CoTrip.org for more information. Remainder of route has minimal shoulder and minimal traffic.

GETTING THERE: Ride starts at Crested Butte Chamber of Commerce at corner of Elk Ave. and 6th St. Free parking, water, restrooms, and a visitor information center.

The long grind up the west side of Cottonwood Pass isn't the toughest climb in the state—but it's damn close. With an approach that's predominantly uphill for 32 miles, a total elevation gain of nearly 4500 feet, and a summit elevation of 12,126 feet, this ride is a beast. And unlike the usual suspects in the hardest-in-the-state conversation—Pikes Peak (Ride 27) and Mount Evans (Ride 35)—Cottonwood Pass is not fully paved. If you want to bag this summit from the west, you're going to have to deal with some dirt.

So why not just ride up and down the fully paved east side from Buena Vista? You absolutely can. It's a beautiful and brutal affair in its own right. But doing so means missing scenic and serene Taylor River Canyon and the spectacularly vast vistas of Taylor Park.

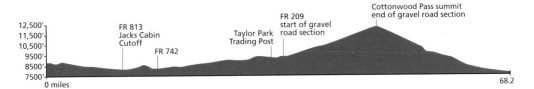

And hey, doing things the hard way is more fun sometimes.

I like to start this ride in Crested Butte, but you can also roll from Gunnison (same total distance) or Almont (11 miles shorter). From Crested Butte, head south on State Route 135 through the East River valley, then turn left at mile 11.7 onto Forest Road 813 (better known locally as Jacks Cabin Cutoff). A mile ahead is the first of the route's two dirt road sections, but it's usually well graded and no problem on a road bike.

Once you're on dirt, you wind gradually uphill 2 miles past grazing cattle and wide-open grassland, then descend for a mile to the end of the dirt and the intersection with FR 742. Turn left and head up Taylor Canyon. This fabulous stretch of quiet road is in great shape since it got a fresh coat of pavement in 2012. Initially, you're out in the open, rolling past hay fields and horse ranches. But soon the red canyon walls and surrounding pine forest close in. The remainder of the climb is in trees, broken only by the occasional glimpse of the Taylor River. The road trends uphill for 16 miles, but the gradient is shallow, 2–3 percent tops. It only gets tough at the approach to Taylor Park Reservoir, elevation 9360 feet.

Here you're treated to one of my favorite views in the state, the giant man-made lake shimmering in the foreground, a wall of granite mountains looming to the northeast. The road levels out for the next 3 miles, as you head north through Taylor Park, passing a marina and then the Taylor Park Trading Post (mile 33.2). If you need water or food, get it now. The real climbing starts just up the road.

Two miles ahead, turn right on FR 209. Over the next 13.7 miles—all unpaved—you gain almost 2800 feet. The pitch is never terribly steep, 4 percent on average. But because you're on a sometimes bumpy surface, progress is slow. In 2012, when the USA Pro Challenge went over Cottonwood Pass, the fastest pros covered this span in about fifty minutes.

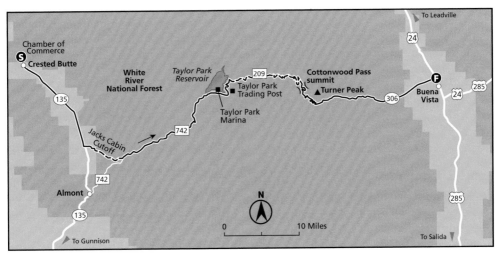

The east side of Cottonwood Pass is paved all the way to the summit, making it a superb stretch of road to climb to—or descend from—the Continental Divide.

Figure it'll take you at least ninety minutes. The first 9 miles of the climb are lined by pine forest, with only the occasional long-distance view. But at tree line (roughly 11,000 feet), things open up with the mighty Sawatch Range dominating the eastern skyline and Taylor Park now far below to the west.

Around mile 46, the road twists back and forth on itself through a series of switch-backs. Here you can finally see the path to the summit, a mile-long stretch of straight road climbing left to right on a narrow shelf about 500 vertical feet above you. A mile and half later, you pass through another set of switch-backs and reach that straight stretch. Now the summit is less than a mile away. Ignore the pain and enjoy the view. It's as good as it gets.

Pavement returns at the summit. Grab a picture in front of the Continental Divide sign, then zoom down the east side. This is a superb descent full of sweeping turns for the first 4.5 miles, then long straight stretches the rest of the way to Buena Vista, 19.3 miles away.

It's also possible (and far less logistically challenging) to turn around at the sum-mit and head back the way you came. But descending the dirt section on a road bike can be dicey unless you catch it after a recent magnesium chloride application when dust is low and the surface hard packed. If you decide to try it, bring spare tubes and a pair of padded cycling gloves.

Route variation: Another great option (without dirt roads) is the aforementioned east side climb of Cottonwood Pass from

Buena Vista. This tough but beautiful 38.7-mile up-and-back route gains 4343 feet and takes two and a half to four hours. The first half of the ascent is mostly flats with a few gentle rollers. The second half is nasty, with a half-mile-long 10 percent pitch around mile 12, and then 7 miles of 6 percent average that gains 2200 feet, all of it above 10,000 feet.

MILEAGE LOG

0.0	From Crested Butte Chamber of Commerce, head south on SR 135
11.7	Left onto FR 813 (Jacks Cabin Cutoff)
12.8	Start gravel road section
15.9	Left onto FR 742 (end of gravel road section)
33.2	Pass Taylor Park Trading Post
35.2	Right onto FR 209 (start of gravel road section)
48.9	Cottonwood Pass summit (end of gravel road section)
49.0	Straight onto SR 306
68.2	Arrive in Buena Vista

47 OHIO CREEK ROAD

Difficulty:	Easy
Time:	1–2 hours
Distance:	31.9 miles out-and-back
Elevation gain:	746 feet
Best seasons:	Spring to fall
Road conditions:	Minimal shoulder, but traffic very light on majority of route.

GETTING THERE: Ride starts at IOOF Park at corner of SR 135 (Main St.) and W. Virginia Ave. in downtown Gunnison. From intersection of US 50 and SR 135, go one block north on Main St., then turn right on W. Virginia Ave. Small park will be on your immediate left. Free on-street parking, bathrooms, and water.

Looped cycling routes are sometimes tough to come by in Colorado. Mountains get in the way. Backroads are often unpaved and rough. The Gunnison area is no exception. That doesn't mean that there's no high-quality road riding. You just need to be willing to embrace the out-and-back, such as this tranquil spin on Ohio Creek Road.

The ride starts at the IOOF Park on West Virginia Avenue in downtown Gunnison. From there, avoid the traffic on Main Street by heading east on West Virginia for two blocks, then take a left onto North Iowa Street (designated bike route). Continue north for five blocks, then take a left onto Denver Avenue. Two blocks later, take a right onto Main Street (State Route 135), which has an ample shoulder.

Continue north out of Gunnison toward Crested Butte, another great out-and-back excursion (Ride 45). At mile 2.6, cross the Gunnison River. A mile later, spot the sign for

One of the hazards of riding bikes in Colorado is the occasional encounter with a cattle drive. Your safest path through is just behind the rear bumper of a car.

Ohio Creek Road (a.k.a. County Road 730). Go left and that's basically it for routefinding. You spend the next 12.4 miles spinning northwest along Ohio Creek. In the distance, spot the flat-faced Anthracite Mountains. Nearer is a mix of rolling hills, wide-open grassland, cottonwood groves, grazing cattle, and the occasional farmhouse, barn, and corral. It's a quintessential western panorama.

The road has a minimal shoulder and a few potholes here and there, but traffic is light—unless you run into a cattle drive, which happened the first time I did this ride.

If that happens to you, wait until a car comes, then tuck yourself in behind it, and follow it through the herd.

Turn around shy of the 16-mile mark where the road forks and pavement gives way to dirt. It's possible to continue on the left fork all the way to Crested Butte via CR 730 to Kebler Pass (34 miles one-way). But the road to Kebler Pass can get pretty rough and is not particularly road bike–friendly. Bring your cyclocross or mountain bike (and a lot of water) if you decide to take on that adventure.

Once you turn around, it's an easy 16-mile

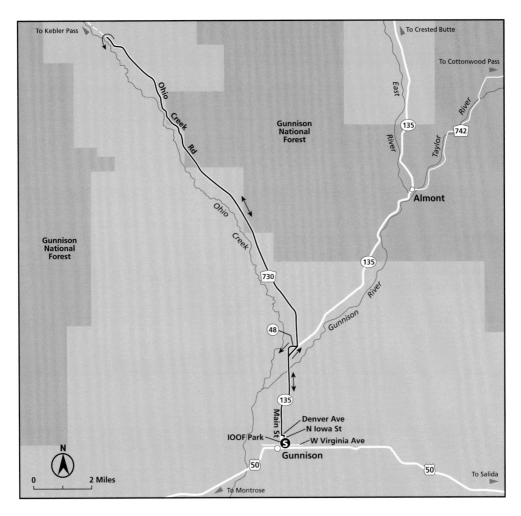

spin back to Gunnison. The road trends downhill and there's often a tailwind. At the 28.3-mile mark, take a right onto CR 48 (Old SR 135), which intersects new SR 135 a mile later. Take a right here, and retrace your route back to the park.

MILEAGE LOG

0.0	From IOOF Park in Gunnison, head east on W. Virginia Ave.
0.2	Left onto N. Iowa St.
0.4	Left onto Denver Ave.
0.5	Right onto SR 135 (Main St.)
3.5	Left onto Ohio Creek Rd. (CR 730)
15.9	Reach turnaround point at end of pavement
28.3	Right onto CR 48 (Old SR 135)
29.0	Right onto SR 135
31.9	Return to start

48 NORTH COCHETOPA PASS

Difficulty:	Challenging
Time:	3½–5 hours
Distance:	62 miles out-and-back
Elevation gain:	2979 feet
Best seasons:	Spring to fall
Road conditions:	Shoulder comes and goes, but traffic is light. Some sections of broken pavement.

GETTING THERE: Ride starts from Saguache Public Library parking lot at 702 Pitkin Ave. in Saguache, which is 180 miles southwest of Denver via US 285 south. Entering Saguache from the north, turn left at intersection of US 285 and Pitkin Ave. Library is on immediate left. Free parking, restrooms, and water.

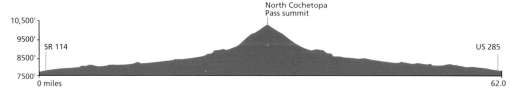

Near the center of the state, there's a stretch of quiet highway most Colorado cyclists have never heard of. To your average Front Range weekend warrior, State Route 114 is merely an obscure line on a map, a lightly traveled road connecting the tiny town of Saguache with US Highway 50.

In between are a handful of ranches, a couple campgrounds, a few dirt road turn-offs, and not much else. Unless you live in the area (few people do), it's unlikely you'd end up here. There are quicker ways to get around this part of Colorado. Of course, that's the allure of this ride—silence, solitude, natural beauty, and the chance to pedal to the summit of 10,135-foot North Cochetopa Pass, which sits on the Continental Divide.

Because it's closer to the Front Range and there's a larger shoulder on the east half of SR 114, I've opted to start this out-and-back route from Saguache. The SR 114 and US 50 intersection—or even nearby Gunnison—

are also viable start points. (See route variations below for more details.) Whichever you choose, bring adequate supplies, food, and drinks. There are no services out here.

From the Saguache Public Library, head one block west, turn right onto US 285, go four blocks north, and turn left onto SR 114. That's it for routefinding. The road is in fair condition, with an occasional crack or seam, and a shoulder that ranges from single-file wide to nonexistent.

The first 7.5 miles are dead straight, as you head into a wide, flat valley, with Sagua-che Creek gurgling on your left. Behind you (make sure to look) is the impressive Sangre de Cristo Range. Up ahead spy the rolling Cochetopa Hills dotted with pine trees, wild-flowers, and fragrant sagebrush. These hills are the creation of the Cochetopa Dome, a volcano that didn't quite make it to the surface but still managed to lift up the surrounding countryside.

The hills that make up North Cochetopa Pass were created by the Cochetopa Dome, a volcano that didn't quite make it to the surface.

The road trends gently uphill for the first 23 miles, then stair-steps for 3 miles before the tough, final 5-mile push to the summit. Along the way, you'll depart the open range, moving into piney forest bordered by walls of hardened lava and remnants of eroded pinnacles that appear as whimsical, odd-shaped rock outcroppings. Up top there's a large pullout with a summit sign commemorating your achievement, plus a few interpretive plaques, one of which explains that mountain lions, bobcats, and lynxes all make their home here in the Rio Grande National Forest. Read up and rest up, then enjoy the mellow spin back to Saguache, experiencing all this great scenery and solitude from a different vantage.

Route variations: To tackle North Cochetopa Pass from Gunnison, pedal east on US 50 for 8 miles, then turn right onto SR 114 and it's 31 miles to the summit. Total elevation

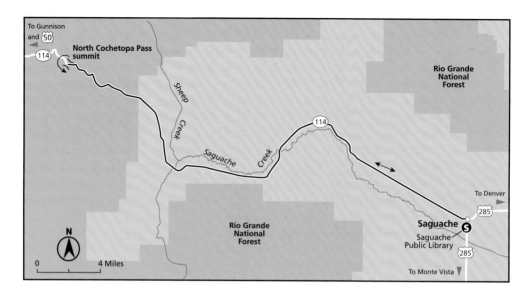

gain is around 2800 feet. Like the east-side approach, the scenery is sublime, highlighted by the 8-mile trip through curvy Cochet- opa Canyon, where Cochetopa Creek cuts through steep walls of pink-hued granite. Shoulder is minimal.

MILEAGE LOG

0.0	Right out of Saguache Public Library parking lot
0.1	Right onto US 285
0.3	Left onto SR 114
31.0	Reach North Cochetopa Pass summit and turn around
61.7	Right onto US 285
61.9	Left onto Pitkin Ave.
62.0	Return to start

49 BLACK MESA

Difficulty:	Challenging
Time:	5–7 hours
Distance:	83.5 miles out-and-back
Elevation gain:	7205 feet
Best seasons:	Spring to fall
Road conditions:	Shoulder comes and goes, but entire route is on lightly traveled secondary highway that is part of the West Elk Loop Scenic and Historic Byway.

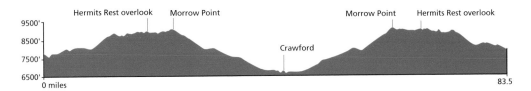

9500'
8500'
7500'
6500'

Hermits Rest overlook   Morrow Point   Morrow Point   Hermits Rest overlook

Crawford

0 miles   83.5

GETTING THERE: Ride starts at Lake Fork Campground, near intersection of US 50 and SR 92, 27 miles west of Gunnison and 200 miles southwest of Denver via US 285 south to US 50 west. From the intersection of US 50 and SR 135 in Gunnison, head west on US 50, then exit onto SR 92. Campground entrance is on immediate right. Free parking, restrooms, and water.

When Dave Wiens talks, people listen—at least when it's about cycling. The longtime pro racer and Gunnison resident won the famed Leadville 100 mountain bike race a record six straight times. He's also a leader in local cycling advocacy efforts and organizes two of the state's best-known bike events, the Gunnison Growler and Dave Wiens West Elk Bicycle Classic (see the route variation below). Wiens has also been riding the trails and roads of Colorado most of his adult life. His favorite road ride? Black Mesa, which is all the endorsement this route needs.

Pedaling the 42-mile section of State Route 92 from US Highway 50 to the small town of Crawford is a truly singular cycling experience, highlighted by stunning views into the depths of the Black Canyon of the Gunnison from atop a buttery smooth road that's blissfully quiet, even during peak summer tourist season.

The ride starts from the Lake Fork Campground, just north of the intersection of US 50 and SR 92, 27 miles west of Gunnison. From the campground overlooking Blue Mesa Reservoir, head west, crossing the Blue

The road between Black Mesa and Crawford is quiet, scenic, and perfect for riding a bike.

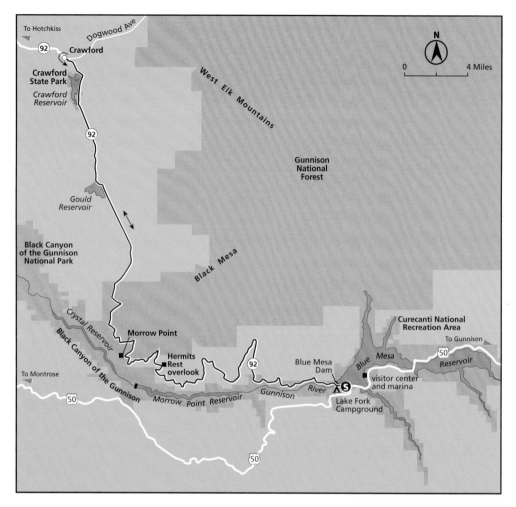

Mesa Dam, then beginning the long, gradual climb up the southwest side of Black Mesa to Hermits Rest overlook.

Early on, you'll catch glimpses into the canyon's dark abyss, before turning northward and heading up a long, open valley lined with fragrant sagebrush and twisted scrub oak. Look left to see the meat of the climb, which starts in earnest when the road switchbacks to the south at mile 8.3. The grade is rarely more than 6 percent, and by mile 12.3 your sustained climbing is over. A series of rollers follows, as you make your way to Hermits Rest overlook at mile 18.1 and then the ride's 9128-foot high point, Morrow Point, at mile

22.6. If you don't have time to ride all day, this is a good place to turn around.

Otherwise, it's basically all downhill for the next 20 miles to Crawford, which, of course, means 20 miles of climbing on the way back. The descent is steep and twisty at first, before leveling out for the long, straight run past Crawford State Park and into Crawford. This, too, is a sublime stretch of quiet road, with cattle ranches, hay farms, and the distant West Elk Mountains conspiring to create a truly beautiful pastoral landscape.

In Crawford you'll find various food and drink options, as well as a little music history. For two decades, the town's best-known resident was Joe Cocker. The famed rock-and-roller of the 1970s and '80s lived in a seventeen-thousand-square-foot mansion on the outskirts of town. Once your fuel stores are topped off, grind back to Morrow Point, then descend to the start at the Lake Fork Campground.

Route variation: For an epic day, tackle the Dave Wiens West Elk Bicycle Classic route (or sign up for the annual September event), a 134-mile ride with 9400 feet of climbing that goes from Gunnison to Crested Butte and includes Kebler Pass (summit elevation 10,007 feet). From Gunnison, roll 27 miles west on US 50 to SR 92 and then follow the main route to Crawford. From Crawford go right on Dogwood Avenue, left on Needle Rock Road, straight on 4200 Road, left on Cottonwood Creek Road, right on Crawford Road, and right on Matthews Lane into Paonia. Follow signs to SR 133, then head north 17 miles to County Road 12. Turn right and it's 31 miles to Crested Butte primarily on gravel road. You can even add the 27-mile spin back to Gunnison to create a monstrous 161-mile loop.

MILEAGE LOG

0.0	From Lake Fork Campground, head west on SR 92
18.1	Arrive at Hermits Rest overlook
22.6	Arrive at Morrow Point
41.8	Arrive in Crawford
65.4	Return to Hermits Rest overlook
83.5	Return to start at Lake Fork Campground

50 SLUMGULLION PASS

Difficulty:	Epic
Time:	7–9 hours
Distance:	102.3 miles out-and-back (shorter options)
Elevation gain:	8120 feet
Best seasons:	Late spring to fall
Road conditions:	Shoulder comes and goes on quiet, rural highway. Some road damage between Slumgullion Pass summit and Spring Creek Pass summit.

GETTING THERE: Ride starts at Lake City Town Park, at corner of 3rd and Silver streets. To get there, take SR 149 to Lake City, then head west on 3rd St. Park will be on your left. Free parking, restrooms, and water.

This ride doesn't have to be a century. Simply pedaling the 21 miles from Lake City to the Slumgullion Pass summit and back is a thoroughly challenging and scenic excursion. But if you're game for a truly grueling test that includes 8120 feet of climbing, prepare for an amazing day in the saddle. The entire route follows State Route 149, one of Colorado's twenty-five designated Scenic and Historic Byways. Along the way, you'll grind up

After passing over the summits of Slumgullion and Spring Creek passes, State Highway 149 descends into the scenic Rio Grande valley.

multiple tough climbs, get a bird's-eye view of the state's second-largest natural lake, cross the Continental Divide, and roll beside the upper reaches of the Rio Grande. The third-longest river in the United States, the Rio Grande begins its 1885-mile journey to the Gulf of Mexico from deep in these surrounding mountains.

The ride starts in Lake City, an old mining town turned quaint tourist draw that's 250 miles southwest of Denver. Within the city limits are more than two hundred historic structures, including Colorado's oldest continually operating courthouse. Before heading out, top off at least two sixteen-ounce water bottles. There's little in the way of civilization between here and the turn-around point in Creede.

Barely a block out of Lake City, you begin climbing. And unlike the majority of the state's highway ascents, this one is legitimately steep. The average gradient for the 7.6-mile

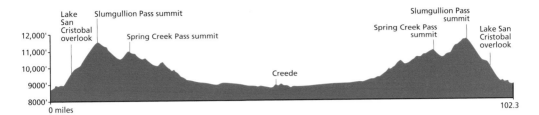

heart of the climb is 7 percent, with numerous pitches steeper than 10 percent. Total elevation gain is north of 2600 feet. Peak elevation is 11,530 feet. If you have a bike outfitted with compact cranks, bring it.

The pass is named after the nearby Slumgullion Earthflow, a massive landslide of yellowish soil that reminded early settlers of slumgullion stew, a hearty blend of beef, macaroni, and tomatoes—sounds like a great recovery meal. This landslide, which still moves up to twenty feet a year, also birthed the enormous Lake San Cristobal by blocking the Lake Fork of the Gunnison River eight hundred years ago. You can check out both natural wonders at the overlook pull-off at

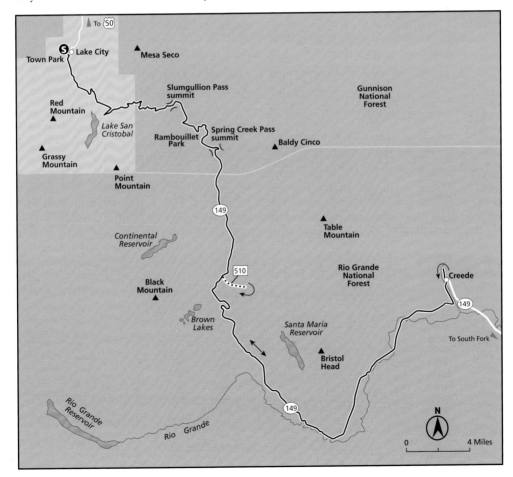

mile 5.3. A little farther up the road is a sign indicating that it's 4 miles to the top. This is the toughest stretch of the climb, with several long straight sections that can be demoralizing if you're not having a good day.

The summit itself feels more like a shoulder. Instead of having wide-open mountain views, you're tucked between rows of tall pine trees. But don't despair. Your hard work pays off just a few miles down the road, where the scenery improves dramatically as you drop into mountain-ringed Rambouillet Park. You'll lose around 1000 feet through here, then quickly regain about half of that vertical during the gentle ascent of Spring Creek Pass, with a summit elevation of 10,898 feet, your crossing point of the Continental Divide.

The next 13 miles trend downhill, save for a short, tough pop around mile 24. Throughout this winding descent, the views open ever wider, unveiling another splendid alpine valley and then expansive Antelope Park. Be sure to check out the small right-side pull-off around mile 25. It has several interpretive signs explaining the area's history as a transport and mining hub in the 1800s. Soon after, the road flattens and the Rio Grande appears, gently wiggling its way down this broad valley. You'll also spot the charred remains of the Papoose wildfire, which burned nearly 50,000 acres of the Rio Grande National Forest in the summer of 2013.

Around mile 37.5, the road and river bend ninety degrees left. A dozen mostly flat miles later, you'll roll into Creede, another old mining town turned tourist locale. Back in the day, Creede was one of the state's wildest little towns with saloons, brothels, and gambling houses lining its main street. More recently, the now much more family-friendly settlement served as a filming locale for Disney's *Lone Ranger* movie starring Johnny Depp.

Once you've refueled and topped off your bottles, it's time to head back. Creede and Lake City have almost identical elevations, meaning that your total vertical gain is essentially the same in both directions. The return trip is far gentler, though, with no horribly steep sections. After the 18-mile trek back through the Rio Grande valley, you'll be pedaling uphill for approximately 18 of the next 33 miles, crossing Spring Creek and Slumgullion passes. The good news is that it's almost all downhill from the final summit to Lake City where, if you're lucky, you'll find a big bowl of slumgullion stew.

Route variation: About 6.5 miles south of the Spring Creek Pass summit, turn left on Forest Road 510. This short detour ends with an amazing view of North Clear Creek Falls as it tumbles into the deep box canyon below.

MILEAGE LOG

0.0	From Lake City Town Park, head east on 3rd St.
0.1	Right onto SR 149
5.3	Lake San Cristobal overlook
10.5	Reach Slumgullion Pass summit
17.4	Reach Spring Creek Pass summit
	North Clear Creek Falls option:
24.0	**Left onto FR 510**
24.7	**Reach overlook and turnaround point**
50.3	Enter Creede
84.7	Return to Spring Creek Pass summit
91.7	Return to Slumgullion Pass summit
102.3	Return to start

51 CUMBRES AND LA MANGA PASSES

Difficulty:	Epic
Time:	5½–7½ hours
Distance:	95.8 miles out-and-back (shorter options)
Elevation gain:	6220 feet
Best seasons:	Spring to fall
Road conditions:	Minimal shoulder on majority of route, but good pavement and light traffic. There are several railroad crossings. Watch for warning signs and slow down. Also watch for trains (and listen for their whistles); no stop gates at crossings.

GETTING THERE: Ride starts at corner of Main St. and 5th Ave. in Antonito, a small town 28 miles south of Alamosa on US 285. Free on-street parking. Nearby grocery store has water and restrooms.

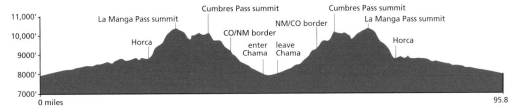

My first encounter with Cumbres and La Manga passes came in the dead of winter about twenty years ago. I was headed from my old hometown of Durango up to the Front Range. A blizzard shut down the normal route on US Highway 160 over Wolf Creek Pass, meaning I had to either abort or head south to New Mexico, then roll northward back into Colorado across these unfamiliar (but less snowbound) side-by-side summits.

My point? Unless you live around here (not many people do) or you're a train buff (more on that shortly), there are not a lot of reasons to drive the lonely stretch of state highway between Chama, New Mexico, and Antonito, Colorado. And that's only one reason why this is such fantastic cycling country. The others are climbing those two passes and all the amazing scenery along the way.

For the sake of doing an almost-century

ride and following roughly the same path as the historic Cumbres and Toltec Railroad, this out-and-back route starts in Antonito. The first 23 miles are essentially one long warm-up. You gain barely 800 feet as you transition from open ranchland to sagebrush country to the pine forests of the Conejos River valley.

This road is part of the Los Caminos Antiguos Scenic and Historic Byway (translation, the old paths). But starting at mile 23 along State Route 17, you might want to call it *Los Caminos Escarpados*. Just moments after you pass through the small community of Horca (which has water and food) and cross the Conejos River, the road pitches upward, signaling the start of La Manga Pass. This is the route's toughest stretch, gaining roughly 1500 feet in 5.5 miles. The average grade is 5 percent with several pitches above 10 percent.

Just after crossing the Conejos River, the road tips upward for the tough climb to the summit of La Manga Pass.

The good news is that the gradient backs off during the last 1.5 miles—and there are great sweeping views of the Conejos valley all the way up.

The summit (elevation 10,230 feet) isn't as dramatic as its above-tree-line cousins to the north—no giant snowcapped peaks jutting into the sky. The beauty here is softer, full of blooming wildflowers in summer and aspens glowing golden in fall. You'll understand quite clearly why the state moniker is "Colorful Colorado."

The ensuing 7 miles trend gently downhill (with a few short ups), as you make your way south past rounded ridgelines toward the base of Cumbres Pass. There's little in the way of civilization up here, but if you need to top off your bottles, try the Cumbres Adventure Center in Los Pinos at mile 31.5.

This is also the first time you're close to the railroad tracks. Don't be surprised if you see a dark plume of coal smoke signaling the approach of this old steam train, which shuttles sightseers back and forth between Chama and Antonito from late May to early October. Four miles of gentle climbing (and occasional descending) later, you'll reach the summit of Cumbres Pass, elevation 10,022 feet and the site of the old Cumbres and Toltec railyard. Be careful crossing the railroad tracks, and watch out for tourists wandering around the side of the road taking pictures.

From here it's 12.5 miles downhill to the turnaround point. At mile 36.8, there's

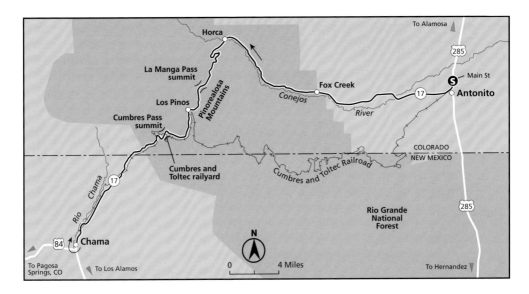

another railroad crossing (there's no need to memorize the mileage because ample signage leads up to every crossing). At mile 39.5, you'll enter New Mexico. At mile 44.5, the road levels out as you roll into the Chama Valley. At mile 46.8, there's another track crossing. And at mile 47.9, you enter Chama proper, a small touristy town with numerous food and drink options.

The return trip to Antonito has almost the same amount of climbing (about 3100 feet), but you gain elevation at a much slower rate. You'll climb about 2100 feet during the 12.5-mile return trip to the Cumbres Pass summit, then another 800 on the rolling return to the La Manga Pass summit. After that, it's almost all downhill or flat, but make sure to save some energy just in case the wind's blowing from the east during your run back into Antonito.

Route variation: Shorten the ride by starting in the tiny town of Fox Creek, which is 13 miles west of Antonito on SR 17. This reduces total out-and-back distance to a little less than 70 miles, but doesn't omit any of the ride's main highlights or climbing.

MILEAGE LOG

0.0	From Antonito, head south on US 285
0.6	Right onto SR 17
22.9	Arrive in Horca
28.4	Summit of La Manga Pass
35.5	Summit of Cumbres Pass
39.5	Enter New Mexico
47.9	Arrive in Chama
57.3	Return to Colorado
61.5	Summit of Cumbres Pass
68.6	Summit of La Manga Pass
95.2	Left onto US 285
95.8	Return to start

SOUTHWEST COLORADO

Variety is the hallmark of the state's sun-splashed southwestern corner. Spin past ancient American Indian ruins and through high desert at Mesa Verde National Park. Trek to towering heights in the San Juans, Colorado's most dramatic mountain range. Or head to Durango for access to desert, mountains, and the rolling hills in between. Spend your off-bike time strolling downtown Telluride or Silverton. Soak your tired legs in the Ouray or Pagosa Hot Springs.

52 WOLF CREEK PASS

Difficulty:	Challenging
Time:	3–5 hours
Distance:	47 miles out-and-back
Elevation gain:	4100 feet
Best seasons:	Spring through fall
Road conditions:	Ample shoulder and good pavement the whole way, but traffic can be heavy.

GETTING THERE: From Main St. in Pagosa Springs, head south on Hot Springs Blvd., then turn left onto San Juan St., arriving at Town Park. Free parking, water, and restrooms, and a visitor center just across street to the west.

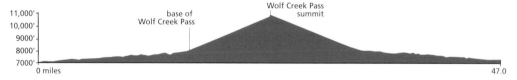

In general, I'm not a big fan of riding bikes on major highways. It can be exceptionally unnerving to have a fully loaded eighteen-wheeler bomb past you at 75 miles per hour. But there are exceptions to every rule, and the ride to the summit of Wolf Creek Pass is one such exception. Though this entire route follows US Highway 160, southern Colorado's main east–west thoroughfare, the enticements of riding to the top of the Continental Divide and back and then soaking in the famed Pagosa Hot Springs are too good to pass up. Plus, there is a wide shoulder and good pavement the whole way.

This ride starts at Town Park in downtown Pagosa Springs, which straddles the San Juan River. There you'll find free parking and bathrooms, and it's just a stone's throw

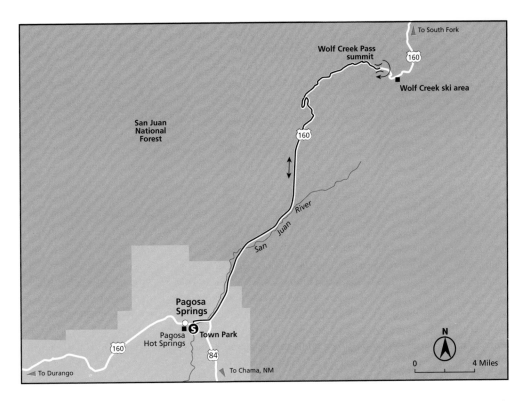

from the hot springs, so after your ride, you can walk over for a well-deserved soak. From the park, pedal one block north to US 160, which doubles as Main Street during its trip through this small touristy town, population 1727. Go right and in 23.5 miles you'll be at the summit of Wolf Creek Pass, elevation 10,856 feet.

At the edge of town, stay left at the intersection with US 84. (A right turn would lead you south to Chama, New Mexico.) The San Juan River is on your left now and stays there for most of the gentle 15-mile approach to the base of the pass. This is a fantastic stretch of road, with rolling hills and wide-open valley views. Around mile 10, your serenity is interrupted when a line of skyscraping mountains, precipitous cliffs, and the climb's first set of switchbacks come into view.

Five miles later, your work begins just as you spin past a sign reading, "Wolf Creek Pass Summit 8 miles." The good news is that since you're on a major highway, the pitch rarely climbs above 7 percent, and it's in the 5 percent range most of the way. The bad news is that even the fastest cyclists take upward of forty-five minutes to pedal to the summit. Also know that there are no services out here, so it's best to bring at least two full sixteen-ounce water bottles, and maybe even stash a third in your jersey pocket if it's a hot day. A light rain jacket is also a good idea. Even in the middle of summer, the weather can turn ugly quickly at this altitude.

Up at the summit, snap a photo in front of the Continental Divide sign, then head back to Pagosa Springs. On the way down the pass, there is a great overlook at the 29-mile mark on the right. But if you don't stop, no one would blame you. The hot springs are waiting.

Route variation: Ride a point-to-point, dropping off the east side of Wolf Creek Pass and descending to the small town of South

The 2013 Ride the Rockies bike tour included a west-to-east grind from Pagosa Springs up and over Wolf Creek Pass.

Fork, which is about 19 miles from the summit. Along the way, you'll pass the Wolf Creek ski area and the Fun Valley RV Park, where the fictional Clark Griswold and his family stayed in the 1983 comedy classic *National Lampoon's Vacation.*

MILEAGE LOG

0.0   From Town Park in Pagosa Springs, go right on Hot Springs Blvd.
0.2   Right on Main St. (US 160)
1.0   Left on US 160
23.5   Reach Wolf Creek Pass summit
47.0   Return to start

53   IGNACIO–BAYFIELD LOOP

Difficulty:	Challenging
Time:	4–6 hours
Distance:	72.2 miles (shorter options)
Elevation gain:	3637 feet
Best seasons:	Early spring to late fall (possible in winter)
Road conditions:	Majority of route is on secondary highway, county roads, and multiuse paths. Shoulder comes and goes, but traffic is typically light. Short section on US 550 has narrow shoulder.

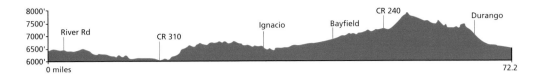

GETTING THERE: Ride starts at Santa Rita Park at 111 S. Camino del Rio in Durango. From downtown Durango, go south on Main Ave., then turn right onto College Dr. At next light, turn left onto Camino del Rio. In 0.85 mile turn right at light, entering park via Santa Rita Dr. Free parking, restrooms, water, and tourist information center.

Two things you should know about cycling in the Durango area: There are a ton of amazing rides and a variety of ways to do them. If you ask a handful of Durango locals about the Ignacio–Bayfield Loop, their explanations are likely to vary. But what won't change is the fact that this ride has mellow country road spinning, a handful of tough climbs, and miles and miles of great scenery. The prescribed route is a melding of personal experience and the wonderful road cycling map produced by La Plata County. (If you're looking for something similar but shorter, check out the Ignacio Loop detailed in the route variation below.)

And make sure to pick up a current copy of the county map at one of the city's many great local bike shops. I especially love Mountain Bike Specialists on Main Avenue, which has a great display of old bikes, vintage jerseys, and various other paraphernalia documenting the city's rich cycling history.

This ride starts at Santa Rita Park on the south end of Durango, adjacent to the Animas River. From here, head south (downstream) on the Animas River Trail, crossing the river twice as you pass behind several shopping plazas on your way out of town. After 3.5 miles of leisurely bike path spinning, exit the trail and turn right onto River Road, which immediately crosses the river. On the other side turn left onto La Posta Road (County Road 213), a mostly flat, quiet country road that parallels the Animas River.

After 13 mellow miles of riverside cruis-ing, enter the tiny town of Bondad. Turn left onto US Highway 550 and jog 1 mile north, before turning right onto CR 310 toward Ignacio. Now it's climbing time. The next 3 miles gain about 550 feet, and the road trends upward through the surrounding high desert. There's no shade out here, so it's best to get an early start if you plan on doing this route in the heat of summer.

Following a half dozen miles on the flats, the route drops into the small town of Ignacio, where you can top off your bottles and grab a snack. From here roll east on State Route 151 for a half mile, then turn left onto Buck Highway (CR 521). The road shoulder is skinny through here, but traffic is usually light—and the westerly views of the far-off La Plata Mountains are spectacular.

At mile 44, CR 521 rolls into Bayfield, your last chance for food and drink until your return to Durango. Once you've refueled, pick up CR 501 and continue north across US 160. Here the scenery transforms from cottonwood-dotted grassland to forests of pine, scrub oak, and aspen. The road itself maintains a consistent uphill trajectory, with the occasional downhill mixed in.

Just after you turn onto CR 240 (mile 53.3) comes the route's toughest climb, a 2.3-mile grind that averages 5 percent and gains 570 feet. Once you're over the top, the road trends downhill for the next 8.3 miles, though there are a few short stingers to keep you honest. The last of those pops brings you up to the Edgemont Ranch area around

From Buck Highway, you're treated to a fantastic view of the distant La Plata Mountains, which border the west side of Durango.

mile 65. From here it's a straight, fast downhill into Durango.

Back in town, continue on CR 240 (Florida Road) to mile 70, then go right at the fork onto East 15th Street. A block later, just after crossing the railroad tracks, turn right onto East 2nd Avenue, which runs into Rotary Park and the Animas River Trail. Turn left (downstream) on the trail, and follow it along the river all the way back to your start point at Santa Rita Park.

Route Variation: Knock about 15 miles and 1000 feet of climbing off this ride by doing what's known locally as the Ignacio Loop. Follow the same route from Durango to Ignacio. But instead of looping north to Bayfield, head directly back to Durango by staying on SR 172. Turn left onto CR 220, right onto US 550 north, left onto US 160 west, and finally left on River Road where you can rejoin the Animas River Trail and pedal back to Santa Rita Park.

MILEAGE LOG

0.0	From Santa Rita Park, head south (downstream) on Animas River Trail
1.5	Continue on Animas River Trail
2.0	Continue on Animas River Trail via footbridge
3.5	Exit trail and turn right onto River Rd.
3.7	Left onto La Posta Rd. (CR 213)
8.8	Right at fork, continuing on CR 213
15.2	Left, continuing on CR 213
16.8	Arrive in Bondad, and turn left onto US 550
17.7	Right onto CR 310 toward Ignacio

20.6   Continue straight on CR 318

23.4   Right on CR 318

32.8   Left on SR 172

34.0   Arrive in Ignacio

Ignacio Loop option:

34.0   **Straight on SR 172**

48.8   **Left onto CR 220**

51.4   **Right onto US 550**

52.2   **Left onto US 160**

53.0   **Left onto River Rd.**

53.1   **Right onto Animas River Trail**

56.5   **Return to Santa Rita Park**

34.3   Right onto Ute St. (SR 151)

34.8   Left onto CR 521 (Buck Hwy.)

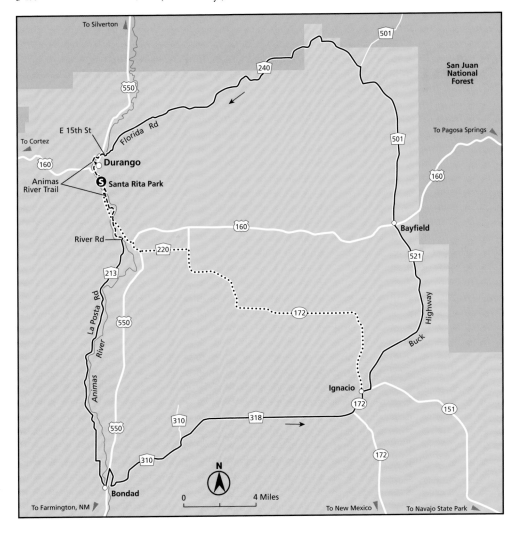

44.0	Arrive in Bayfield
44.4	Right onto Bayfield Pkwy.
44.5	Left onto CR 501, and cross US 160
44.8	Straight on CR 501
52.6	Right on CR 501
53.3	Left onto CR 240
67.0	Arrive in Durango, and continue on CR 240 (Florida Rd.)
69.5	Straight through roundabout, continuing on CR 240 (Florida Rd.)
70.0	Right at fork onto E. 15th St.
70.1	Cross railroad tracks, then take immediate right onto E. 2nd Ave.
70.2	At Rotary Park, turn left onto Animas River Trail
70.6	Right onto footbridge, continuing on Animas River Trail
70.9	Left onto footbridge, continuing on Animas River Trail
71.8	Right, continuing on Animas River Trail
72.2	Return to start

54 TEXAS CREEK LOOP

Difficulty:	Moderate
Time:	3–5 hours
Distance:	42.4 miles
Elevation gain:	4221 feet
Best seasons:	Spring to fall
Road conditions:	Includes 14.5 miles of gravel road. Shoulder comes and goes.

GETTING THERE: Ride starts at Santa Rita Park at 111 S. Camino del Rio in Durango. From downtown Durango, go south on Main Ave., and turn right onto College Dr. At next light, turn left onto Camino del Rio. In 0.85 mile, turn right at light, entering park via Santa Rita Dr. Free parking, restrooms, water, and tourist information.

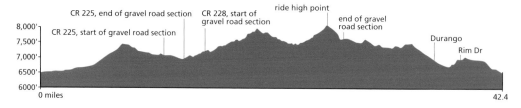

Every good cycling locale needs a Roubaix-style ride. In Durango, that ride is the Texas Creek Loop, which includes great scenery, several stiff climbs, and two extended sections of hard-packed gravel road. Neither segment is particularly rough, but as always, make sure to pack an extra tube and pump just in case.

This route starts at Santa Rita Park on the south end of town, which allows plenty of warm-up time before the real work begins.

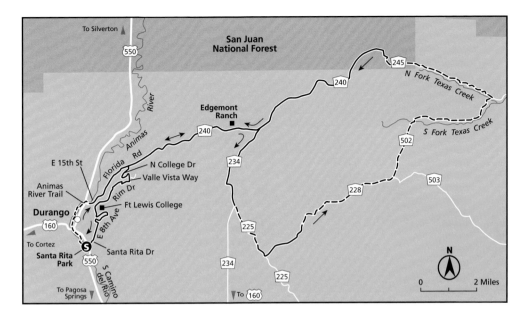

From the park, jump on the Animas River Trail and head upstream. Along the way, you pass Smelter Rapid, a rollicking stretch of Class III whitewater inundated with rafters and kayakers in the summertime. The red and blue gates hanging over the river are part of a kayak slalom course.

Continue on the path as it crosses the river twice, then ducks underneath Main Avenue and heads into Rotary Park at mile 2.2. Here turn right off the path and onto East 2nd Avenue (if you get to the footbridge parallel to a railroad bridge, you've gone too far). Next turn left onto East 15th Street, and then go left at the fork, continuing gradually uphill on what's now County Road 240 (Florida Road). Ahead you'll pass the city's ice rink and Chapman Hill, which over the years has hosted a variety of pro-level mountain bike races.

Soon, the din of Durango fades, as CR 240 heads out of town. The opening climb of consequence comes around mile 5, as the road rises up to Edgemont Ranch. A quick descent follows. Then turn right onto CR 234. Three miles ahead, take the left fork onto CR 225, and begin the first gravel section, a flat, 2-mile stretch through quiet wooded countryside.

Stay left at mile 13.3, continuing on CR 225 back onto pavement.

Then go left again a tenth of mile later, turning onto CR 228. Two miles ahead, stay straight on CR 228, heading back on gravel, this time for a dozen miles. Climbing also renews, as the road stair-steps up to nearly 8000 feet about 1.5 miles after the left turn onto CR 502.

The ensuing 5 miles are mostly downhill, as the road parallels the south fork of Texas Creek before dropping into a beautiful small valley. At mile 23.7, make a sharp left onto CR 245. (Keep your eyes open. It's easy to miss this turn.) Now climb again, grinding along the north fork of Texas Creek for 2.6 miles, with an average gradient of 5 percent and the steepest pitches near the summit. Over the top, keep your speed in check for the steep descent on gravel road.

Pavement returns at mile 27.8. You cross the Florida River, then immediately turn left onto CR 240. The road trends downhill all the way back to Durango, but there are a handful of leg burners along the way, including the return climb to Edgemont Ranch. By mile 36 you're back in Durango. Two miles

For maximum traction when climbing steep dirt roads, try to keep weight evenly balanced on both wheels.

ahead it's decision time. Either head back the way you came via Florida Road to the Animas River Trail, or go left onto North College Drive for the side trip up to Rim Drive and the Fort Lewis College campus.

Unless you're pressed for time or completely out of energy, I strongly recommend the latter, which includes several great overlooks of the city and surrounding mountains. After cresting the stiff North College Drive climb, turn right on Rim Drive, and wind past a golf course and then around the perim-eter of the small liberal arts school arguably best known for having one of the nation's premier competitive cycling programs. They even offer athletic scholarships to talented bike racers.

After taking in the sights, continue south along Rim Drive, then turn right onto East 8th Avenue, which drops down into Durango. At the bottom of the hill, continue straight on 8th, then turn right on Santa Rita Drive, which delivers you back to the start at Santa Rita Park.

MILEAGE LOG

0.0   From Santa Rita Park, right (upstream) on Animas River Trail
1.3   Cross river via footbridge, continuing on Animas River Trail
1.6   Cross river via footbridge, continuing on Animas River Trail
2.2   Just after crossing under Main Ave. and entering Rotary Park, turn right off trail onto E. 2nd Ave.
2.3   Left onto E. 15th St. (CR 240)

2.4	Left, continuing on CR 240 (Florida Rd.)
8.6	Right onto CR 234
11.4	Left onto CR 225 (start of gravel road)
13.3	Left at fork, continuing on CR 225 (end of gravel road)
13.4	Left at fork on CR 228
15.2	Straight on CR 228 (start of gravel road)
18.6	Left at fork onto CR 502
23.7	Left onto CR 245
26.4	Ride high point
27.8	End of gravel road
27.9	Left onto CR 240
36.4	Return to Durango
37.7	Left onto N. College Dr. (CR 239)
38.4	Continue on Valle Vista Way
38.7	Right onto Rim Dr.
40.9	Right onto E. 8th Ave.
42.0	Right onto Santa Rita Dr.
42.4	Return to start

55 ANIMAS VALLEY LOOP

Difficulty:	Easy
Time:	1–2 hours
Distance:	27.1 miles
Elevation gain:	841 feet
Best seasons:	Early spring to late fall (possible year-round)
Road conditions:	Shoulder comes and goes, but primarily on quiet roads.

GETTING THERE: From downtown Durango, go north on Main Ave., turn right on E. 15th St., and then left onto Florida Rd. Proceed 2 miles, then turn left onto CR 250. Ample parking in small shopping plaza on immediate right.

Every cycling hotbed needs a mellow, scenic ride for those days when you just don't feel like suffering. In Durango, that ride is the Animas Valley Loop (also known as Bakers Bridge or simply the Valley Loop or Long Valley, depending on who you talk to). Whatever you call it, this is a sublime, mostly flat ride that traces the perimeter of the wide, red rock wall–lined Animas Valley situated just north of Durango.

You could start just about anywhere in town, but I've chosen the shopping plaza just north of the intersection of Florida Road and County Road 250 primarily because that's typically where local group rides meet. A small bakery here called Bread has reverential status among Durango's large cycling populace. After you've grabbed a snack and a cup of coffee, head north out of town on CR 250, paralleling the Animas River on your left. The

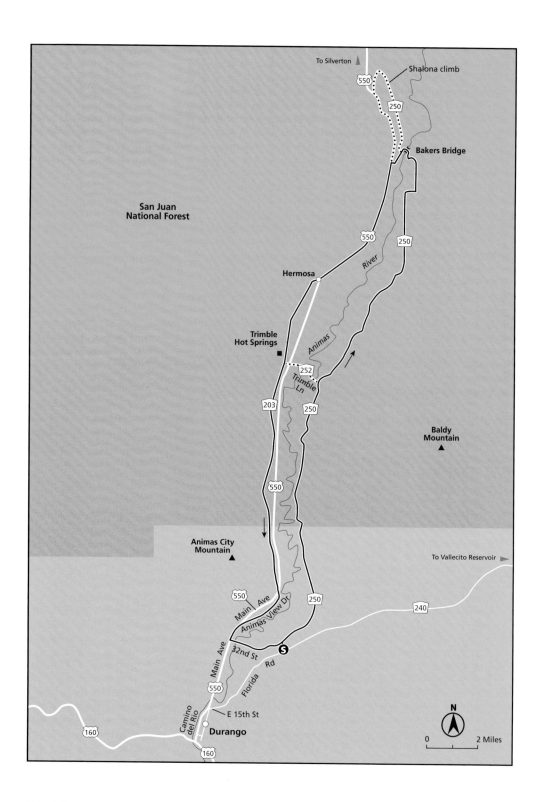

To Silverton

Shalona climb

550

250

Bakers Bridge

San Juan
National Forest

550

250

River

Hermosa

Animas

Trimble
Hot Springs

252

Trimble
Ln

203

250

Baldy
Mountain

550

550

Animas City
Mountain

To Vallecito Reservoir

550

Main Ave

Animas View Dr

250

240

Main Ave

32nd St

S

Florida Rd

550

Camino del Rio

E 15th St

160

Durango

160

N

0   2 Miles

On hot days, the Animas River is a great place to cool off mid-ride. Other times just taking in the view is enough.

road has a few tiny rollers but is essentially flat all the way to Bakers Bridge at mile 12.8, which comes just after CR 250 turns left, then right, then left again.

Pause for a moment to take in the beautiful downriver view. On hot summer days, expect to see swimmers jumping from riverbank rocks—and occasionally the bridge. Now continue across the bridge, following CR 250 to the intersection of US Highway 550 at mile 13.6. (Note that just before this intersection, you'll pass through a smaller intersection, which accesses a slightly longer route with more climbing that's described below.)

At US 550, turn left and head south, passing Honeyville, a beekeeping and honey bottling business that's been around since the 1920s. At mile 16.7, just after you cross the tracks of the famed Durango & Silverton Narrow Gauge Railroad, turn right, then left,

merging onto CR 203. Now you're officially on the other side of the valley for the equally tranquil trip back to Durango.

The views are a little more wide open on this side, as you pass a mix of residential areas, open spaces, small ranches, and Trimble Hot Springs, a great spot for a post-ride soak. At mile 23.6, you'll reach the end of CR 203. Cross US 550, and take an immediate right onto Animas View Drive. Continue for another 1.5 miles, rolling back into town. At mile 25, turn left onto Main Avenue, then take a left onto East 32nd Street. A half mile later go back across the Animas River and return to CR 250. Take a right here, and the starting point will be on your left.

Route Variation: For an easier ride, known locally as the Short Valley or Trimble Loop, take a left from CR 250 onto CR 252 (also called Trimble Lane) at the 6.5-mile mark.

You run straight into CR 203. Go left here, and head back to town for what will be a 16-mile loop.

For a longer ride that includes the 2.2-mile Shalona climb, stay right on CR 250 just before reaching US 550 at mile 13.3. This leads to an ascent that gains about 550 feet with an average grade of 4.8 percent. Follow CR 250 to the top of the climb where you wrap around to the left and intersect US 550. Turn left, heading downhill, and rejoin the main route in about 1.5 miles.

MILEAGE LOG

0.0	From shopping plaza, go right onto CR 250
	Trimble Loop option:
6.5	**Left onto CR 252 (Trimble Ln.)**
7.5	**Left onto CR 203, rejoining main route**
12.8	Cross Animas River at Bakers Bridge
	Shalona climb option:
13.0	**Right, staying on CR 250**
15.7	**Left onto US 550, rejoining main route**
13.3	Straight, toward US 550
13.6	Left onto US 550
16.7	Right, then quick left onto CR 203
23.6	Cross US 550, then immediate right onto Animas View Dr.
25.0	Left onto Main Ave.
25.5	Left onto E. 32nd St.
27.0	Right onto CR 250
27.1	Return to start

56 IRON HORSE CLASSIC

Difficulty:	Challenging
Time:	3–5 hours
Distance:	47.5 miles one-way
Elevation gain:	5812 feet
Best seasons:	Spring through fall
Road conditions:	Ample shoulder on majority of route. Use caution at railroad crossing at mile 9.6.

GETTING THERE: To stay true to the official road race route and distance, park on the street near Durango High School at 2390 Main St., then start riding from the high school parking lot.

Every spring since 1972, cyclists have lined up for the Iron Horse Bicycle Classic, then raced (or just ridden) the mountainous 47.5-mile trek from Durango to Silverton. The event traces its roots to a pair of brothers, one a conductor for the Durango & Silverton Narrow

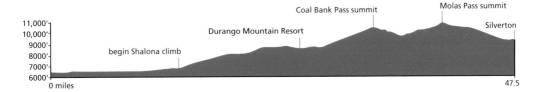

Coal Bank Pass summit

Molas Pass summit

Durango Mountain Resort

Silverton

begin Shalona climb

11,000'
10,000'
9000'
8000'
7000'
6000'

0 miles

47.5

Gauge Railroad (a.k.a. the Iron Horse), the other a cycling enthusiast. One day they bet on who could make the Durango–Silverton trip faster. Surprisingly, the cycling brother won. Flash forward to 1972, when thirty-six Durango locals commemorated the feat by racing bikes to Silverton. That gathering has been repeated nearly every year since, growing into an iconic cycling event that sells out its roughly four thousand entries.

Whether you sign up for the event or just ride the route on your own, the Durango to Silverton journey is a true cycling classic with epic high mountain challenge and *Sound of Music*–worthy scenery. Just remember you'll need to have a return trip plan. If you're feeling ambitious, ride up and back. It's a nearly 100-mile effort with around 10,000 feet of climbing. Other options include shuttling a car to Silverton beforehand, having a friend

From the summit of Molas Pass, it's a rapid descent to the old mining town of Silverton at 9308 feet.

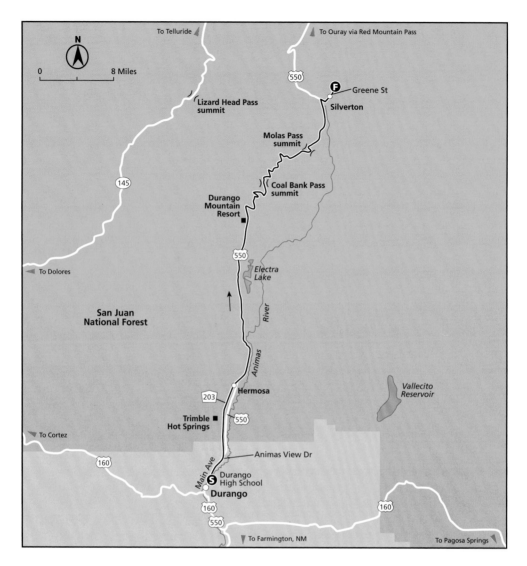

pick you up, or taking the train from Silverton back to Durango. If you choose the latter, buy your one-way ticket in advance, and let the ticket agent know you'll be bringing a bike on board.

To trace the official race route, this ride starts at Durango High School at 2390 Main Avenue. From there, head north on Main, rolling out of town on what becomes US Highway 550. You can stay on US 550 the whole way, but there's less traffic if you bear right at mile 1.3 and get onto Animas View Drive. This residential road parallels US 550. At mile 2.8, cross the highway and pick up County Road 203, which parallels the other side of the highway. (The race route stays on US 550, but the total mileage is nearly identical.)

Seven miles down CR 203, pass Trimble Hot Springs, a great post-ride recovery destination. At mile 9.6, enter the small town of Hermosa, which has a general store if you need food or water. Just past Hermosa, merge back onto US 550, which takes you the rest of the way to Silverton. Watch out for the railroad tracks just after you reenter the highway; they're at an odd angle. Also keep an eye out for the train, which takes about three and a half hours to complete its journey to Silverton. See if you can beat it.

The next couple miles are generally flat, allowing you ample time to take in the ever-improving scenery. Look for hawks flying overhead, and marvel at the giant aspen groves lining the road. At mile 13, your work begins in earnest, as you turn slightly left and head up the Shalona climb. This stiff 1.7-mile ascent serves as a warm-up for the much bigger challenges ahead. For the ensuing 14 miles, the road continues its gradual, rolling ascent into the heart of the San Juan Range. At mile 23, just after a short descent, there's a gas station and deli on your left. Make sure to top off your bottles here; it's your last chance before Silverton.

The next 4.6 miles are mostly flat as you roll past Durango Mountain Resort. By now, you'll have spotted the looming figure of Engineer Mountain jutting into the northern skyline. It is your constant companion during the climb up Coal Bank Pass. At mile 27.8, cross Cascade Creek on your way around a tight right turn. At the apex, the start of Coal Bank Pass comes into full view. All by itself, it's not overly difficult. The grade never gets much above 7 percent, the pavement is smooth, and there's decent-sized shoulder most of the way. But by now, your legs are probably getting a little tender, and over the next 5.4 miles, you'll gain a couple thousand feet on the way to the 10,640-foot summit.

Take a break at the top, then jump back on your bike for the first of two extended high-speed descents. You drop about 800 feet over the next 3 miles before the day's final climb begins at mile 36. Like Coal Bank, Molas Pass is not overly steep (average grade is 5.5 percent). But it's far more exposed than its predecessor, meaning the wind can be a factor. Wind or no wind, the views remain stellar as you switchback your way from 9749 feet up to the ride's high point at 10,910.

There's only 7.2 miles left in the ride now, and nearly all of it is downhill. Just be watchful for the occasional crack in the pavement, and mind the right side of the road. It drops off steeply and is only intermittently protected by a guardrail. At mile 46.9, stay right, exiting US 550 and merging onto Greene Street, which takes you into downtown Silverton. Roll to the Handlebars Restaurant and Saloon at the corner of 13th Street. They serve a mean bacon cheeseburger, and the walls and ceiling are cluttered with artifacts from this old town's fascinating mining history.

MILEAGE LOG

0.0	From 2390 Main St., head north on Main Ave.
1.3	Right onto Animas View Dr.
2.8	Cross US 550, then right onto CR 203
9.5	Left onto US 550
9.6	Railroad track crossing
25.3	Pass Durango Mountain Resort ski area
27.8	Begin Coal Bank Pass climb
33.1	Summit Coal Bank Pass
36.0	Begin Molas Pass climb
40.3	Summit Molas Pass
46.9	Right, merging onto Greene St.
47.5	Finish in downtown Silverton

57 DEEP CREEK TELLURIDE

Difficulty:	Moderate
Time:	1½–3 hours
Distance:	28.7 miles
Elevation gain:	2687 feet
Best seasons:	Spring to fall
Road conditions:	Bike lane leaving Telluride has some cracks and seams. Shoulder on SR 145 comes and goes. Two gravel road sections (6 miles and 4 miles).

GETTING THERE: From downtown Telluride, go west on Colorado Ave., then take a left onto S. Tomboy Dr. Follow S. Tomboy Dr. to W. Pacific Ave., cross San Miguel River, and enter Carhenge parking lot. Free parking and restrooms.

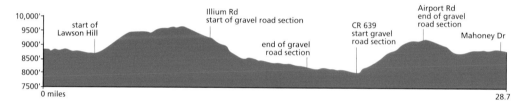

If you want to pedal a loop in the Telluride area, you have to mix in a little dirt. But in the case of the Deep Creek loop, that's certainly not a bad thing. The ride's two gravel sections (6 miles on Illium Road and 4 miles on Deep Creek and Last Dollar roads) are usually in good shape during the summer, and they get you away from traffic and into the beautiful backcountry.

Just remember to avoid these roads after recent rain when they may be muddy. It's also a good idea to get updated road condition beta from one of the local bike shops. The transportation department uses magnesium chloride to harden the surface and keep dust down, which is great for cyclists as long as you don't head out right after the chemical's application when the road is still damp.

Like the Lizard Head Pass ride (Ride 58), this ride starts at Telluride's Carhenge parking lot, where large slabs of red sandstone replace

standard cement car stops. From here, roll across the San Miguel River, and head north for two blocks. Then take a left onto State Route 145 Spur, and roll out of town on the road or adjacent bike path. At mile 3.3, turn left, joining SR 145 proper.

Right away, you grind up one of two significant climbs on this route. Lawson Hill is a 2.4-mile kick in the stomach that averages a leg-burning 7.4 percent. The pain subsides just as you pass the turn for Mountain Village and the Telluride Ski Resort, but you're gradually heading uphill until you reach mile 8. Next comes a speedy 2-mile descent. Check your speed as you near the bottom and prepare for a sharp right-hand turn onto Illium Road at mile 10.4. This begins the ride's first gravel section. The road continues downhill for another 2 miles, before leveling off in a small idyllic valley. Here the south fork of the San Miguel River gurgles on your left, the San

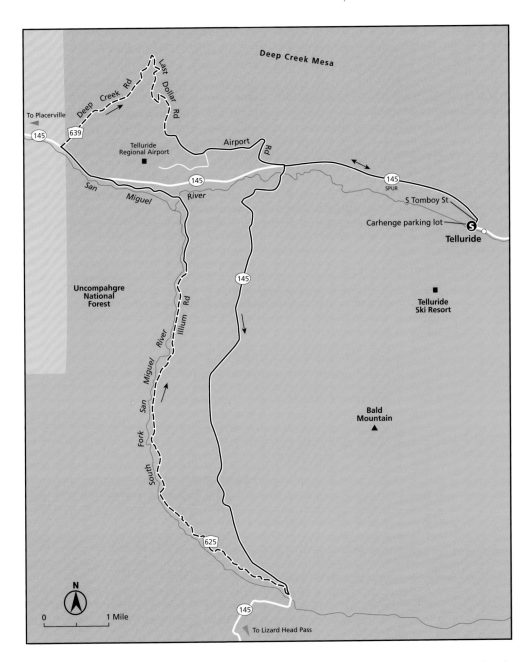

Juan Mountains tower in the distance, aspen trees are all around, and cars are nowhere to be found.

At mile 16.4, gravel gives way to pavement. Two miles farther, just after passing the Illium Hotel (a.k.a. the county jail), turn left on SR 145 heading west. There's not much shoulder, but in less than a mile, you're back on dirt, after turning right off the highway and onto tree-lined Deep Creek Road. Begin the ride's second and more difficult climb, a 4.3-mile grind up a sometimes loose gravel road that gains 1270 feet with an average grade of 6 percent. The pitch is steepest during the first 2 miles, then levels off slightly after you make a right onto Last Dollar Road. Find a gear that allows you to pedal while seated for improved rear-wheel traction.

Around the 22-mile mark, the trees part, unveiling another massive mountain vista. A mile and a half later, at the top of Deep Creek Mesa, Last Dollar Road merges with Airport Road and you're back on pavement. On your right is Telluride Regional Airport, North America's highest commercial airport at 9070 feet. Its slogan ("Where the best pilots land") is a testament to the tricky nature of guiding small airplanes around the surrounding peaks. From here it's a quick trip down Airport Road to SR 145. Turn left here, and Telluride is 2.7 miles down the road. If it's a hot day, finish your ride with a dip in the San Miguel River. Nothing soothes tired legs like an ice bath. After that, go wander around Telluride. It's one of Colorado's most well-preserved little mountain towns.

MILEAGE LOG

0.0	From Carhenge parking lot, head north on S. Tomboy St.
0.2	Left onto Colorado Ave. (SR 145 Spur)
0.4	Straight through traffic circle and continue west on SR 145 spur or adjacent bike path
3.3	Left on SR 145
10.4	Right onto CR 625 (Illium Rd.), start of gravel road
16.4	End of gravel road
18.6	Left on SR 145
19.5	Right on CR 639 (Deep Creek Rd.), start of gravel road
21.5	Right onto Last Dollar Rd.

With the south fork of the San Miguel River gurgling on your left and the majestic San Juan Mountains filling the northern horizon, the spin north along Illium Road is hard to beat.

23.6	Merge onto Airport Rd. (end of gravel road)
25.6	Left onto SR 145 Spur
28.3	Right out of traffic circle to Mahoney Dr.
28.5	Left on W. Pacific Ave.
28.7	Right turn back to Carhenge parking lot

58 LIZARD HEAD PASS

Difficulty:	Challenging
Time:	3–5 hours
Distance:	55.4 miles out-and-back
Elevation gain:	5203 feet
Best seasons:	Spring through fall
Road conditions:	Bike lane on way out of Telluride has some cracks and seams. Shoulder comes and goes on SR 145 (good pavement).

GETTING THERE: From downtown Telluride, go west on Colorado Ave., then take a left onto S. Tomboy Dr. Follow S. Tomboy Dr. to W. Pacific Ave., cross San Miguel River, and enter Carhenge parking lot. Free parking and restrooms.

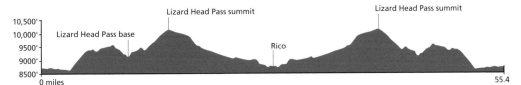

Pedaling up mountain passes is integral to the Colorado cycling experience. The combination of physical challenge and amazing high-alpine scenery is an allure most cyclists simply cannot resist. So which of these trips up—and sometimes over—the various Rocky Mountain roads is the best? There is no one right answer. Each cycling summit offers its own unique experience. If you ask me, they're all amazing.

But if you were forced to choose just one high mountain ascent from within the colorful confines of the thirty-eighth state, the ride up Lizard Head Pass would surely make the short list of classic classics. Situated along the 28-mile stretch of State Route 145

between Telluride and Rico, this enchanting road doles out an intoxicating mix of smooth, bike-friendly pavement, tough (but not onerous) climbing, and postcard-perfect scenery. Speaking of intoxicating, sharp-eyed riders will notice that Wilson Peak, the four-teener looming to the southwest on the way toward Lizard Head's north face, looks a lot like the mountain on the Coors beer label. It's not a coincidence.

This ride starts at Telluride's Carhenge parking lot, where large slabs of red sandstone replace standard cement car stops. From here, pick up SR 145 Spur, then head south out of town on the road or adjacent bike path. At mile 3.3, turn left, joining SR 145 proper.

Almost immediately the climbing begins, as you grind your way up Lawson Hill, a 2.4-mile wake-up call with an average grade of 7.4 percent. The pitch relents as you pass the turn for Mountain Village and the Telluride Ski Resort, but the road keeps climbing gradually all the way to mile 8. Next comes a rapid descent to the turnoff for Illium Road (part of Ride 57).

Here SR 145 makes a sweeping right turn, and it's essentially all uphill for the next 4.5 miles. You know you're getting close to the

summit when Sheep Mountain and Vermilion Peak begin to fill the eastern skyline and you pass Trout Lake on the left. At the summit (elevation 10,222 feet), there's a small parking lot and restrooms. You'll also catch your first glance of unmistakable Lizard Head Peak to the west.

If you're smoked, turn around and head back to Telluride. If not, keep riding to Rico. From here, it's about 12 miles, all of it downhill. At mile 18, the Dolores River flows in from the east, then runs parallel with SR 145

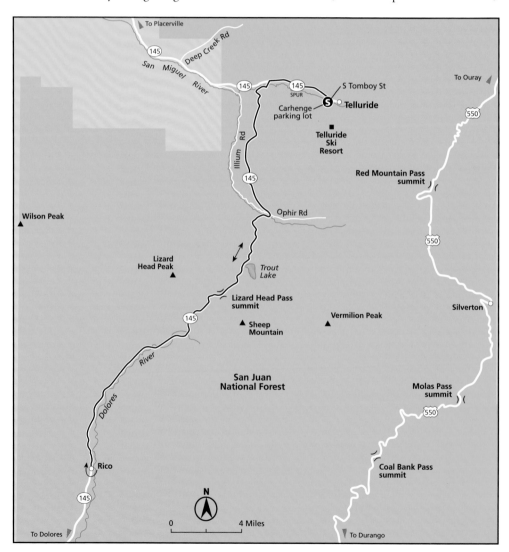

The grind to the summit of Lizard Head Pass will take your breath away—in more ways than one.

down the aspen-lined valley. In Rico, at mile 27.7, you'll find everything you need to fuel up for the trip back to Telluride. Last time I pedaled through, during the 2013 Ride the Rockies charity bike ride, I spent a few minutes chatting with the owner of the Mine Shaft Inn. He said that at present Rico had a population of "a couple hundred on a good day" and that there were "three bars, a post office, a trucking company, and a great Fourth of July parade." It's a cool and funky spot that's definitely worth a visit.

On the trip back to Telluride, hug the guardrail just outside Rico, and peer down at the rushing waters of the Dolores. Then knuckle down for the longer but more gradual southern ascent of Lizard Head Pass. The heart of the climb is 5.6 miles with a 3 percent grade. From the summit, it's 15 mostly downhill miles back to Telluride. Back at Carhenge, kick off your cycling shoes, and head to the nearby bank of the San Miguel River. There's a little wading spot just across the bridge that's perfect for soaking tired legs.

MILEAGE LOG

0.0	From Carhenge, head north on S Tomboy St. to SR 145 Spur
0.1	Left on SR 145 Spur, heading west on road or adjacent bike path
3.3	Left, heading south on SR 145
15.0	Reach Lizard Head Pass summit
27.7	Arrive in Rico
40.4	Reach Lizard Head Pass summit
52.1	Right on SR 145 Spur to Telluride
55.4	Return to start

Difficulty:	Challenging
Time:	4–6 hours
Distance:	69.2 miles out-and-back
Elevation gain:	6190 feet
Best seasons:	Late spring to early fall
Road conditions:	Shoulder comes and goes. Steep drop-off, narrow shoulder, and no guardrail on portions of Red Mountain Pass ascent.

GETTING THERE: Ride starts at Hartwell Park at intersection of Sherman St. (SR 62) and Railroad St. in small town of Ridgway, a thirty-minute drive south of Montrose, an hour north of Telluride, and ninety minutes south of Grand Junction.

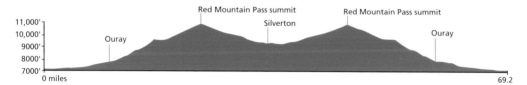

Few stretches of tarmac elicit more intrigue than the notorious mountain road that connects Ouray and Silverton. Known alternatively as the "Million Dollar Highway" and one of the world's most dangerous roads (as proclaimed by *USA Today* in 2013), this 23-mile stretch of US Highway 550 that crosses Red Mountain Pass is brutal, breathtaking, and a little bit scary. And that applies whether you're on a bike or in a car. Why the notoriety? For starters, it's truly *Sound of Music* scenic here in the heart of the San Juans. Jagged peaks thrust high into the sky, waterfalls plunge down sheer rock faces, and the gaping Uncompahgre Gorge disappears into the distant shadows. Million-dollar views abound.

But it's that roadside gorge, dark and deep, along with the lack of a guardrail and avalanche and rockslide exposure that have led to US 550's infamy. Countless puckered tourists have been frightened by the fact that at times this section of narrow road cut into the side of the mountain has little more than a shoulder separating their car from the abyss. And over the years, there have been six avalanche-related fatalities. The reality, though, is that as long as you're not drunk, texting, or otherwise overly distracted, there's nothing to worry about. The last fatal avalanche incident was in 1992; a variety of mitigation protocols have since been put into place. (There are no guardrails so that plow drivers have somewhere to push snow during winter.) Besides, you're not going to tackle this ride in the winter. What you should be worried about is the 6190 feet of climbing.

I like to start in Ridgway, which means a flat, 10-mile warm-up spin to Ouray and the start of the climb. But this stretch of US 550 has a small shoulder and can get a little busy. If that makes you nervous, start at the base of the pass. It's easier to catch a post-ride soak in the famed Ouray Hot Springs that way. Once you're past Ouray, you'll be headed uphill for 13 miles, gaining 3300 feet with an average

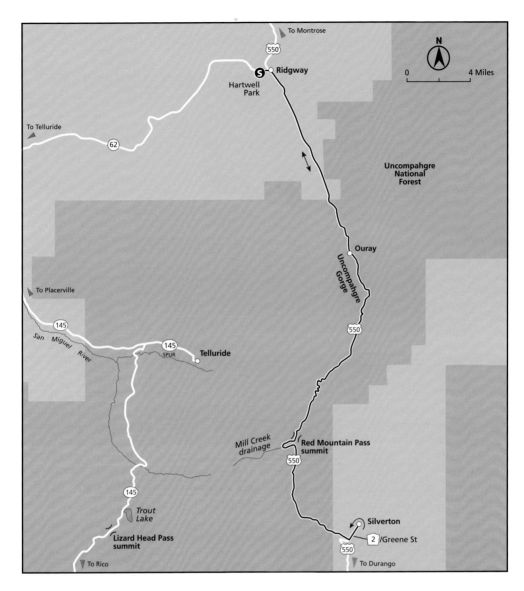

To Montrose

To Telluride

Hartwell Park

S Ridgway

550

To Placerville

62

145

145
SPUR

Telluride

San Miguel River

Uncompahgre Gorge

Ouray

Uncompahgre National Forest

N

0   4 Miles

550

Mill Creek drainage

Red Mountain Pass summit

550

550

145

Trout Lake

Lizard Head Pass summit

To Rico

Silverton

2 /Greene St

550

To Durango

grade of 5 percent. This is also the section of greatest "exposure," with the road's sometimes precipitous drop-off looming on your right. Stop and take a look. The view into the gorge is amazing—and it's really not that scary. The shoulder is plenty wide.

Around mile 17, the road levels out, as you roll across a majestic high-alpine valley, sky-scraping mountains lining either side. Soak in the scenery and enjoy the respite. Two miles

later, the road kicks again, grinding to the 11,018-foot summit at mile 23.7. Now it's decision time. If you're feeling flat, it's best to turn around and head back.

Otherwise, keep rolling to Silverton, which is another 10 miles south, nearly all of it downhill on smooth pavement with an ample shoulder. It's a fabulous descent, highlighted by the view up the Mill Creek drainage, which is on your right as you whip around

The road up Red Mountain Pass has been called one of the world's most dangerous roads. It's easy to see why.

a tight switchback near mile 26. Just keep in mind that you'll soon be riding back up this road. Save some energy.

At mile 33.3, turn left off the highway and onto County Road 2, which merges with Greene Street and takes you into Silverton. Roll to the end of town, and you'll reach the finish line of the famed Iron Horse Bicycle Classic (Ride 56). Grab a snack, top off your bottles, and listen for the whistle of the Durango & Silverton Narrow Gauge Railroad, which used to haul precious metals out of these mountains but now delivers sightseers to this summertime tourist hub.

When you're rested and ready, head back the way you came. From this side, the more gradual Red Mountain Pass ascent is just shy of 10 miles and gains 1787 feet at an average grade of 3 percent. About two miles past the summit, check out the scenic overlook on the left side of the road. There's a great view of Red Mountain (it is indeed red), plus several interpretive signs loaded with interesting tidbits about the area's mining history. (In the ground below you is a 5.5-mile tunnel that runs all the way to Telluride.)

On the way down, the steep drop-offs are a lane away; just as well since you'll be going much faster. Keep your eyes peeled for the occasional pothole or rock in the road, and enjoy the ride. It really is a million-dollar cycling experience.

MILEAGE LOG

0.0 From Hartwell Park at the intersection of Sherman St. (SR 62) and Railroad St. in Ridgway, head east on Sherman St.

0.4 Right onto US 550

10.0 Arrive in Ouray

10.7	Begin Red Mountain Pass climb
23.7	Reach Red Mountain Pass summit
33.3	Left on CR 2, and arrive in Silverton
33.4	Merge onto Greene St.
34.3	Reach turnaround point
35.4	Right onto US 550
45.0	Reach Red Mountain Pass summit
58.7	Arrive in Ouray
69.2	Return to start

60 MESA VERDE NATIONAL PARK

Difficulty:	Moderate to Challenging
Time:	3–5 hours (shorter options)
Distance:	53 miles
Elevation gain:	5310 feet
Best seasons:	Year-round
Road conditions:	Majority of route has little or no shoulder. Obey single-file law. Best avoided during summer weekends when traffic is heavy. Bicycles must have white headlight and red taillight or reflector for tunnel. Mesa Verde National Park charges cyclists a $5 or $8 entrance fee, depending on time of year.

GETTING THERE: Ride starts just off US 160 at Mesa Verde National Park Visitor and Research Center, 10 miles east of Cortez, 8 miles west of Mancos, and 36 miles west of Durango. Free parking, bathrooms, and water.

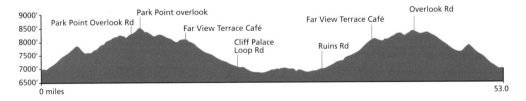

In 2009, *National Geographic Traveler* named Mesa Verde one of its "50 Places of a Lifetime," lauding America's first World Heritage Site for both its high-desert beauty and historic significance. Within the 52,000-acre national park are more than 4500 archaeological sites, including 600 stone-and-mortar cliff dwellings built by Ancient Puebloans. Some of the ruins date back 1400 years. It's a truly amazing place worth at least a day trip. Make that two days. The bike ride through Mesa Verde is equally magical. During this 53-mile out-and-back, you're treated to rolling roads, panoramic views, and cliff-edge overlooks of precipitous red rock canyons and even some of the park's ancient dwellings. If you have time, toss a bike lock and a pair of flip-flops in a backpack so that you can walk around a little.

The ride starts just off US Highway 160 at the park's visitor and research center. Fill your bottles. This is arid and nearly shadeless country. Triple-digit temperatures are common during the summer months. Exit the visitor center parking lot, then turn left on Ruins Road. A mile later, reach the entrance station, and pay the fee. You'll also need to show that you have a white headlight and red taillight, which are required for passage through an unlit tunnel farther up the road.

The road heads uphill for the next 3.9 miles, crawling along the side of this massive mesa. A notch in the hillside marks the end of

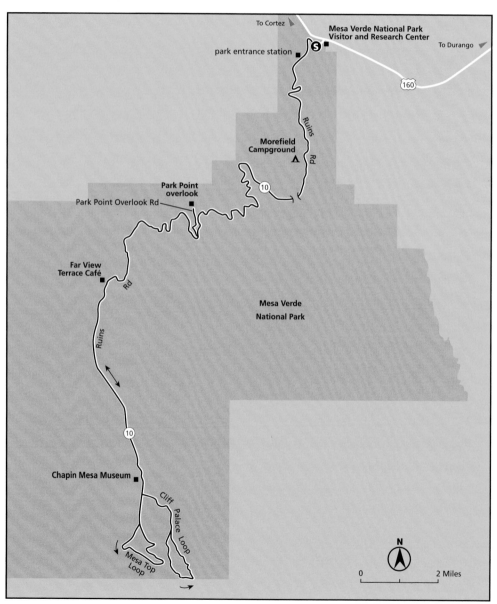

From this ride's high point at Park Point overlook, the entire Four Corners region spreads out before your eyes.

the first climb. Immediately, you drop down into a secluded valley surrounded by a stunning patchwork of red rock, green grass, and piñon and juniper trees. Some are healthy and full of needles, while others are scarred black from forest fires that ravaged the area in the early 2000s. You'll also pass Morefield Campground on your right, which has water and restrooms.

Another mile up the road is the aforementioned tunnel. It's about two city blocks long. Turn on your lights, and take the full lane. The road is fairly narrow. Once you're back in daylight, you climb again, but it's gradual. Soon the views open up. Spot the towering La Plata Mountains and fertile Mancos Valley to the east, the distant desert to the west, and an

array of smaller mesas that make up the massive Mesa Verde in between. One more small climb brings you to the 10.5-mile mark and the road's high point at 8365 feet.

To reach the park's high point, turn right onto Park Point Overlook Road, and follow it a half mile to a parking lot. Now walk your bike up the short footpath on the right, which leads to a fire lookout, elevation 8572 feet. On a clear day, visibility extends for 100 miles in all directions, allowing you to see the entire Four Corners region.

Back on Ruins Road, it's mostly downhill to the Far View Terrace Café and gift shop at mile 16.6. This is a good spot to get out of the sun, grab a snack, and top off your bottles. It's also a good turnaround point. Continuing onward means giving away almost all the elevation you've gained, and then having to climb out on the way back. But it also brings you to the cliff dwellings.

If you continue, go left at the stop sign at mile 21.6. A half mile later, turn left for the Cliff Palace Loop or continue straight for the Mesa Top Loop. Both are 6-mile string-and-balloon roads with one-way traffic. Ride them both if you can. But if you must pick one, opt for Cliff Palace, which has overlooks of Cliff Palace and Balcony House, two of the park's largest and most spectacular cliff dwellings. Just know that you must have a ticket to walk down into the sites and that this is not ideal bike shoe terrain. Once you're done with the loops, top off your bottles at the Chapin Mesa Museum (just left of Ruins Road at the stop sign) or after you climb back to the Far View Terrace Café. Tackle four short ascents to reach the final, blissful downhill back to the starting point.

MILEAGE LOG

0.0   From Mesa Verde National Park Visitor and Research Center, left onto Ruins Rd.
0.9   Pass entrance station
5.1   Go through tunnel
10.5   Right on Park Point Overlook Rd.
11.1   Walk up footpath to Park Point overlook
11.8   Right back onto Ruins Rd.
16.6   Reach Far View Terrace Café
21.6   Left at stop sign to Mesa Top Loop
22.0   Left on Cliff Palace Loop Rd.
27.6   Left on Ruins Rd. toward Mesa Top Loop
30.9   Left on Mesa Top Loop
31.6   Right on Ruins Rd. to begin return trip
53.0   Return to start

61 PARADOX VALLEY

Difficulty: Challenging
Time: 4–6 hours
Distance: 79.2 miles out-and-back
Elevation gain: 5323 feet
Best seasons: Year-round
Road conditions: Shoulder comes and goes, but entire route on lightly traveled roads. Some road damage on final climb approaching turnaround point. Take caution during descent.

GETTING THERE: Ride starts in Naturita, a small town an hour's drive west of Telluride. Park free at the Naturita Visitor Center, located at intersection of SR 141 and W. 2nd Ave. Restrooms and water in visitor center, as well as a small grocery store directly across highway.

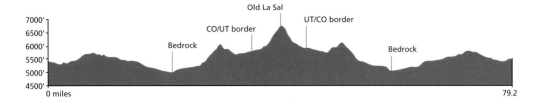

The Paradox Valley ride is a lot like the place it's named after. At times it simply doesn't make a lot of sense. But while I can't explain why the Dolores River bisects (instead of runs through) this lonely valley (thus the paradox), I can tell you that, though far off the beaten path and occasionally mind-numbing, this is a truly unique cycling experience. There is challenging climbing (more than 5000 feet), stunning beauty (the valley's red rock cliff walls rise 2000 feet), and eerie solitude (my last time through, I encountered a half dozen vehicles—in four and a half hours). Just make sure to bring basic roadside repair tools and ample food. On that same ride, the only store along the route—the old general store in tiny Bedrock—was shuttered and up for sale.

The ride starts at the visitor center in Naturita, another one of western Colorado's quiet, no-stoplight towns that's seen its fortune ebb and flow with the tides of the fickle mining industry. From here, head west on State Route 141, spying the San Miguel River on your right. At mile 2.2, turn left onto SR 90, and your routefinding is over. It's a shade more than 37 miles to the turnaround point, which is at the top of the Old La Sal climb just across the Utah border.

Initially the road is tucked inside a small canyon. But by mile 4, the view opens up, growing ever wider as you head into the heart of the Wild West. About now, you'll likely start asking yourself why the hell you're out in this barren, desolate place. Have patience. It'll

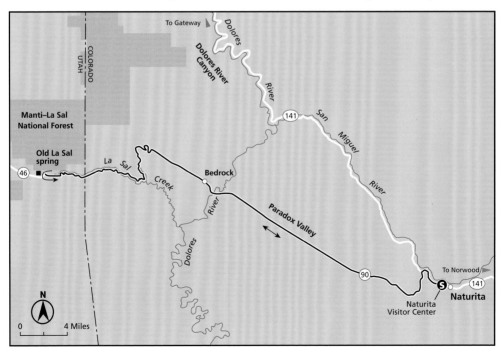

You'll have plenty of time to think during the long, lonely spin through the Paradox Valley.

make sense soon. Around mile 7, as you roll over the top of a gradual climb, the Paradox Valley and Utah's distant La Sal Mountains are revealed. It's a magical place, with towering walls of red sandstone stretching as far as the eye can see.

This javelin-straight stretch of tarmac trends gently downhill to mile 20.8, where it crosses the Dolores River in the midst of its wrong-way journey across the valley. Less than a mile later is the aforementioned town of Bedrock, whose postmaster still receives a steady stream of mail addressed to Fred and Wilma Flintstone. The general store may or may not have reopened when you roll through. At the very least, its front porch provides welcome shade, and there's a spigot out back. Top off your bottles. It's your last water supply until the turnaround point.

At mile 26.4, the road swings left, climbing up the valley's southern edge. The 3-mile ascent averages 5 percent, gaining about 850 feet. The views are terrific, as is the rapid descent down into a smaller valley on the other side. Here the scenery changes. Red rock formations remain, but an infusion of water courtesy of La Sal Creek supports a much greener landscape. Scrub oak, native grasses, piñon, and juniper line the narrow road and dot nearby hillsides.

At mile 36.1, you enter Utah. A mile and a half later, the ride's toughest climb begins. The ensuing 2.3 miles average 7 percent and gain 820 feet. The payoff at the top is the most valuable of desert resources, a spring on the right side of the road near what's left of Old La Sal, a cow town abandoned long ago. Look for a three-foot length of black hose hanging over a small concrete basin in a pull-out on the north side of the road. The water is crystal-clear, ice cold, and supremely refreshing. And yes, it's safe to drink. Dunk your head while you're at it.

Now turn around and head back the way you came, preparing for a second look at all this amazing beauty—and another trek through the Paradox Valley, this time trending gently uphill most of the way. Soak in the scenery, contemplate this geologic conundrum, and pray there isn't a headwind.

MILEAGE LOG

0.0	From Naturita Visitor Center, head west on SR 141
2.2	Left on SR 90
20.8	Cross Dolores River
21.2	Arrive in Bedrock
36.1	Enter Utah
39.6	Reach Old La Sal, turnaround point
43.2	Return to Colorado
58.0	Arrive in Bedrock
77.0	Right on SR 141
79.2	Return to start

WESTERN SLOPE

At the "grand junction" of the Gunnison and Colorado rivers is the Western Slope's Grand Valley, home to the state's most fertile soil and some of its best cycling terrain. Pedal through red rock wonderlands in Colorado National Monument or Unaweep Canyon, climb the distant summit of Grand Mesa, or simply enjoy a leisurely spin past the farms, vineyards, and orchards that dot the lands around Fruita, Palisade—and Grand Junction.

62 UNAWEEP CANYON

Difficulty:	Challenging
Time:	5–7 hours
Distance:	88.5 miles out-and-back
Elevation gain:	5589 feet
Best seasons:	Spring through fall (possible in winter)
Road conditions:	Narrow shoulder on majority of route, but traffic is light and pavement is in good condition.

GETTING THERE: Ride starts at Gunnison Bluffs trailhead parking area in Whitewater. From downtown Grand Junction, head south on 5th St., which becomes US 50. Continue on US 50 for 9 miles, then take a right onto 1st St. in the small town of Whitewater. It is an easy turn to miss; if you get to the SR 141 junction, you've gone too far. Follow 1st St. to intersection with Coffman Rd., then bear right, continuing on Coffman Rd. for about a mile. Just after road bends right, parking area will be on your left. Parking is free. No bathrooms or water.

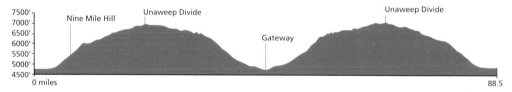

In the language of the Ute Indians who roamed these lands hundreds of years ago, Unaweep means "canyon with two mouths." And indeed, this area is a geological oddity: a canyon with no beginning, just a divide in the middle and streams running out each end. The real conundrum, though, is how the canyon got here in the first place. Some geologists believe the Gunnison River cut the deep Unaweep channel before changing course and moving to its present, more northward locale. Others credit the Dolores River, which now flows farther south.

Either way an uplift of the surrounding Uncompahgre Plateau left Unaweep Canyon high and dry. Also not in question is the grandeur of this place. Another of the Colorado Scenic and Historic Byways, it's a straightforward out-and-back from Whitewater to Gateway and features a long grind up to the remote Unaweep Divide, plus a lot of towering rock wall views and a slew of spectacular high-desert scenery. Though the shoulder is tiny and the climbs are long, this lightly traveled road provides a cutaway look at this sprawling plateau where one of the two aforementioned rivers carved into the radiant red sandstone.

From the starting point at the Gunnison Bluffs trailhead parking lot just outside Whitewater, turn right and head 1.6 miles east on Coffman Road to the intersection with State Route 141. Turn right and you're essentially done with routefinding.

Almost immediately after turning onto SR 141, you cross the Gunnison River, then start the gradual ascent of Nine Mile Hill, the first half of the ride's outbound climb. Initially, you're tucked into a small canyon with the seasonal East Creek drainage on your right. But soon the view opens up, revealing a broad high-desert landscape dotted with cactus, piñon pines, juniper, sagebrush, and varying shades and shapes of sandstone. It's a George Hayduke kind of place. (If you've never heard of George, pick up a copy of Edward Abbey's *The Monkey Wrench Gang*. It's a riotous read.)

By the 10-mile mark, the grade backs off, but you'll still trend uphill for another 11 miles, as you begin rolling into the tall-walled Unaweep Canyon. At the summit, which doesn't feel like one, a sign heralds your arrival at Unaweep Divide, elevation 7048 feet, and the transition from the East Creek drainage to the West Creek drainage; mouth to mouth, if you will. If you're feeling spry, the trip to Gateway is well worth the effort. There's more great scenery, and you'll get a fresh look at where you've come from (plus another long climb) during the trip back. But if 88.5 miles and almost 5600 feet of altitude gain are beyond your reach, ride to the divide, then head back to Whitewater. This option reduces your total distance to 43 miles with

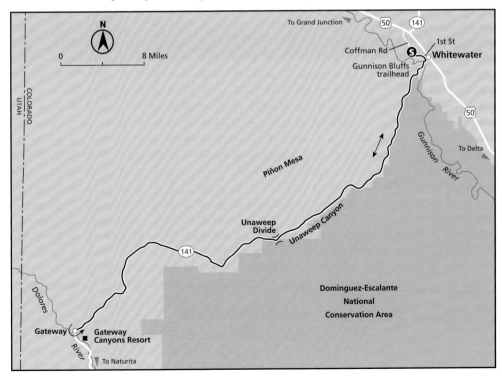

This canyon road with "two mouths" climbs above 7000 feet during its ever-scenic trip from Whitewater to Gateway.

2400 feet of climbing, and you still get to see the most spectacular sections of the canyon.

If you go on, the descent to Gateway starts gradually, before picking up speed around the 34-mile mark. It's a steady 4 to 6 percent grade the rest of the way down, but since it has no tight turns, you can go as fast as your nerves allow. Just as you roll into town, there's a small general store on the right side of the road. Or continue another half mile to swanky Gateway Canyons Resort, which is owned by Discovery Channel founder (and cycling fan) John Hendricks. Either way, make sure to top off your bottles and fuel reserves. The west side climb is tough for the first 10 miles before it backs off around the 55-mile mark.

Route Variation: The Unaweep Canyon route accounts for roughly a third of the Unaweep Tabeguache Scenic and Historic Byway, which also includes the 51 miles of SR 141 between Gateway and Naturita through the Dolores River Canyon. If you have the time and resources to put together a point-to-point tour, this is another must-do ride. You'll pass the infamous Hanging Flume and ascend a steady 3.5-mile climb that averages 4 percent, topping out near the confluence of the Dolores and San Miguel rivers. If you run low on water, there's a natural spring tucked behind the trees in the small pull-out on the right side of the road 19.5 miles south of Gateway.

0.0	Right out of Gunnison Bluffs trailhead parking lot onto Coffman Rd.
1.6	Right onto SR 141
21.3	Reach Unaweep Divide
44.3	Arrive in Gateway
67.3	Return to Unaweep Divide
86.9	Left onto Coffman Rd.
88.5	Return to start

63　FRUITA FARMS LOOP

Difficulty:	Easy
Time:	1½–3 hours
Distance:	37 miles
Elevation gain:	835 feet
Best seasons:	Spring to fall (possible in winter)
Road conditions:	Minimal shoulder on majority of route, but these flat, rural farm roads generally have very little traffic.

GETTING THERE: Ride starts at Canyon View Park, just off I-70 on 24 Rd. between Fruita and Grand Junction. Take I-70 west from Grand Junction (3.5 miles) or I-70 east from Fruita (8.5 miles), then take exit 28 for 24 Rd. toward Redlands Pkwy. At traffic circle, take first exit onto 24 Rd. Proceed 0.2 mile and park will be on your left. Free parking, restrooms, and water.

If you're looking for a flat spin on quiet rural roads, the Fruita Farms Loop (created by my friend John Hodge) is perfect. There's just a tiny bit of climbing, the scenery is fabulous, and it's easy to shorten or lengthen the ride depending on wind, weather, or whim. Like the annual Rose Hill Rally charity ride held each May, this loop starts at Canyon View Park. From there, you alternate between number roads and letter roads, as you make a counterclockwise trip around the farmland north of Interstate 70 between Fruita and Grand Junction.

Along the way, enjoy rural tranquility and take in the nearly constant long-distance views of Colorado National Monument to the south, Grand Mesa and Mount Garfield to the east, and the towering Book Cliffs due north. It's big sky country at its finest. And you'll likely have it all to yourself, save for the cows, horses, chickens, and cornfields. All told, there are twenty-two turns during this 37-mile loop. Your best bet for routefinding is to simply write out this sequence, then tape it to your top tube and go: *Right out of south end of park onto G Road, R23, LL, R20, LN, R19, LO, L18, RN³/₁₀, R17, LP, L16, LM, R17, LK, R19, LJ, R24, LI, R24½, and RG. Right back into park.*

The first letter indicates the direction you turn; the second letter or number is the name of the road. So R23 is a right turn on 23 Road, and LI is a left on I Road, etc. In case you're curious, the number roads indicate the

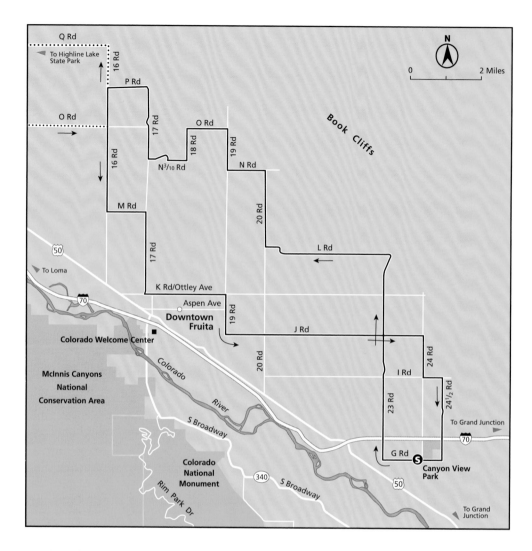

number of miles due east from the Colorado-Utah state line, while letter roads are also 1 mile apart with A Road serving as the center line. Anywhere north of A Road (such as this entire route) the roads are labeled B Road, C Road, D Road, etc. Anything south of A Road includes an S, for example CS Road or BS Road (the most frequently stolen sign in Mesa County). Fractions are also mileage indicators and are sometimes used for both number and letter roads, including N$\frac{3}{10}$ Road and 24½ Road on this route.

The whole system, while not particularly imaginative, is great for cyclists trying to figure out how far from home they are on a windy, cold day. And yes, if this ride has a downfall, it is the wind. It doesn't blow all the time, but when it does, there's nowhere to hide. Just hope it's coming out of the west, which means that no matter when you decide to turn around, you'll have a tailwind blowing you back to Canyon View Park.

As for refueling stops, your best bet is downtown Fruita, which is three blocks south just after the left onto K Road. Within a four-block span on Aspen Avenue, you'll find a

The Grand Valley's elementary road-naming system makes navigating the tranquil countryside as easy as 1-2-3 and A-B-C.

grocery store, coffee shop, a few burger joints, and one of my all-time favorite bike shops, Over the Edge Sports. Once you're satiated, continue east on Aspen Avenue until you run into 19 Road. Take a right here, and you're back on the main route.

Route Variation: You can add about 13 miles by heading farther west to Highline Lake State Park (free to cyclists), where you can top off your bottles, rest up in the shade, and even take a swim. To get there, go right instead of left on 16 Road at the 18.8-mile mark, then take a left on Q Road, and finally a right on 11⁸⁄₁₀ Road, which will lead you into the park. To get back on the main route, ride back out 11⁸⁄₁₀ Road, go left on Q Road, right on 12 Road, left on O½ Road, right on 14 Road, left on O Road, and finally right on 16 Road, which is the western border of the main Fruita Farms Loop.

MILEAGE LOG

0.0	From Canyon View Park, right onto G Rd.
1.0	Right on 23 Rd.
6.1	Left on L Rd.
9.3	Right on 20 Rd.
11.2	Left on N Rd.
12.2	Right on 19 Rd.
13.2	Left on O Rd.
14.1	Left on 18 Rd.
14.9	Right on N³⁄₁₀ Rd.
16.1	Right on 17 Rd.
17.8	Left on P Rd.
18.8	Left on 16 Rd.

Highline Lake State Park extension:

18.8	**Right on 16 Rd.**
19.8	**Left on Q Rd.**
24.0	**Right on 11⁸⁄₁₀ Rd.**
25.2	**Arrive Highline Lake State Park, turnaround point**
26.4	**Left on Q Rd.**
26.6	**Right on 12 Rd.**
28.1	**Left on O½ Rd.**
30.1	**Right on 14 Rd.**
30.6	**Left on O Rd.**
32.6	**Right on 16 Rd. to return to main route**

21.8	Left on M Rd.
22.8	Right on 17 Rd.
24.8	Left on K Rd. (Ottley Ave.)
26.8	Right on 19 Rd.
27.8	Left on J Rd.
32.8	Right on 24 Rd.
33.8	Left on I Rd.
34.3	Right on 24½ Rd.
36.3	Right on G Rd.
37.0	Right back into Canyon View Park

64 COLORADO NATIONAL MONUMENT

Difficulty:	Moderate to Challenging
Time:	2½–4 hours
Distance:	39.5 miles
Elevation gain:	3518 feet
Best seasons:	Year-round
Road conditions:	Majority has smooth pavement, but narrow shoulder within Colorado National Monument. Three short tunnels require a headlight and taillight. Monument charges cyclists a $5 entrance fee, good for a week.

GETTING THERE: Ride starts from Riverside Park at 675 W. Colorado Ave. From downtown Grand Junction, head west on Ute Ave., make a right onto 1st St. and then a left onto Grand Ave., which becomes Broadway. Proceed a half mile, then turn left onto West Ave. Riverside Park is directly ahead. Free on-street parking, bathrooms, and water.

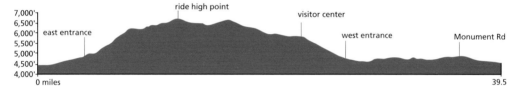

Only the most hardcore Kevin Costner fans likely remember his role in the 1984 film *American Flyers*. But for cyclists, the campy coming-of-age tale is must-see cinema, one of the rare occasions Hollywood has shined its bright lights on the two-wheeled world. Among the movie's most famous scenes is extensive race footage shot along Rim Rock Drive inside Colorado National Monument. The idea was to mimic the Coors Classic bike race's famed Tour of the Moon stage, which traced a twisting path through this red rock wonderland. I'll skip delving deeper into the plotline. This wasn't exactly Costner's finest work. But suffice to say, there are some spectacularly scenic scenes in the movie—and along this route.

The ride starts at Riverside Park, which is about a mile west of downtown Grand Junction. Before heading to the park, make sure

to check out the eclectic downtown street art. The collection is a mix of permanent and temporary pieces, ranging from whimsical metal sculptures to amphibian statues. Also make sure your water bottles are full. This is arid country, and once you're out of town, the lone refilling spot is 22.4 miles into the ride.

From the park, get on the bike path that runs along the nearby Colorado River, and head west (downstream) under the underpass. Take an immediate right on the far side of the underpass, which will lead you to a bike lane running south along Broadway (State Route 340) as it crosses the river.

At the half-mile mark, turn left onto Monument Road. Now the full scope of Colorado National Monument appears, giant walls of red rock filling the southern border of the Grand Valley. Mile 3.9 brings you to the monument's east entrance, where you'll pay

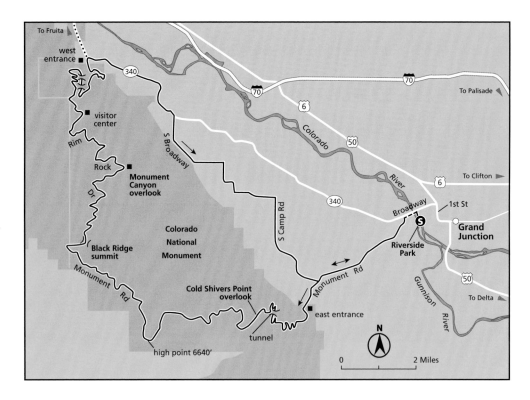

an entrance fee. You'll also need to show that you have a white headlight and red taillight, which are required for passage through three short tunnels along the route. This is strictly a safety measure, so the lights need only be bright enough to make you visible to drivers, not illuminate your path. A couple small blinkies suffice.

Just past the entrance station, it's time to climb. It's not a terribly difficult ascent, 7.8 miles with an average grade of 4.1 percent. But expect to pedal uphill for at least forty minutes. Pause for a moment at the Cold Shivers Point overlook at mile 7.6 to take in the expansive view of the aptly named Grand Valley, then continue along Rim Rock Drive, passing more overlooks along the way.

Near mile 12, the bulk of the climbing is done, as you reach the road's high point at 6640 feet. At mile 19.4, pass the Monument Canyon overlook. The distant rock spires and sheer sandstone cliffs are a true marvel of

Mother Nature. Make sure to stop and take it all in. Three miles later, you arrive at the visitor center, where you can top off your water bottles and grab a snack. Next up is another 4 miles of steeper descending, as you make your way down to the park's west entrance at mile 26.5.

Less than a half mile later, intersect with State Route 340, and turn right to head back to Grand Junction. At mile 29.5, take a slight right onto South Broadway, following the bike route signs. It keeps you out of traffic while you continue to meander along the base of the monument, taking in yet another perspective of this natural wonder. Keep a sharp eye on the road signs for the next 4 miles to stay on South Broadway through several turns. Finally at mile 33.6, turn right onto South Camp Road. Two and half miles later, turn left onto Monument Road, and retrace your route back to Riverside Park.

You can also do this ride in the opposite

Whichever entrance you choose (this is near the east side), the climb into Colorado National Monument is a ride you'll never forget.

direction, traversing the base of the monument first, then climbing up the west side. This ascent is longer but shallower (10.4 miles, average grade 3.3 percent, total elevation gain 1800 feet). Some argue the scenery is better here, so it's better to be moving slower. I say try both and decide for yourself.

Route Variation: Start this ride from Fruita, which is about 13 miles west of Grand Junction. From Interstate 70 westbound, take exit 19, then turn left on SR 340, and park at the Colorado Welcome Center on the south side of the highway on the left (see map for Ride 63, Fruita Farms Loop). The welcome center has free parking, water, and restrooms.

Once you're pedaling, continue on SR 340 away from the interstate for 2.5 miles, then either pick up the prescribed route (traversing the base of the monument, then climbing the east side), or turn right onto Rim Rock Drive and climb the west side, following the turn-by-turn directions in reverse order.

An alternative to the on-street route at the base of the monument is the Colorado Riverfront Trail. Completed in fall 2014, this multiuse path connects Grand Junction to Fruita, running east–west along the Colorado River. Pick up the trail at the Colorado Welcome Center in Fruita or at Riverside Park in Grand Junction. Just know that there are many spur trails in the Grand Junction section, so take a look at the map on the Colorado Riverfront Commission's website before you attempt it.

MILEAGE LOG

0.0	From Riverside Park, turn right onto bike path adjacent to Colorado River
0.1	Follow path below underpass, then take an immediate right, joining bike lane paralleling Broadway (SR 340)
0.5	Turn left onto Monument Rd.
3.9	Enter Colorado National Monument via its east entrance
7.6	Arrive at Cold Shivers Point overlook
19.4	Arrive at Monument Canyon overlook
22.4	Arrive at visitor center
26.5	Exit Colorado National Monument
26.8	Right on SR 340
29.5	Right on S. Broadway
33.6	Right on S. Camp Rd.
36.1	Left on Monument Rd.
39.5	Return to start

65 LITTLE PARK ROAD LOOP

Difficulty:	Moderate to Challenging
Time:	1½–3 hours
Distance:	26.3 miles
Elevation gain:	2937 feet
Best seasons:	Spring through fall (possible in winter)
Road conditions:	Minimal shoulder on majority of route, but traffic is very light and pavement is good. Descent includes a short, unlit tunnel, which requires a headlight and taillight. You don't have to pay the entrance fee if you visit only the lower portion of Colorado National Monument.

GETTING THERE: This ride starts at Riverside Park, located at 675 W. Colorado Ave. From downtown Grand Junction, head west on Ute Ave., and make a right onto 1st St. and then a left onto Grand Ave., which becomes Broadway. Proceed about a half mile, then turn left onto West Ave. Riverside Park is directly ahead with free parking, water, and restrooms.

If Colorado National Monument (Ride 64) is the Grand Junction area's crown jewel ride, Little Park Road is the less heralded diamond in the rough. The climb is tougher, the road is quieter, and the high-desert scenery is stunning in its own right. Plus the final third travels through the east side of the monument, so you get to see some of the sights but don't have to pay the entrance fee (more on that in a moment.)

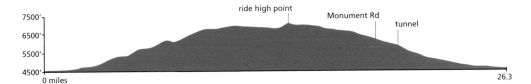

ride high point

Monument Rd

tunnel

7500'

6500'

5500'

4500'

0 miles

26.3

The ride starts at Riverside Park, about a mile west of downtown Grand Junction. Before rolling out, make sure your water bottles are full. This is arid, shadeless country, and there are no spots to refill along the way. From the park, hop on the bike path that parallels the nearby Colorado River, and head downstream below the underpass. Take an immediate right, and loop up to the path running south along Broadway (State Route 340) over the river.

At the half-mile mark, turn left onto Monument Road. A block later, go left on D Road. This takes you through one of Grand Junction's more "eclectic" neighborhoods before the road Ts. Next, go right on Rosevale Road, and a mile later turn right on Little Park Road. Now it's time to climb. The bulk of the next 8 miles are uphill on a grade that averages 6 percent with several painful pitches above 10 percent. It's a fun, stair-stepping ascent with views of Grand Mesa to the east, Colorado National Monument to the west, and the sprawling Grand Valley behind you.

Around the 9.5-mile mark, the road levels out, as you turn southwest and roll along the northern edge of the massive Uncompahgre Plateau. Catch your breath. There are two

Once the climbing is done, Little Park Road rolls gently along the edge of the massive Uncompahgre Plateau, offering great long-distance views of the Book Cliffs to the north.

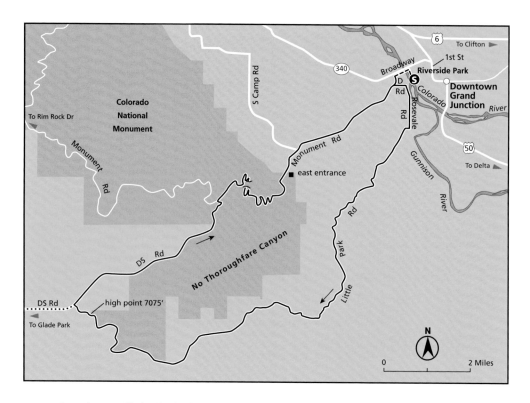

more short but stiff climbs before the long downhill back to the start. The first begins at the 13.2-mile mark and takes you to the ride's high point at 7075 feet, or roughly 2500 feet higher than where you started.

But your work isn't over just yet. At mile 14.3, immediately after you turn right off Little Park Road and onto DS Road, the road pitches up once more. It's a short climb, though, and your reward is another spectacular panorama. On a clear day, you can see Utah. Follow DS Road to its terminus at the intersection with Monument Road, then turn right heading into Colorado National Monument. As long as you head down, there's no fee. The hitch is that while you may be tempted to go left here and check out the upper section of the monument, unless you've already paid the entrance fee, you'll be subject to a fine. The closest place to pay that fee is at the bottom of the road you're about to go down. Bottom line: if you want to combine this ride with a trip through the main section of the monument, it's best to detour to the east entrance station and pay the fee before backtracking to Little Park Road.

Now that that's cleared up, enjoy the descent down the east side of the monument. It has a shallow grade with a handful of sweeping turns and countless breathtaking views. There's a tunnel at the 20.1-mile mark, and as per park rules, your bike must be equipped with a red taillight and white headlight. (Small blinkies suffice.) Continue downhill another 4.8 miles, leaving the monument and returning to Broadway (SR 340). Go right here and head back to Riverside Park.

Route Variation: Double the length of this ride and increase your climbing by 1000 feet by adding an out-and-back on DS Rd. Go left at the intersection of Little Park Rd. and DS Rd., then ride 13.6 miles to the end of the pavement, turn around and head back to the main route.

0.0   From Riverside Park, right onto bike path adjacent to Colorado River

0.1   Follow path west under underpass, then take immediate right, joining bike lane that parallels SR 340, and cross Colorado River

0.5   Left on Monument Rd.

0.7   Left on D Rd.

0.9   Right on Rosevale Rd.

1.8   Right on Little Park Rd.

7.1   Right on Little Park Rd.

14.3   Right on DS Rd.

          DS Rd. extension:

          14.3   **Left on DS Rd.**

          16.1   **Arrive at Glade Park (food and water available)**

          27.9   **Reach end of pavement and turn around**

          41.5   **Rejoin main route**

18.7   Right on Monument Rd.

20.1   Enter short, unlit tunnel

25.9   Right onto Broadway (SR 340), and retrace route back to start

26.3   Return to start

66   PALISADE FRUIT AND WINE BYWAY

Difficulty:	Easy
Time:	1–2 hours
Distance:	23.2 miles
Elevation gain:	695 feet
Best seasons:	Spring through fall (possible year-round)
Road conditions:	Intermittent shoulder, but entire route is on quiet rural roads, save for small section of multiuse path.

GETTING THERE: Ride starts at Veterans Memorial Park at intersection of Main St. and 8th St. in downtown Palisade. From I-70, take exit 42 for Palisade, proceed south for a third of a mile, and then turn left onto 1st St. In another half mile, turn right onto Main St., and park will be on your right a half mile down the road. Free parking, water, and restrooms.

Why do this ride? The best answer comes in the form of a question from John Hodge, a Palisade local who showed me around his cycling neighborhood. "Where else can you stop along the way and get a fresh, juicy peach or even sample some wine?" he asked. Well said. Sure, you can hammer out this mostly flat 23.2-mile loop and call it a workout. But it's far better to lollygag, soaking in views of (and possibly stopping at) the various orchards, farm stands, lavender gardens, and yes, wineries that line much of this route.

The orchards surrounding Palisade provide a bounty of fruit in summer and a safe haven come fall.

The ride starts at Veterans Memorial Park in downtown Palisade, then follows the well-signed Palisade Fruit and Wine Byway loop. Either direction works fine, the only real consequence being whether you ascend or descend what the locals call Puke Hill. John wasn't 100 percent sure where that name originated, but it's not hard to imagine what could happen if you combined too much wine and fruit with this short but very steep climb. I've chosen the counterclockwise (downhill) version—less chance of an incident.

There are a handful of turns along the route, but if you follow the byway signs, routefinding is generally easy. At mile 7.6, as you're heading south on 33½ Road, look for the gap in the guardrail just before the road bends right. Exit here onto a multiuse path. The first

100 feet are gravel, but it's paved after that, tracing the Colorado River with good views of Mount Garfield, the prominent outcropping in the Little Book Cliff Mountains just north of the interstate.

A mile and half after you roll onto the path, turn left onto the bridge across the river, which spills you onto C½ Road. Turn left, and you're back on the byway for the return leg. (In case you're wondering, the numbered roads indicate the number of miles due east from the Colorado-Utah state line, while the letter roads are also 1 mile apart.) Once you're on C½ Road, continue following the signs, which keep you on the main road across East Orchard Mesa. At mile 17.7, arrive at the Puke Hill descent. Be careful.

A mile later, turn right onto State Route

6, which runs along the base of Grand Mesa (Ride 67). This is a particularly spectacular section, with the massive mesa towering directly above on your right and the Colorado River rolling along your left. At mile 20.9, turn left, crossing the river on North River Road, to head back to downtown Palisade. Turn left on Main Street, and the park is a few blocks ahead.

As for where to stop along the way, by my count, there are eight wineries and nine fruit stands and orchards. All have something worth sampling, especially during peach season. If you want more detailed information, pick up a copy of the Fruit and Wine Byway Tourist Map from the Palisade Chamber of Commerce, which is just up the road from Veterans Memorial Park at 319 South Main Street.

MILEAGE LOG

0.0   From Veterans Memorial Park, turn left on Main St.
0.4   Left onto 1st St., which becomes G⁴/₁₀ Rd.
2.1   Left onto 36¹/₁₀ Rd.
2.6   Right on G Rd.
3.6   Left on 35 Rd.
4.6   Right onto F Rd.
5.6   Left on 34 Rd.
6.3   Right on E¼ Rd.
6.8   Left on 33½ Rd.
7.6   Go through gap in guardrail, merging onto multiuse path

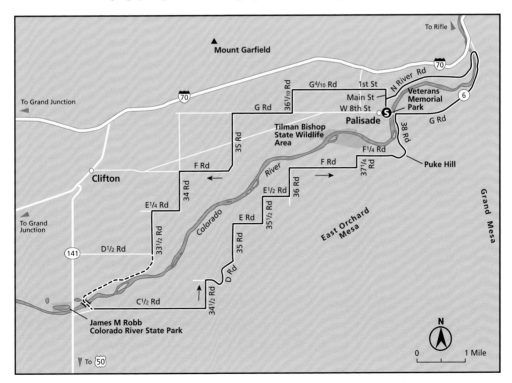

9.2	Left onto footbridge across Colorado River
9.5	Leave bike path and turn left onto C½ Rd.
11.6	Left on 34½ Rd.
12.1	Right on D Rd.
12.9	Left on 35 Rd.
13.5	Right on E Rd.
14.0	Left on 35½ Rd.
14.5	Right on E½ Rd.
15.0	Left on 36 Rd.
15.5	Right on F Rd.
16.7	Left on 37¼ Rd.
16.9	Right on F¼ Rd.
17.7	Descend steep hill, joining 38 Rd.
18.7	Right on SR 6
20.9	Left at bridge onto N. River Rd.
22.9	Left on Main St.
23.2	Return to start

67 GRAND MESA

Difficulty:	Epic
Time:	4½–7½ hours
Distance:	68.2 miles up-and-back
Elevation gain:	6747 feet
Best seasons:	Spring to fall
Road conditions:	Shoulder comes and goes, but traffic is generally light, especially past turnoff for SR 330. Sections of broken pavement on road above Powderhorn Mountain Resort.

GETTING THERE: Ride starts from roadside pull-out on SR 65, less than a half mile from I-70. From Grand Junction, take I-70 east about 18 miles to exit 49 for SR 65. Park in pull-out on right. No water or bathrooms.

By numbers alone, the Grand Mesa ride lives up to its name: 21 miles of continuous climbing, nearly 6000 feet of elevation gain. But this is more than just a protracted uphill death march. From the start just south of Interstate 70 to the turnaround point at the Grand Mesa Visitor Center, you'll spin through four ecological zones, take in dozens of spectacular long-distance views, and pass a handful of the three-hundred-plus lakes that dot the lush landscape of the world's largest flat-top mountain.

Your ride starts just south of I-70 at the pull-out on the right side of State Route 65 (a.k.a. Grand Mesa Scenic and Historic Byway). There's no water or restrooms here, so come ready to ride. Grand Mesa is a great place to escape the searing summer heat typical along

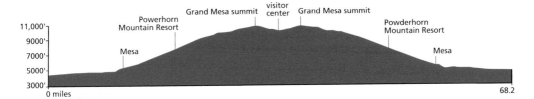

Colorado's mostly arid Western Slope, but you're still going to need plenty to drink and eat. The first 10 miles are fairly mellow, as you roll ever so slightly uphill through the towering red sandstone canyon walls that border Plateau Creek. This is typically the route's busiest stretch of road, but there's an ample shoulder. Traffic usually abates after you pass the SR 330 intersection at mile 10. Mile 10 is also where those aforementioned 21 miles of climbing begin. The grade is generally in the 4 to 5 percent range, but there are a handful of leg-searing sections, especially closer to the top. Expect to grind uphill for at least two hours.

At mile 11.3, roll into the small town of Mesa. Fill your bottles here. The next water stop is 13 steep miles up the road. Just ahead is Powderhorn Mountain Resort, a great little family-friendly ski area. The road bends east here, crawling up the side of the mesa. Look left for your first real taste of the sprawling views that reach far across the Grand Valley. There's a huge stand of aspen here, too, making this a spectacular fall ride.

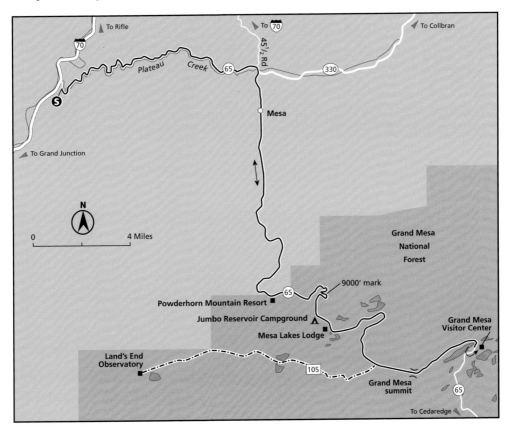

The ride up Grand Mesa passes through four distinct ecological zones, but the bounty of amazing long-distance views are likely to leave the most lasting impression.

Around mile 22.2, the road winds through a series of four steep switchbacks, passing the 9000-foot mark along the way. (The start's at 4796 feet.) The grade backs off for about a half mile, then ramps up again as the road traverses a narrow shelf cut into a steep cliff wall. This is arguably the route's most stunning stretch of road. Mile 24.4 brings you to the Jumbo Reservoir Campground, which is open seasonally and has potable water. You can also fill up at the Mesa Lakes Lodge (open year-round), just ahead on the right. From here, it's 6.5 miles (and 1000 feet of climbing) to the summit.

As you'd expect, the top of Grand Mesa isn't a jagged peak. If not for the sign on the right side of the road at mile 31.1, you might not realize you are now 10,839 feet above the sea (and more than 6000 feet higher than the start point). Turn around here if you like, or continue 3 miles down the south side to the Grand Mesa Visitor Center (open Memorial Day through the end of September), which has restrooms, water, and a vibrant outdoor wildflower garden.

Route Variation: If you still have gas in your tank and want to see one of the most amazing views on Grand Mesa, add the mostly flat, 20-mile out-and-back dirt road detour to the Land's End Observatory. The turnoff is on the west side of SR 65, 1.5 miles north of the summit. On a clear day, you can see from Utah to central Colorado without turning your head.

For a great point-to-point encompassing the entire Grand Mesa Scenic and Historic Byway, continue from the summit down the south side of SR 65 to Cedaredge (50 miles one-way) or on to Delta and the intersec-

tion of US Highway 50 (65 miles one-way). Just like on the north side, the views through here are tremendous, with the entire San Juan Mountain range stretching out in the distance.

If you're a true masochist and comfortable riding on a busy highway, do a 125-mile loop starting and finishing in Grand Junction. Just know that this route includes an unavoidable 5-mile section on I-70 and at least 32 miles on US 50.

MILEAGE LOG

0.0	From pull-out, turn right onto SR 65
10.0	Right, continuing on SR 65
11.3	Arrive in Mesa
19.1	Pass Powderhorn Mountain Resort
24.4	Pass Jumbo Reservoir Campground
24.6	Pass Mesa Lakes Lodge
31.1	Reach Grand Mesa summit
34.1	Reach Grand Mesa Visitor Center and turnaround point
37.4	Return to Grand Mesa summit
68.2	Return to start

EASTERN PLAINS

Colorado is most famous for its Rocky Mountains, but the Great Plains occupy roughly a third of the state. Out east, you'll almost always encounter more cows than cars. Some roads are dead flat. Others roll endlessly. Faint outlines of distant peaks hover on the western skyline. Prairie grass sways in the wind. Bring what you need. Bike shops are few and far between.

68 SOUTH PLATTE RIVER TRAIL

Difficulty:	Easy
Time:	1–2 hours
Distance:	19.4 miles
Elevation gain:	156 feet
Best seasons:	Early spring to late fall (possible year-round)
Road conditions:	Includes 6.8 miles of gravel road. US 138 has narrow shoulder and broken pavement.

GETTING THERE: Ride starts just off Julesburg exit of I-76 at Colorado Welcome Center, 181 miles from Denver and 3 miles from the Nebraska-Colorado border. Free parking, coffee, twenty-four-hour restrooms, water, and tourist information.

Few people will drive to Julesburg for an easy ninety-minute bike ride. But if you're heading into or out of Colorado on Interstate 76 near the Nebraska border, the South Platte River Trail Scenic and Historic Byway is a great spot to spin out your legs. This 19.4-mile mixed-surface route is the shortest of the state's twenty-three scenic and historic byways. Besides the fresh air and peaceful prairie scenery, a series of interpretive signs lines the route. Each details a piece of the area's rich Old West history, including Fort Sedgwick (mile 7.2).

The former military outpost was established in 1864 to protect the transcontinental telegraph route as well as travelers on the famed Overland Route, and later became famous thanks to the Kevin Costner drama *Dances*

with Wolves. (Costner's fictional character mans the fort by himself for a time.) Today a flagpole and plaque are all that remains. All the buildings were packed up and shipped to Nebraska when the fort closed down in 1871.

Pedaling begins at the Colorado Welcome Center, just off I-76 on County Road 28. Head left out of the parking lot, heading west on CR 28. At mile 1.0, pavement gives way to gravel. It's well graded and no problem on a road bike. Just try to avoid the road's shoulder. This is prime goathead country, and the closer to the edge of the road you ride, the greater your chance of a puncture from the plant's thumbtack-like seeds. As with any ride, bring a pump and extra tube.

At mile 7.8, pavement returns as you turn right onto CR 27.8. The next 1.3 miles trend

Around the 9-mile mark, you'll roll into Ovid, a tiny agricultural town that straddles the Union Pacific rail line.

slightly downhill as you cross the South Platte River and roll into Ovid, a tiny agricultural town that sits on the Union Pacific rail line. Be careful crossing the tracks at mile 9.1. Just after you enter Ovid, turn right onto US Highway 138. Less than a mile farther, pass a shuttered sugar beet processing plant with a few old cars and a bunch of vintage farm equipment parked out front. It's worth a look. The next few miles bring more tranquil spinning, as you pass fields of corn, hay, and soy.

At mile 13.5, US 138 merges with US 385. Two miles later, you enter Julesburg, the fourth town with that name in the area. The first burned down, the second was abandoned, and the third was only temporary, erected for the workers laying the Transcontinental Railroad line. The current iteration has a few shops and restaurants. At mile 17.3, just after you exit Julesburg, stay right, following US 385 toward the welcome center. At mile 19.1, turn right onto CR 28, and you've completed the loop.

MILEAGE LOG

0.0	From Colorado Welcome Center, left on CR 28
1.0	Start of gravel road
7.8	Right onto CR 27.8 (end of gravel road)

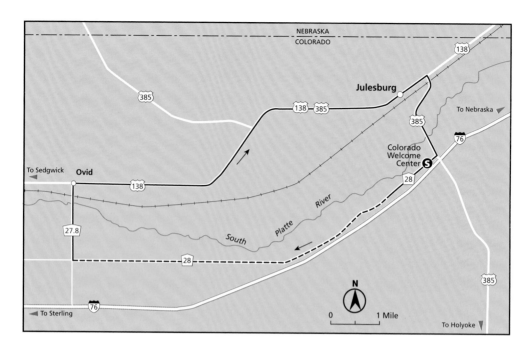

9.3	Right onto US 138
17.3	Right onto US 385
19.1	Right onto CR 28
19.4	Return to start

69 TWO TIME ZONES, THREE STATES

Difficulty:	Challenging
Time:	4½–6 hours
Distance:	88 miles
Elevation gain:	2918 feet
Best seasons:	Early spring to late fall
Road conditions:	Shoulder comes and goes, but entire route on secondary highways. Rumble strips alongside road in some spots.

GETTING THERE: Ride starts from Municipal Park at corner of 3rd St. (US 34) and Blake St. in Wray, 170 miles east of Denver. Free parking, water, and bathrooms.

This route is courtesy of former Colorado state senator Greg Brophy, an avid cyclist who grew up on a farm near Wray. When I asked him to share the best rides in the area, this 88-mile loop that includes three states and two time zones was at the top of his list. "The scenery

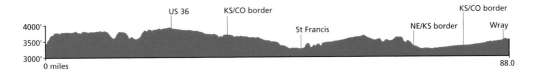

is beautiful. The roads are quiet. But don't be fooled," he warned. "This ride is anything but flat." Indeed, with 2900 feet of climbing and the likelihood that at some point you'll battle wind, this loop can be every bit as challenging as its high mountain brethren farther west.

From downtown Wray, head west on 3rd Street, then turn left onto US Highway 385. Almost immediately, the road pitches upward for a steady 2-mile climb out of this small agricultural community surrounded by cliffs and bluffs on three sides. At the summit, a big wind turbine on the side of the road serves as a not-so-subtle reminder of the potential suf-

fering to come. The next 9.5 miles are mostly flat, as you head south passing fields of corn and hay, and then a giant feedlot that you'll likely smell before you see. The road's shoulder is narrow, but the pavement is good and traffic light.

At mile 11.5, the horizon is interrupted by a string of testing rollers. Up and down you go for the next 8.5 miles, crossing several cottonwood-lined creek beds. Around mile 20, the road levels out again. Four miles later, turn left on US 36, and begin the gradual downhill leg into Kansas and the central time zone. You cross the border at mile 35 and,

There's a common misconception that Colorado's Eastern Plains are completely flat. But as you'll see along this route, that is definitely not the case.

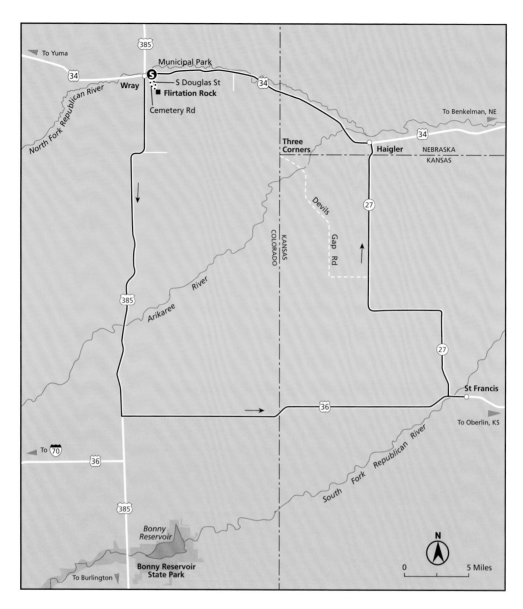

soon after, descend more steeply, dropping into the Republican River basin. The turn for the ride's northbound leg, Kansas State Route 27, is at mile 47. But if you need water or food, add the quick out-and-back into St. Francis, about 1.5 miles ahead on US 36. There's a truck stop cafe on your left as you roll into town.

Now turn around and head back to Kansas

SR 27; turn right and grind up a stiff climb away from the river basin. The ensuing 22 miles are some of the ride's toughest. Pass the turnoff for Three Corners (where a rough dirt road leads to the spot where you can touch Colorado, Kansas, and Nebraska at the same time), and then roll into Nebraska, and back to mountain time. At mile 71.6, turn left onto US 34 in Haigler, Nebraska, which has a small café where you can get water and a snack. The final 16-plus miles trend gently uphill, as you reenter Colorado and then roll back into Wray on 3rd Street.

Head back to the start point, or for a little extra climbing and a great bird's-eye view of the town and surrounding countryside, turn left on South Douglas Street and climb to Flirtation Rock, site of the first Masonic meeting in eastern Colorado. After taking in the view from the overlook, continue up the hill, then turn right on Cemetery Road, which passes the town cemetery before looping around and descending into downtown Wray.

MILEAGE LOG

0.0	West on 3rd St. (US 34)
0.1	Left on Dexter St. (US 385)
5.2	Continue on US 385
24.0	Left on US 36
35.0	Enter Kansas
47.0	Pass intersection with Kansas SR 27
48.3	Arrive in St. Francis, Kansas
49.5	West on US 36 (Kansas SR 27)
49.6	Right on Kansas SR 27
70.6	Enter Nebraska
71.6	Turn left on US 34, and arrive in Haigler, Nebraska
78.8	Enter Colorado
88.0	Arrive in Wray

70 HUGO RACE LOOP

Difficulty:	Moderate
Time:	3½–5 hours
Distance:	80 miles
Elevation gain:	1823 feet
Best seasons:	Early spring to late fall (possible in winter)
Road conditions:	Majority of route on country roads with no shoulder. Light traffic and sections of rough pavement. Single-file shoulder on SR 71 and SR 94.

GETTING THERE: Ride starts adjacent to Lincoln County Clerk's Office at 103 3rd Ave. in Hugo. Free parking.

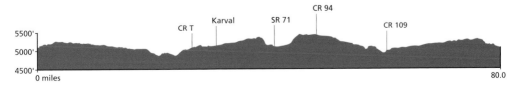

The desolate countryside around the small town of Hugo was once the site of one of Colorado's most challenging amateur road races.

From 2003 to 2011, the Hugo Road Race was a rite of spring. Each May, amateur bike racers from across Colorado battled for bragging rights on the quiet country roads that surround this small cattle ranching community 100 miles east Denver. It was tough, tactical racing, where relentless rollers and whipping winds detonated fields. Get dropped (I always did), and it was a lonely solo push to the finish line. Alas, registration numbers dwindled in later years (maybe it was simply too hard), and the event was cancelled in 2012. This ride traces the old race route, an 80-mile string-

and-balloon configuration with about 1800 feet of climbing.

From the intersection of 3rd Avenue and 1st Street adjacent to the County Clerk's Office, head south out of town on 3rd, which quickly becomes County Road 109. Here (and on the majority of the route), you'll be on a narrow farm road with no divider line, no shoulder, and almost no traffic. It's peaceful, quiet country—unless the wind is blowing.

CR 109 trends gently uphill for the opening 3.5 miles, then crests a small rise where you get your first view of what's to come.

Ahead the road stretches out like a knife blade, a train of rollers disappearing in the distance. To your right (if it's a clear day), make out the faint outline of the Rocky Mountains. To your left, it's great plains and big sky as far as the eye can see. Mile 26.8 brings your first turn, a sweeping right onto CR T (just stay on the pavement). A mile later, turn back to the south on CR 31. A mile after that, go right toward Karval on CR S, beginning the route's main westbound leg.

By now, you understand the route's key characteristics: there is very little shade; the pavement is bumpy in spots; and if the wind is blowing, you need to be on the lookout for tumbleweeds. This is especially true during times of drought, when these thorny menaces seem to be everywhere. Beware, lest you end up with punctured tire(s) or a mangled rear derailleur. (In case you're curious, the lack of precipitation reduces cattle herds, which usually eat the plants before they become a nuisance.)

Mile 30.7 brings you to the tiny town of Karval. There's a water spigot in front of

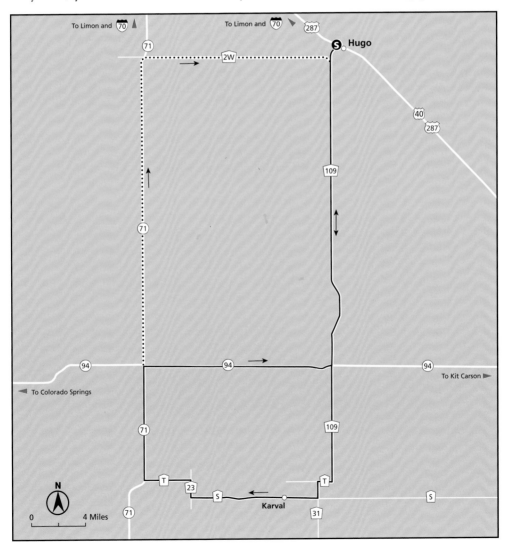

the church on the left side of the main road and a Gatorade machine in front of the fire station across the street. (It doesn't always accept bills, so bring a handful of quarters just in case.) Both were working the last time I rode through, but there are no guarantees. On a hot day, I recommend that you carry three water bottles.

Six miles ahead, turn right onto CR 23. A mile later, go left on CR T. Up ahead is a half-mile, sustained downhill and one of the ride's most stunning views, with this arrow-straight road literally disappearing into the horizon. Fortunately, you don't have to go that far. At mile 40.7, turn right onto State Route 71 heading north, the busiest road on the route. But even here, expect cattle to outnumber cars ten to one. At mile 47.7, turn right onto SR 94 just after you pass

the unincorporated community of Punkin Center. In the 1920s and 1930s, all the area buildings were painted the color of pumpkins (thus the name).

SR 94 trends downhill for the next dozen miles as you head east, crossing Brush Creek just before reaching the intersection of CR 109. Go left here, and it's 20 mostly uphill miles to the finish in Hugo. Once you're back in town, head over to Hines Park, and take a dip in the vintage swimming pool that was built in the 1930s and is listed on the National Register of Historic Places.

Route Variation: Early versions of the race were held on a 64-mile rectangular route that cut out the trip to Karval. From Hugo, head south on CR 109, then west on SR 94, then north on SR 71, and finally east back to Hugo on CR 2W.

MILEAGE LOG

0.0	Head south (away from town) on 3rd Ave., which becomes CR 109
26.8	Right onto CR T
27.8	Left onto CR 31
28.8	Right onto CR S
30.7	Enter Karval
36.7	Right onto CR 23
37.7	Left onto CR T
40.7	Right onto SR 71
47.7	Right onto SR 94
59.9	Left onto CR 109
80.0	Return to start

71 PAWNEE BUTTES ROUBAIX

Difficulty:	Epic
Time:	5–8 hours
Distance:	56.5 miles
Elevation gain:	1649 feet
Best seasons:	Early spring to late fall

The distinctive Pawnee Buttes are the result of uneven erosion: the surrounding landscape was worn down by wind and water, but this pair of pillars survived thanks to a harder layer of caprock.

Road conditions: Includes 46 miles of gravel roads that are rough and loose in spots. Do not attempt after recent rainfall. Bring extra tubes. Cyclocross bike recommended. Final 10.5 miles of loop is on paved state highway with ample shoulder.

GETTING THERE: Ride starts at intersection of SR 14 and CR 129 in New Raymer. Free parking. Water is available at restaurant (closed Sundays) on south side of highway.

Warning: As the title of this ride implies, this route is not for the faint of heart, ill equipped, or under prepared. This is a true Roubaix-style adventure across the rugged Colorado Piedmont that's almost entirely on wind-whipped gravel roads. Some sections are rough, others loose and sandy. I strongly recommend wide tires, or preferably a cyclocross

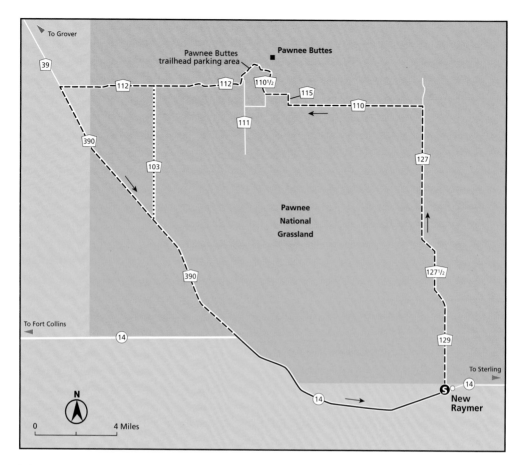

bike. Bring multiple spare tubes and a patch kit. And do not attempt this ride if there's even a slight chance of rain. Moisture will turn the road into impassable muck.

You'll also need two twenty-ounce water bottles and a hydration pack, or a well-stocked support vehicle. There are no services or water available anywhere along this shadeless route. It can be scaldingly hot in the summertime. Finally, make sure to bring a camera. The payoff for all this suffering and hardship is a close-up look at two of the most unique natural rock formations in Colorado—the distinctive Pawnee Buttes.

The ride starts in New Raymer (or just Raymer on some maps), which has a liquor store and restaurant but little else. The closest source of supplies, including a bike shop, is Fort Morgan, 26 miles south via State Route 52. Also know that many businesses in this part of the state are closed on Sundays. From New Raymer, head north on County Road 129, which is part of the Pawnee Pioneer Trails Scenic and Historic Byway. These opening miles are on constantly rolling hard-packed dirt road, which besides leading into the Pawnee National Grassland, is a main thoroughfare for energy exploration truck traffic. Be cautious and courteous.

Through here, you get the first glimpses of the Pawnee Buttes, two three-hundred-foot-tall fortress-like mesas that rise from otherwise level land. These peculiar twin pillars are the product of uneven erosion where the surrounding high plains were worn away by water and wind, but the buttes persevered thanks to outer caps of harder sandstone and conglomerate rock.

At mile 12.9, turn left onto CR 110, and begin the ride's main climb, a stair-stepping affair that rises 725 feet on the way to the Pawnee Buttes trailhead parking area at mile 21.5. The pitch is never particularly steep (and occasionally downhill), but the road's condition deteriorates the closer you get to the parking area. At the trailhead, there's a restroom (but no water), a handful of shaded picnic tables, an overlook, and several interpretive signs explaining that this vast expanse of shortgrass prairie has been occupied by humans for more than twelve thousand years, and that each of the white-washed wind turbines planted behind the buttes produces enough energy to power three hundred homes.

Heading out of the parking lot, turn right toward Grover. Just ahead on the right is another great overlook, followed almost immediately by the descent to CR 112. Turn right here, and continue to drop away from the buttes on a gravel road that has some sections of rough washboard but is otherwise in decent shape. At mile 25.7, make a quick right and then a left to continue on the historic byway (CR 112). If you do run into problems, there are a couple ranch houses around mile 31.

At mile 32.2, turn left on CR 390, and begin the final flat push to the finish. It's 13 miles to SR 14 and another 10.5 miles on a paved road with a wide shoulder back into New Raymer.

Route Variation: You can shorten the route by about 6 miles by turning left off CR 112 onto CR 103 at mile 28. Follow CR 103 south for 6 miles, then turn left onto CR 390, continuing on main route toward SR 14 and on to New Raymer.

MILEAGE LOG

0.0	From New Raymer, head north on CR 129 (start of gravel road)
3.9	Continue on CR 127½
6.2	Left on CR 127
12.9	Left on CR 110
18.8	Right on CR 115
19.3	Left on CR 110½
20.3	Right at fork toward Pawnee Buttes
21.5	Arrive at Pawnee Buttes trailhead parking area
21.6	Turn right out of parking lot, toward Grover
23.7	Right onto CR 112
25.7	Quick right and left, continuing on CR 112
	CR 103 shortcut:
28.0	**Left on CR 103**
34.0	**Left on CR 390, rejoining main route**
32.2	Left onto CR 390
41.3	Left, continuing on CR 390
46.0	Left onto SR 14 (end of gravel)
56.5	Return to New Raymer

72 SANTA FE TRAIL TRIANGLE

Difficulty:	Easy
Time:	1½–2½ hours
Distance:	32 miles
Elevation gain:	505 feet
Best seasons:	Early spring to late fall (possible in winter)
Road conditions:	Shoulder comes and goes, but majority of route is on lightly traveled rural roads.

GETTING THERE: Ride starts at Potter Park at corner of Grant Ave. and 5th St. in La Junta. From intersection of US 50 and US 350, head east on US 50, then turn right on Grant Ave. Park is two blocks ahead on right. Free parking.

Among the best reasons to ride Colorado's Eastern Plains is the sheer number of possibilities and permutations. Unlike the state's more mountainous regions where the low number of passable roads makes it difficult to craft loops of a reasonable length, the options

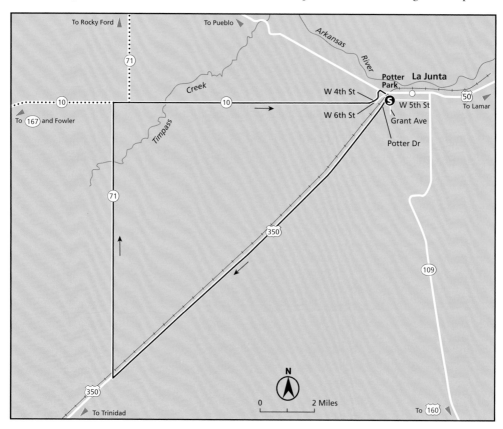

Long shadows, curious cloud shapes, and soft late-day light make a trip to the Eastern Plains a worthwhile endeavor.

out east are almost limitless. Take this outing on quiet rural roads south and west of La Junta. As constructed, it's a mellow 32-mile loop along portions of the Santa Fe Trail Scenic and Historic Byway. But if that's too short, check out the route variations below, which include 40- and 86-mile options. You can also go even shorter by mixing in one of the many gravel roads that crisscross the area.

This ride starts at Potter Park, then rolls southwest out of town on US Highway 350. You'll spend the next 13 miles on roughly the same route as the famed Santa Fe Trail, once part of an important 1800s-era trade network that linked Europe and the East Coast with Santa Fe and Mexico City. The wagon trains are long gone, but on a clear day, you're treated to stunning distant views of the Spanish Peaks and Sangre de Cristo Mountains.

Closer in is a tranquil mix of verdant cropland and sweeping shortgrass prairie dotted with cottonwood groves and ranch houses.

At mile 13.1, be mindful of the railroad tracks as you turn right onto State Route 71 for this route's 9-mile northward leg. Don't be surprised if you have this quiet stretch of road to yourself. Enjoy the peace and solitude, but make sure to come prepared in case you encounter mechanical issues. Punctures caused by goathead can be an issue in these parts, for instance. Next, turn right at the intersection with SR 10, which takes you on a dead-straight eastern path back to La Junta. If the wind is coming from the west, which it often is, you'll have no problem ripping along at 25 miles per hour. If it's blowing in your face, get ready to work. There's no place to hide out here.

On the outskirts of La Junta, around mile 31, stay right, merging onto 6th Street. Follow this left and then right, crossing US 350. Then turn right on Potter Drive and left on 5th Street, and you'll be back where you started.

Route Variation: For a 40-mile loop, follow SR 71 north to Rocky Ford, then take US 50 back to La Junta. To up the distance to 86 miles, turn left on SR 10, then take this quiet state highway west about 19 miles before turning north on SR 167 toward Fowler. In Fowler, pick up US 50 east for the straight run back to La Junta.

MILEAGE LOG

0.0	From Potter Park, head west on 5th St.
0.1	Left onto US 350 (Potter Dr.)
13.1	Right onto SR 71
22.2	Right onto SR 10
30.8	Right, merging onto 6th St.
31.3	Left, continuing on 6th St.
31.6	Right to cross US 350, then right onto Potter Dr.
31.8	Left onto 5th St.
32.0	Return to start

MULTIDAY ROUTES

Creating manageable cycling routes in Colorado can be tricky. The scarcity of passable roads and abundance of impassable mountains often makes getting from here to there an exercise in circuitousness. Sometimes, there is no path of least resistance. But that changes when your available ride time exceeds the standard sunrise-to-sunset constraint. With multiple days, options for excellent adventure increase exponentially.

73 CENTRAL SUMMITS CHALLENGE

Difficulty:	Epic
Time:	2–4 days
Distance:	234.4 miles
Elevation gain:	16,104 feet
Best seasons:	Summer to fall
Road conditions:	Independence Pass, Kebler Pass, and Cottonwood Pass are all closed seasonally (typically from early November to late May). Check CoTrip.org for status. Shoulder ranges from wide to nonexistent. Gravel road on Kebler Pass (29 miles), Jacks Cabin Cutoff (3.1 miles), and Cottonwood Pass ascent (13.7 miles)—all best avoided after recent rain. Use extreme caution during single-lane section of Independence Pass descent.

GETTING THERE: Ride starts at intersection of Main St. and US 24 in Buena Vista. Free on-street parking, as well as water and food nearby.

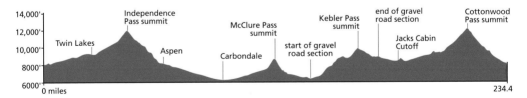

Independence Pass, McClure Pass, Kebler Pass, and Cottonwood Pass are each typically ridden as out-and-backs. Unless you string together massive loops, there's no easy way to get up, over, down, and back without retracing your pedal strokes. But if time is not tight, you're in for a treat that includes four amazing climbs, two trips above 12,000 feet, two Continental Divide crossings, plus an endless barrage of tranquil valley vistas, rushing river overlooks, and soaring mountain scenery.

But how many days? Where to start? Which direction to ride? Counterclockwise, for starters. Because the west side of Cottonwood Pass

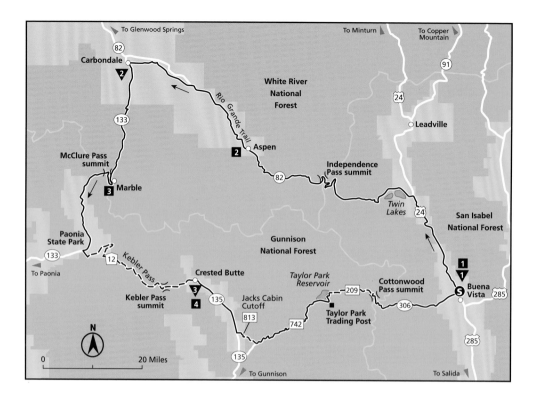

includes 13.7 miles of dirt road, it's better to climb west to east, avoiding a potentially bone-jarring descent. The start point is a matter of convenience. If you live in Aspen, start there. Same goes for Crested Butte or Carbondale. I chose Buena Vista primarily because of its proximity to Denver. It also means your final 19 miles are a 4000-foot descent down the east side of Cottonwood Pass—not a bad way to finish.

The duration of your trip depends on how much vacation time you can take and your personal pain threshold. In the summer of 2013, my buddy Zack did the whole loop in a day. But he has a very high pain threshold (and used to race professionally). For the rest of us, it's a two-day ride at minimum. And even that's a stretch. If forty-eight hours is all you have, you'll need to get as far as Marble on Day 1 (113 miles, plus a 6-mile detour; 7151 feet of climbing). Or if you don't mind

camping, consider Paonia State Park (132 miles; 8132 feet), which is as close to halving this ride as you can get.

But three or even four days is the sweet spot. On a three-day outing, aim for Carbondale on Day 1 (91 miles; 4900 feet). On Day 2, spin over McClure Pass and Kebler Pass, spending the night in Crested Butte (72.5 miles; 6752 feet). Then finish with the climb of Cottonwood Pass and descent back to Buena Vista (70.8 miles; 4452 feet). With one more day to play, finish Day 1 in Aspen (61.1 miles; 4898 feet). Get to Marble on Day 2 (50.1 miles; 2254 feet). Roll over Kebler to Crested Butte on Day 3 (52.5 miles, 5105 feet). And again finish with the big grind over Cottonwood on your last day.

Whichever option you choose, remember that Independence Pass (Ride 41) and Cottonwood Pass (Ride 46) both extend above tree line, which means heeding the two cardinal

On a clear day the summit of Independence Pass serves up a stunning array of high mountain scenery, including views of Mount Elbert, the tallest mountain in the state.

rules of high-altitude bike riding: Start early to avoid afternoon thunderstorms, and carry adequate foul-weather gear.

The opening 19 miles of Day 1 trend uphill on US Highway 24 from Buena Vista to State Route 82. This is the busiest leg of the route, but the shoulder is wide, and busy is a relative term in these parts. On your right, spy the rushing waters of the Arkansas River. To your left, catch views of the skyscraping Collegiate Peaks. A left turn on SR 82 commences the long approach to Independence Pass. After 20 miles of gentle rolling, the road turns 180 degrees left and pitches skyward. The next 4.5 miles average 5 percent on the way to the 12,095-foot summit. The descent to Aspen is fast, twisty, and a tad treacherous. Be careful.

In Aspen, pick up the Rio Grande Trail, which gets you off the highway for the westerly spin through the Roaring Fork Valley to Carbondale. Now, turn south on SR 133, which is part of the West Elk Loop Scenic Byway. If you opt to stop in Marble for a night (which I highly recommended), look for County Road 3 on your left around mile 113.

Just down the road on the main route is McClure Pass, which gains 1200 feet in 3.5 miles (peak elevation 8755 feet). It's a relatively easy ascent compared to this route's other primary obstacles, but still no pedal in the park. From the McClure Pass summit, it's 14.5 mostly downhill miles to Paonia State Park, and another 3 miles to the left turn for CR 12 and Kebler Pass. The road morphs to gravel almost immediately, but it's usually hard-packed and little problem on a road bike. The climb stair-steps, with a false summit around the 150-mile mark, then a longer push to the actual high point at 9980 feet (mile 158.5). The grade is never too steep, 7–8 percent at its worst. The pass is home to one of the largest aspen groves in the United States. Come in fall to see the state's best leaf show.

Pavement returns at mile 163.2. Two miles later, you roll into Crested Butte, an old mining town turned year-round tourist hub. Lodging options run the gamut. From Crested Butte, head south on SR 135 for the mostly flat 12-mile spin to Jacks Cabin Cutoff (Forest Road 813). The road's paved to start, then turns to gravel for 3 mellow miles. Watch out for the cattle guards.

At mile 181.6, pavement returns at the left turn onto FR 742. Next is the steady ascent up Taylor Canyon. The only truly steep pitch comes during the last mile, when you roll past the dam and arrive on the shores of Taylor Park Reservoir, elevation 9360 feet. The road levels for the next 3 miles. If you need water or food, stop at the Taylor Park Trading Post (mile 198.9). It's your last chance before Buena Vista.

Two miles ahead, turn right on Forest Road 209, and begin the final climb. In 13.7 miles, you gain 2800 feet, all of it on dirt road. The pitch is never too steep, but the soft surface will make progress slower. Figure on at least ninety minutes to the summit of Cottonwood Pass (elevation 12,126 feet). Now snap a picture in front of the Continental Divide sign, and descend to Buena Vista, 19.3 miles and nearly 4000 feet below.

MILEAGE LOG

0.0	From Main St. in Buena Vista, take US 24 west
18.7	Left onto SR 82
42.7	Reach Independence Pass summit
51.6	Start of narrow road section
55.0	End of narrow road section
61.1	Arrive in Aspen, and continue on SR 82
63.4	Right onto Cemetery Ln.
64.6	Left onto Rio Grande Trail multiuse path
91.2	Arrive in Carbondale, and left onto Main St.
91.8	Left onto Weant Blvd.
92.1	Left onto SR 133
116.8	Reach McClure Pass summit
134.2	Left onto CR 12 (start of gravel road)
158.5	Reach Kebler Pass summit
163.2	End of gravel road section
165.0	Arrive in Crested Butte
165.1	Stay straight on Whiterock Ave.
165.8	Right onto 6th St. (SR 135)
177.4	Left onto Jacks Cabin Cutoff (FR 813)
178.5	Start of gravel road section
181.6	Left onto FR 742 (end of gravel road)

198.9 Pass Taylor Park Trading Post
200.9 Right onto FR 209 (start of gravel road)
214.5 Reach Cottonwood Pass summit (end of gravel road)
214.6 Straight onto SR 306
234.4 Arrive in Buena Vista

74 SAN JUAN SCENIC SKYWAY

Difficulty:	Epic
Time:	2–4 days
Distance:	226 miles
Elevation gain:	17,030 feet
Best seasons:	Summer to fall
Road conditions:	Route has everything from smooth, wide shoulder to no shoulder at all.

GETTING THERE: Ride starts at Santa Rita Park at 111 S. Camino del Rio in Durango. From downtown, head south on Main Ave., turn right onto College Dr., and then left on Camino del Rio. In less than a mile, turn right at traffic light, entering park via Santa Rita Dr. Free parking, restrooms, water, and tourist information.

This mountainous route's name is borrowed from the fine folks at the Colorado Department of Transportation, who've bestowed these magical 226 miles with Scenic and Historic Byway status. Not to be outdone, in 1996 the US Department of Transportation labeled the loop an All-American Road, the highest designation American pavement can receive. The San Juan Scenic Skyway route, which traverses the mighty San Juan Range, is also called the Death Ride, an homage to its 17,000 feet of climbing and the band of crazies who gather annually to tackle it all in a day. I recommend a more relaxed approach. Better to suffer less and enjoy more.

Like the Central Summits Challenge (Ride 73), this route has feasible two-, three-, and four-day itineraries, and you can start wherever is most convenient. Unlike that ride, this entire loop is paved, so spin in either direction without worrying about having to go downhill on dirt. There are reasonable arguments

for a variety of permutations, but Death Riders typically go counterclockwise starting in Durango, so that's what I've chosen. Itinerary options break down as follows:

» **Two days:** Durango to Telluride (114 miles; 11,150 feet of climbing); Telluride to Durango (112 miles; 5880 feet). Or Durango to Ridgway (83 miles, 7798 feet); Ridgway to Durango (143 miles; 9232 feet).
» **Three days:** Durango to Ouray (72 miles; 7616 feet); Ouray to Rico (72 miles; 6003 feet); Rico to Durango (82 miles; 3411 feet).
» **Four days:** Durango to Silverton (48 miles; 5812 feet); Silverton to Telluride (73 miles; 5504 feet); Telluride to Dolores (61 miles; 2761 feet); Dolores to Durango (44 miles; 2953 feet).

All these towns have their own distinct charm. Mountain-ringed Silverton is full of

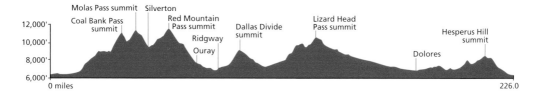

12,000'
10,000'
8,000'
6,000'
0 miles   226.0

Molas Pass summit   Silverton
Coal Bank Pass   Red Mountain   Lizard Head
summit   Pass summit   Pass summit
                                     Ridgway   Hesperus Hill
                                     Ouray   Dallas Divide   summit
                                                     summit
                                                                                 Dolores

mining history. Ouray is home to some of the best hot springs in the state. Rustic Ridgway feels plucked from a John Wayne western. Telluride has luxury accommodations, great restaurants, and superb scenery. Rico is laid-back and affordable. Dolores is just twenty minutes from Mesa Verde National Park (Ride 60). And Durango is a Colorado cycling mecca, blessed with countless road and mountain bike possibilities, plus a full spectrum of lodging and dining options. Honestly, you can't go wrong.

The first 48 miles trace the Iron Horse Classic route (Ride 56), which is flat and scenic for the first 13 miles heading north on US Highway 550, and then gradually uphill to mile 30 before finishing with two demanding high mountain climbs, Coal Bank Pass (summit elevation 10,640 feet) and Molas Pass (10,910 feet). Once you're over Molas, it's

Scenes such as this one near the summit of Lizard Head Pass reveal why the 226-mile San Juan Scenic Skyway has been proclaimed an All-American Road.

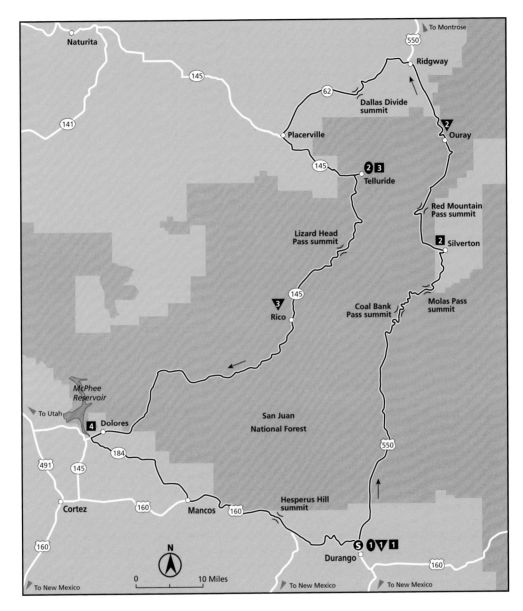

a rapid—and otherworldly scenic—descent into Silverton.

Just outside Silverton, you grind to the 11,017-foot summit of Red Mountain Pass (Ride 59). This stretch is known as the Million Dollar Highway, a nod to the spectacular mountain panoramas and the road's precarious hillside perch. Despite precipitous road-side drop-offs, there are no guardrails in many places so that plow drivers have somewhere to push snow in the winter. Fortunately, you'll be descending on the rock wall–lined inside lane, not next to the cliff's edge.

Mile 72 brings you to Ouray and its rejuvenating hot springs. From here, it's a flat 10 miles to the left turn for State Route 62.

Pass through Ridgway, then pedal up Dallas Divide (summit elevation 8983 feet). The views of the jagged Sneffels Range are as good as it gets. Now descend gently for about a dozen miles to the left turn for SR 145. Just ahead is Placerville, which has a general store. Here the road slants subtly upward for the gradual 12-mile ascent toward Telluride. Be careful: There are several blind corners, and the shoulder is narrow.

If Telluride's a resting point, follow SR 145 Spur east for 3.3 miles. On the way in, spot Bridal Veil Falls at the far end of the valley. It's the state's tallest free-falling waterfall (365 feet). If you're continuing south to Rico, turn right to stay on SR 145 southbound. Just ahead is Lawson Hill, a nasty 2.4-mile dig past the entry of the Telluride Ski Resort. The road levels for the ensuing couple miles. Then

just after a fast descent and hard right turn, you begin climbing Lizard Head Pass (Ride 58). This is the route's final big challenge: 4.7 miles, 1000 feet of elevation gain, an average gradient of 4 percent, and a summit elevation of 10,222 feet.

Up top, catch a glimpse of the unmistakable Lizard Head Peak to the west. Now descend, paralleling the Dolores River as it slices downvalley to Rico where you'll find a handful of basic food and sleep options. From Rico, the road continues its downhill trend to Dolores (mile 178.7). Just past town, pick up SR 184 toward Mancos, and begin the eastbound leg. In Mancos, turn left onto US 160. Now only 28 miles, Hesperus Hill (elevation 8423 feet), and maybe a headwind stand between you and the finish back in Durango.

MILEAGE LOG

0.0	Pick up Animas River Trail going north (upriver)
3.1	Reach end of path, and merge onto E. 32nd Ave. northbound
3.5	Left onto 32nd St.
3.6	Right onto Main Ave. (US 550)
35.9	Reach Coal Bank Pass summit
42.9	Reach Molas Pass summit
48.0	Arrive in Silverton
59.5	Reach Red Mountain Pass summit
72.0	Arrive in Ouray
82.4	Left onto SR 62
82.5	Arrive in Ridgway
93.7	Reach Dallas Divide summit
105.7	Left onto SR 145
106.1	Arrive in Placerville
118.5	Right, continuing on SR 145 (or SR 145 spur 3.3 miles to Telluride)
130.4	Reach Lizard Head Pass summit
142.7	Arrive in Rico
178.7	Arrive in Dolores
180.7	Left onto SR 184
198.0	Arrive in Mancos
198.2	Left onto US 160
212.5	Reach Hesperus Hill summit
225.3	Return to Durango, and pick up Animas River Trail going south (downriver)
226.0	Return to start

75   PLAINS TO PUEBLOS

Difficulty:	Epic
Time:	6–9 days
Distance:	515 miles
Elevation gain:	27,236 feet
Best seasons:	Late spring to fall
Road conditions:	Everything from smooth, wide shoulder to no shoulder at all.

GETTING THERE: Ride starts at Willow Park in Lamar. From Denver take I-25 south to exit 100A, then follow US 50 east. In 120 miles, turn right, continuing on US 50 and US 385 into Lamar. Then turn left onto Forest St., and park is two blocks ahead. Free parking, restrooms, and water.

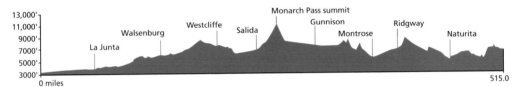

There's no absolute right way to cross Colorado by bike. In 2012, Race Across America took the far southern route, staying on US Highway 160 most of the way and traversing the Continental Divide at Wolf Creek Pass. The Adventure Cycling Association's Western Express route pushes farther north, adding more time in the mountains via US 50 and 550. Both are viable options worth exploring.

Yet another alternative is this "Plains to Pueblos" route, a 515-mile trek that begins along the windswept Eastern Plains and finishes in the heart of the high-desert lands once occupied by the Ancient Puebloans. In between are endless rural roads, sweeping mountain valleys, skyscraping peaks, stunning red rock canyon country—and more than 27,000 feet of climbing. Potential itineraries range from six to nine days. But anything less than eight, and you'll be pushing hard. The average daily mileage on the nine-day plan is just a shade under 60 miles, and each day ends in a town where you could

sleep inside or under the stars. If time is tight, I suggest trimming from the east. While stunning in their sheer vastness, the route's first 130 miles are fairly repetitive.

Our journey starts in Lamar, an old frontier town on the famed Santa Fe Trail trade route, 31 miles east of the Kansas border. Pick up US 50, and begin your westward trek across the rolling plains. This road gets busy at times, but the shoulder is wide. After 35 miles of easy spinning, turn right onto State Route 194. If it's a clear day, you can spot the faint outline of the Spanish Peaks, which feature prominently in the Highway of the Legends route (Ride 30).

At mile 48.8, pass Bent's Old Fort National Historic Site. Once a major 1800s-era trading hub, it's a fascinating peek into frontier history. Next stop is La Junta (mile 55.9). You can either spend the night here (as part of the nine-day plan), or push on another 74 miles to Walsenburg via SR 10. There's nothing but big sky, prairie grass, and tumbleweeds

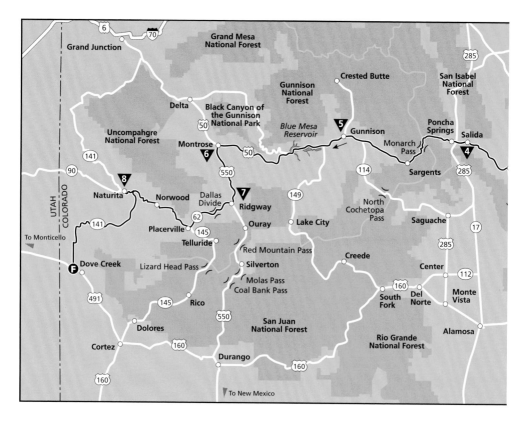

out here, so make sure you're fully committed before taking on this gently uphill stretch of road. Walsenburg has a smattering of basic lodging options, or you can camp at nearby Lathrop State Park.

Now head north on the business route of Interstate 25 through town. Then pick up SR 69 for the spectacular run through the Wet Mountain Valley with the massive Sangre de Cristo Range standing sentinel on your left and the Wet Mountains filling the eastern skyline. This is among the best cycling country in the state, with its mouse-quiet roads, jaw-dropping scenery, and a gentle uphill grade that tops out around 8600 feet before tilting downward for the descent into Westcliffe (mile 191). Grab a room in town, or camp in nearby San Isabel National Forest.

The next morning, continue the spectacular spin across the Wet Mountain Valley,

which is also part of the Hardscrabble Century route (Ride 29). But instead of heading down the Texas Creek drainage, turn left onto seldom used County Road 1A, then drop into the Arkansas River Canyon at Cotapaxi. Here rejoin US 50, heading west toward Salida and Poncha Springs. Be careful; sightlines are short, and traffic can get heavy on this stretch of road.

Get a good night's sleep in Salida or Poncha Springs (both have camping and lodging options), then wake up ready to climb. This leg starts with the long grind up to the Continental Divide and the summit of Monarch Pass (elevation 11,312 feet). The heart of the climb is 10.7 miles and gains 2900 feet with an average grade of 5 percent. There's a gift shop up top if you need to top off your bottles.

Ten miles of speedy downhill and 20 miles of valley rollers bring you to Gunnison, a

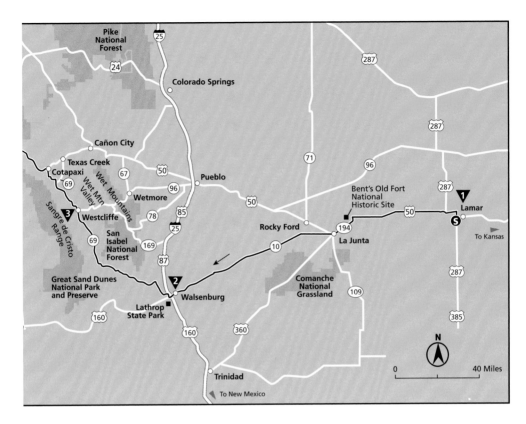

classic Colorado cowboy town that features in Rides 45 and 47. Spend the night in town, or roll a few miles west to one of the campgrounds along the Gunnison River. Start your next day with a westerly spin along Blue Mesa Reservoir; its 20-mile length and 96-mile shoreline make it the largest body of water in the state. At the lake's western tip, commence a blitzkrieg of rollers as you pass through tiny Cimarron (which has food and water), ascend Cero Summit, and finally drop into Montrose, the second-largest city on Colorado's Western Slope (population 19,132). Lodging and food options run the gamut.

Now turn south on US 550, spinning along the Uncompahgre River, with the mighty San Juan Range filling the distant skyline. If you want to get a closer look at these menacing mountains, check out Rides 56, 58, 59, and 74. This route steers clear of all that climb-ing, instead bending west on SR 62, which passes through Ridgway, a small rustic town 27 miles from Montrose. Stop here and spend the rest of the day relaxing at Ridgway State Park. Or press on for the tough ascent of Dallas Divide. Up top is one of the state's most spectacular mountain views.

Eight miles past the summit, turn right onto SR 145 and continue westward. Initially, this narrow two-lane road is tucked tightly between a red rock wall and the San Miguel River. But the terrain soon opens, as you climb up and out of San Miguel Canyon and onto Wrights Mesa, then roll into Norwood (which has food and water). Continue on SR 145 as it jogs north and west past cattle ranches and fields of hay. On a clear day, you can spot eastern Utah's La Sal Range towering in the distance. Fifteen miles west of Norwood, the landscape begins its final

This east–west route across the state includes extensive time on the quiet roads of the Wet Mountain Valley, which is bordered to the west by the massive Sangre de Cristo Range.

metamorphosis, growing ever drier and more desertlike. Continue west at the intersection of SR 141, rolling into Naturita Canyon and on to tiny Naturita (or its neighbor Nucla) for the final night of this cross-state tour.

These tiny boom-bust mining towns have seen better days, but you're still guaranteed to encounter friendly folk who'll point you toward a good meal. At last check, there were several lodging options and some primitive camping nearby. But it's best to call ahead to be sure. The final leg begins with a 4-mile backtrack, then a right turn to stay on SR 141

heading south. You'll start with a gradual climb to Dry Creek Basin and on to Gypsum Gap (elevation 6139 feet). Now drop into lonely Disappointment Valley where you may spot a herd of wild horses running near the road.

At mile 491, cross the Dolores River, then immediately begin the final climb, a 7-mile grunt toward the tiny town of Egnar (which does not have any services). Ten miles due south, turn left on US 491, and Dove Creek is 2 miles ahead. Now head for home—or continue west. The Utah border is only 8 miles away.

0.0	In Lamar, head west on Forest St.
0.1	Right onto US 385 and 287 (Main St.)
2.0	Left, continuing on US 287 and 50
7.9	Straight, continuing on US 50
35.2	Right at fork, merging onto SR 194
44.9	Left, continuing on SR 194
55.1	Left onto SR 109 (Main St.)
55.9	Arrive in La Junta, and right onto US 50
57.9	Left onto SR 10
129.7	Stay straight, merging onto US 160
129.8	Arrive in Walsenburg
130.6	Right onto Main St. (I-25 Business)
130.8	Stay straight, merging onto Walsen Ave. (I-25 Business)
132.7	Left onto SR 69
191.0	Arrive in Westcliffe, and continue north on SR 69
207.1	Left onto CR 1A
214.1	Arrive in Cotapaxi, and left onto US 50
237.1	Arrive in Salida, and continue on US 50
242.0	Arrive in Poncha Springs
242.1	Right, continuing on US 50
249.4	Left onto US 50
260.4	Reach Monarch Pass summit
301.9	Arrive in Gunnison
365.0	Arrive in Montrose
365.1	Left onto South Hillcrest Dr.
366.5	Right onto East Niagara Rd.
367.0	Left onto US 550
392.0	Arrive in Ridgway, and right onto SR 62
415.4	Right onto SR 145
432.4	Arrive in Norwood
448.0	Right, merging onto SR 141
451.9	Arrive in Naturita
451.9	Backtrack on SR 141 south
456.0	Right, continuing on SR 141
512.7	Left on US 491
515.0	Arrive in Dove Creek

The famed Red Rocks Park and Amphitheatre, just west of Denver,
is a great place to see a concert or go for a mellow bike ride.

RESOURCES

ADVOCACY GROUPS
Bicycle Aurora: www.coloradocycling.org
Bicycle Colorado, Denver:
    www.BicycleColorado.org
Bicycle Douglas County:
    www.bicycledouglascounty.org
Bicycle Longmont:
    www.bicyclelongmont.org
Bike Denver: www.bikedenver.org/advocacy/
Bike Depot, Denver: www.thebikedepot.org
Bike Fort Collins: www.bikefortcollins.org
Community Cycles, Boulder:
    www.communitycycles.org
    /bicycle-advocacy.html
Montrose Area Bicycle Alliance, Montrose:
    www.montrosebicycle.org
Routt County Riders, Steamboat Springs:
    www.routtcountyriders.org
Summit Biking, Summit County:
    www.summitbiking.org

NATIONAL PARKS
Mesa Verde National Park:
    www.nps.gov/meve
Rocky Mountain National Park:
    www.nps.gov/romo

BIKE MAPS
Colorado Department of Transportation:
    www.cotrip.org. *Up-to-date road
    conditions.*

CITY, COUNTY, AND REGION
Boulder:
    www.bouldercolorado.gov/goboulder/bike
Boulder County: www.bouldercounty.org
    /doc/transportation/bikemap.pdf
Breckenridge: www.townofbreckenridge
    .com/index.aspx?page=983
Colorado Riverfront Trail:
    www.riverfrontprojects.org
Colorado Springs: www.springsgov.com
    /Page.aspx?NavID=4175
Denver: www.denvergov.org
    /bicyclingindenver/denverbikemaps
    /tabid/438249/Default.aspx
Fort Collins:
    www.fcgov.com/bicycling/bike-maps.php
Grand Junction: www.tomorrowhillfarm
    .com/JohnHodgebicycleMaps.html
Jefferson County:
    http://bikejeffco.org/riding-in-jeffco
    /overview-of-jefferson-county-riding
La Plata County: www.co.laplata.co.us/sites
    /default/files/departments/engineering/
    documents/lpc_areabikemap.pdf
Mesa County:
    http://riverfrontproject.org/trails
Montrose: http://co-montrosevcb2.civicplus
    .com/156/Road-Biking
Pueblo:
    http://activepueblo.net/maps/bike/city
Roaring Fork Valley:
    www.rfta.com/trails.html

STATE
Colorado Bicycle & Byways:
    http://dtdapps.coloradodot.info/bike

BIKE SHARING
Aspen: www.we-cycle.org
Boulder B-Cycle: http://boulder.bcycle.com
Denver B-Cycle: http://denver.bcycle.com
Fort Collins Bike Library: www.fcgov.com
    /bicycling/library.php

CYCLING EVENTS

Note: The month-by-month listings are a tiny fraction of the cycling events that take place in Colorado every year. Check the statewide calendars for more exhaustive lists.

STATEWIDE EVENT CALENDARS

Bicycle Colorado: http://bicyclecolorado
.org/events/2014-event-calendar
Bicycle Racing Association of Colorado:
www.coloradocycling.org/calendar/menu
303Cycling: http://303cycling.com
/colorado-cycling-calendar/month
USA Cycling: www.usacycling.org
/events/?state=CO

MAY

Café Velo Gran Fondo, El Paso County:
www.cafevelobikes.com/granfondo
Iron Horse Bicycle Classic, Durango:
http://ironhorsebicycleclassic.com
Superior Morgul Classic, Superior:
www.withoutlimits.com
The L'Eroica, Grand Junction:
www.browncycles.com/leroica.htm

JUNE

Bicycle Tour of Colorado, statewide:
www.bicycletourcolorado.com
Black Forest Classic, Colorado Springs:
http://crclub.org/Default
.aspx?pageId=1596902
Buena Vista Bike Fest, Buena Vista and
Leadville: http://bvbf.org
Denver Century Ride, Denver:
http://denvercentury.com
Elephant Rock Cycling Festival, Douglas
County: http://elephantrock.com
Guanella Pass Hill Climb, Georgetown:
http://guanellapasshillclimb.com
North Boulder Park Classic, Boulder:
http://boulderclassic.com
Ride the Rockies, statewide:
http://ridetherockies.com

JULY

Bob Cook Memorial Mount Evans Hill
Climb, Idaho Springs:
http://bicyclerace.com
Tour de Ladies, Parker:
www.tourdeladies.com
Tour de Steamboat, Steamboat Springs:
http://tourdesteamboat.com
Triple Bypass, Evergreen to Avon:
http://teamevergreen.org/triple-bypass

AUGUST

Copper Triangle, Copper Mountain:
http://coppertriangle.com
Durango 100 Gran Fondo, Durango:
www.durango100.com
Lookout Mountain Hill Climb, Golden:
http://coloradobikelaw.com
New Belgium Tour de Fat, Fort Collins:
www.newbelgium.com
Red Rocks Century, Morrison:
http://redrockscentury.com
Steamboat Stage Race, Steamboat Springs:
http://bikesteamboat.com
Venus de Miles, Boulder:
http://colorado.venusdemiles.com
West Elk Bicycle Classic, Gunnison:
http://westelkbicycleclassic.com

SEPTEMBER

Bikes and Brews, Cañon City:
www.bikesandbrews.org
Durango Fall Blaze, Durango:
www.fortlewis.edu/cycling
/DurangoFallBlaze.aspx
New Belgium Tour de Fat, Denver:
www.newbelgium.com
Pedal the Plains, Eastern Plains:
www.pedaltheplains.com
Salida Bike Festival, Salida:
http://salidabikefest.com

OCTOBER

Tour of the Moon, Grand Junction:
http://tourofthemoon.com

HELPFUL WEBSITES

Bicycling magazine: www.bicycling.com. *The world's leading cycling magazine.*

Bicycle Racing Association of Colorado: www.coloradocycling.org. *Statewide race governing body, which also sponsors numerous clinics.*

Bike the Byways Colorado: www.bikebyways.org/Byways/index.php. *Cycling information on all twenty-five of the state's scenic and historic byways.*

RoadBikeReview.com: *Helpful bike and gear reviews, as well as the latest cycling news.*

Strava: www.strava.com. *Allows cyclists to track their rides via a smartphone or GPS device and share their results with the Strava community.*

303 Cycling: http://303cycling.com. *Information on races, group rides, and other cycling news with an emphasis on the Boulder and Denver areas.*

CLUBS AND TEAMS

Alpha Bicycle Co-Vista Subaru, Centennial: www.alphabicycle.com

Altitude Cycling, Evergreen: www.altitudecycling.org

Aspen Cycling Club, Aspen: www.aspencyclingclub.org

Avout Racing, Littleton: http://avoutracing.com

Be the Beast Racing, Boulder: www.bethebeastracing.com

Black Sheep Junior Cycling, Lakewood: www.blacksheepcycling.org

Boulder Junior Cycling, Boulder: www.boulderjuniorcycling.org

Boulder Orthopedics, Lafayette: www.bouldermasterscycling.com

COBRAS, Littleton: www.cobrascycling.org

Colorado Riders Club, Englewood: www.crclub.org

Colorado School of Mines, Golden: http://recsports.mines.edu/REC-club-sports-cycling

Colorado Springs Cycling Club: www.bikesprings.org/

CP Racing, Colorado Springs: www.cpracingteam.com

Cross Propz Racing, Nederland: www.crosspropz.com

DBC Events, Boulder: http://dbcevents.com

Denver Bicycle Touring Club, Denver: www.dbtc.org/

Denver 38 Racing, Denver: http://denver38racing.com/

Durango Wheel Club, Durango: www.durangowheelclub.com

Evol Elite Racing, Boulder: www.plainstopeaksracing.com

Excel Sports Boulder, Boulder: www.excelsportscycling.com

Feedback Sports Racing, Golden: www.feedbacksports.com

Fort Collins Cycling Team, Fort Collins: www.fccyclingteam.com

Fort Follies, Fort Collins: http://fortfollies.com

Fort Lewis College Cycling Team, Durango: http://cycling.fortlewis.edu

Foxtrot Racing, Lafayette: http://foxtrotracingteam.com/

Front Rangers Cycling Club, Littleton: www.frontrangersdenver.org

Front Rangers Junior Cycling, Colorado Springs: http://frontrangers.org

Green Mountain Sports Velo, Arvada: www.greenmountainsports.com/contact.html

GS Boulder Cycling, Golden: www.gsboulder.com

GS CIAO, Boulder: www.horizonpanachecycling.com

Heart Cycle Bicycle Touring Club, Denver: www.heartcycle.org

Littleton Masters Bicycle Racing Club, Timnath: www.limabeanscycling.com

Local Velo, Littleton: http://localvelo.com

Louisville Velo Club, Denver: www.louisvillecyclery.com

LTR Sports, Grand Junction: www.livetrainrace.com

Mile High Cycling Society (sponsored by Lathram Financial Group), Englewood: http://milehighcycling.org

Naked Women's Racing, Grand Junction: http://nakedwomensracing.com

Natural Grocers Cycling Team, Denver: http://naturalgrocerscycling.com

Old School Racing, Niwot: www.racerxcycling.com

Outdoor DIVAS Cycling, Arvada: www.outdoordivascycling.com

Panorak Racing, Westminster: www.panorak.com

Peak to Peak Training Systems, Denver: www.peaktopeaktraining.com

Pedal Racing, Lakewood: http://pedalraceteam.com

Peloton-Specialized Cycling Team, Littleton: www.peloton-specialized.com

Primal-Audi Denver, Lakewood: www.haulnass.com

Pro Peloton Pinarello Racing Team, Lakewood: www.propeloton.com

PSIMET/Zilla Racing, Boulder: www.psimetzillaracing.com

Rally Sport Cycling Team, Thornton: www.leadoutvelo.com

RealD-Amgen Masters Cycling, Boulder: http://reald-amgencycling.org

RLW Cycling Team, Denver: www.routinelegworks.com

Rocky Mountain Cancer Centers Cycling Team, Lakewood: www.boulderveloracing.com

Rocky Mountain Road Club, Greenwood Village: www.rockymountainroadclub.com

Schwab Cycles Racing Team, Littleton: www.schwabcycles.com

Sonic Boom Racing, Lakewood: http://sonicboomracing.com

South Central Racing, Louisville: www.southcentralracing.com

Southern Colorado Velo, Salida: www.socovelo.com

Sports Optical Racing Team, Colorado Springs: www.sportsoptical.com

Spradley Barr Wind Chill Cycling, Denver: www.windchillcycling.com

St. Vrain Velo, Cheyenne: www.blueskyvelo.com

Steamboat Velo, Boulder: www.bikesteamboat.com

Team Body Sync, Boulder: http://bodysync.blogspot.com

Team Cycleton, Morrison: www.teamcycleton.com

Team Evergreen Cycling, Denver: www.teamevergreen.org

Team Rio Grande, Denver: www.riograndecycling.com

Team Rocky Mountain Health Plans, Fort Collins: www.teamrmhp.com

Team Small Batch, Parker: www.teamsmallbatch.com

The Cyclist-Lawyer.com, Colorado Springs: www.TheCyclist-Lawyer.com/team

The Natural Way Racing Team, Golden: www.tnwrt.com

Tough Girl Cycling, Highlands Ranch: www.toughgirlcycling.com

Twin Peaks Cycling, Inc., Arvada: www.twinpeaksracing.com

In 2014, Colorado was ranked the nation's sixth most bike-friendly state by the League of American Bicyclists. Signs such as this one on Lizard Head Pass near Telluride are part of the reason why.

INDEX

A

Adventure Cycling Association, 279
Air Force Academy, 11, 108
Air Force Academy Loop, 11, 108
Almont, 45, 187
Alpine Park, 177, 180
Alpine Visitor Center (Rocky Mountain National Park), 65
American Flyers, 104, 243
America's Mountain, 123
Animas River, 29, 208–216, 278
Animas River Trail, 208–212, 278
Animas Valley, 213–215
Animas Valley Loop, 12, 29, 213
Antonito, 201–203
Arkansas River, 11, 27, 124–131, 168, 178–181, 273, 280
Arkansas River Canyon, 129–131, 280
Arkansas River Trail, 11, 27, 124–128
Armstrong, Lance, 86, 167
Aspen, 29, 166, 170–175, 272–273

B

Bakers Bridge, 12, 29, 213–216
Balanced Rock, 117
Balcony House, 232
Bates, Katherine Lee, 123
Battle Mountain, 161
Bayfield, 12, 206–210
Bear Creek Trail, 49
Bedrock, 233–235
Bedrock Store, 233–234
Bent's Old Fort National Historic Site, 279
Bergen Park, 44–46
best rides, 27–30
Beverly Heights Park, 34–36
Big Thompson Canyon, 10, 65, 69
Bike Town USA, 142, 143
Black Canyon, 12, 28, 195
Black Mesa, 12, 28, 194–197
Blue Mesa Reservoir, 195–196, 281
Bob Cook Memorial Mount Evans Hill Climb, 152, 286

Boulder, 11, 23, 27, 29, 30, 68, 70–75, 77–106
Boulder Bike Paths, 11, 27, 100–101
Boulder County, 77–78, 80–81, 97, 104–105
Boulder Creek Path, 21, 27, 100–103
Bow Mountain, 80–84
Brainard Lake, 10, 28, 73–77
Breckenridge, 157–160
Brooklyn neighborhood, 146
Brophy, Greg, 258
Buckhorn Canyon, 57–60
Buena Vista, 179, 186–189, 271–275
Buffalo Bill's Grave, 35–36

C

C-470 Trail, 43, 47, 49
Cache la Poudre River, 57, 61
Camp Hale, 163
Cañon City, 128–132
Canyon View Park, 239–242
Carbondale, 271–274
Carhenge parking lot, 220–224
Carter Lake, 10, 62–64, 69–73
Cascade, 121–124
Castle Creek Road, 175
Cedaredge, 255
Central Summits Challenge, 13, 271–275
Chama, New Mexico, 201–205
Chatfield State Park, 43, 47–49
Chautauqua Park, 94–100
Cheesman Park, 54–56
Cherry Creek Reservoir, 10, 51
Cherry Creek State Park, 10, 50–54
Cherry Creek Trail, 10, 27, 50–53
Cheyenne Cañon, 11, 29, 117–120
Cheyenne Mountain Zoo, 120
Cinnamon Roll Century, 69
City Park, 53–57
Cliff Palace, 232
Cliff Palace Loop, 232
Coal Bank Pass, 217–219, 276–278
Coal Creek Canyon, 98–99

Coal Mine–Oak Creek Loop, 33, 143–145
Cochetopa Dome, 12, 192–193
Colorado Front Range Trail, 111
Colorado laws, 18
Colorado National Monument, 13, 27, 243–248
Colorado River, 68, 164–166
Colorado Riverfront Trail, 245, 246
Colorado Springs, 24, 28, 29, 30, 108, 111–121
Colorado Welcome Center, 245, 256–257
Confluence Park, 10, 47–53
Continental Divide, 12, 13, 30, 68, 123, 140, 163, 171, 188, 192, 198, 205, 271, 274, 279
Coors Classic, 17, 94, 104, 106, 243
Copper Mountain Resort, 163
Copper Triangle, 11, 160–164
Costner, Kevin, 104, 243, 256
Cotapaxi, 280, 283
Cottonwood Pass, 12, 30, 186–189, 271–275
Crawford, 195–197
Crawford State Park, 196
Creede, 198, 200
Crested Butte, 12, 183–186, 186–189, 197, 272–274
Crested Butte Chamber of Commerce, 183, 186
Crested Butte Mountain Resort, 184
Crested Butte to Gunnison, 12, 183–186
Crystal Creek Reservoir Visitor Center, 124
Cuchara, 133–136
Cuchara Mountain Resort, 133
Cucharas Pass, 133, 135, 136
Cumbres and Toltec Railroad, 201, 202
Cumbres Pass, 12, 201–203
cyclocross, 101, 113, 265

D
Dakota Stonewall, 136
Dallas Divide, 278
Dams Road to Pinewood Climb, 10, 60–64
Danielson, Tom, 34, 118, 152
Dave Wiens West Elk Bicycle Classic, 195, 197

Death Ride, 275
Deep Creek Steamboat Springs, 11, 30, 140–143
Deep Creek Telluride, 12, 220–223
Deer Creek Canyon, 10, 40–44, 47
Deer Trail Road, 83, 84
Dolores, 275–278
Dolores River, 224, 225, 233, 234, 236, 238, 278, 282
Dolores River Canyon, 238
Delta, 255
Denver, 10, 27, 31, 40, 46, 50, 53–56
Denver City Parks, 10, 27, 53–56
Denver Metro, 31–56
Denver Museum of Nature and Science, 53, 56
difficulty ratings, 23–25
Dillon, 11, 157–160
Dinosaur Ridge, 38
Disappointment Valley, 282
Dotsero, 166, 167
Dove Creek, 282, 283
Drake, 68
Durango, 30, 206–219
Durango & Silverton Narrow Gauge Railroad, 215, 228
Durango High School, 216, 218
Durango Mountain Resort, 219

E
East Orchard Mesa, 250
East River, 183, 185
Eastern Plains, 256–270
east–west cross-state route, 279
Eben G. Fine Park, 87, 90, 91, 93, 100, 102
Echo Lake, 46, 152, 153
Echo Lake Lodge, 46, 152, 153
Echo Lake Park, 152
Eldora Mountain Resort, 98
elevation accuracy, 25
Elk Mountain (Sleeping Giant), 117, 142, 144, 148
Elk Range, 173, 185
Elk River, 142
Emerald Loop, 11, 29, 146–149
Emerald Mountain, 144, 147

Estes Park, 65, 68, 69, 79

F

family rides, 27
Far View Terrace Café, 231, 232
Flagstaff Road, 10, 29, 94–96, 97, 99
Flatirons, 94, 97
Flirtation Rock, 260
floods (2013), 23, 57, 60, 65, 73, 77, 80, 87
Florence, 128, 129, 131
Fort Collins, 57–65, 72
Fort Lewis College, 212
Fountain Creek, 111, 113, 114, 127, 128
Fountain Creek Regional Park, 111,
    113, 114
Fountain Creek Regional Trail, 111, 114,
    127, 128
Fox Creek, 203
Franz Lake, 182
Fremont Pass, 161
Frisco, 157–159
Front Range North, 57–107
Fruita, 13, 239–242, 245
Fruita Farms Loop, 13, 239–242
fueling, 21

G

Garden of the Gods, 11, 115–117
Gateway, 237–239
Gateway Canyons Resort, 238
Gateway Visitor Center, 153, 155, 156
Georgetown, 153, 155, 156
getting started, 17
Glen Cove Inn, 124
Glen Haven, 68, 69
Glenwood Canyon, 11, 28, 164–167
Glenwood Canyon Recreation Trail, 164,
    166, 167
Glenwood Springs, 164, 166
Gold Camp Road, 118, 120
Gold Hill, 10, 30, 87–91
Gold Hill Loop, 10, 30, 87–91
Gold Run Road, 86, 87, 89, 90
Golden, 31, 34
Golden Gate Canyon, 10, 31–33
Golden Gate Canyon State Park, 10, 31–33

Goose Creek Greenway Trail, 101–103
Grand Junction, 236, 239, 243, 246, 252
Grand Lake, 68
Grand Mesa, 13, 252–255
Grand Mesa Scenic and Historic Byway,
    252, 255
Grand Mesa Visitor Center, 252, 254, 255
Grand Valley, 28, 241, 243, 244, 247, 253
Grant, 155, 156
gravel road riding, 22
Great Plains, 256, 263
Green Ridge Glade Reservoir, 61, 72
Gross Dam Loop, 10, 97–100
Gross Reservoir, 96, 97, 98, 99
Guanella Pass, 11, 153–156
Guanella Pass Road, 153, 155
Gunnison, 12, 183–186, 189–191, 195, 197
Gunnison Bluffs trailhead, 236, 237, 239
Gunnison River, 185, 189, 236, 237, 281
Gypsum Gap, 282

H

Haigler, Nebraska, 260, 261
Hardscrabble Century, 11, 128–132
Hardscrabble Pass, 130
Hartwell Park, 226, 228
Helen Hunt Falls, 118, 121
Hermits Rest overlook, 196, 197
Hermosa, 218
Hesperus Hill, 278
Highline Canal Trail, 52
Highway of the Legends, 11, 133–136
Horca, 201, 203
Horsetooth Reservoir, 57, 58, 59, 61, 63,
    67, 72
how to use this book, 23
Hugo Race Loop, 13, 261–264
Hugo Road Race, 262
Hygiene, 70, 71, 72

I

Idaho Springs, 149, 151, 152, 153
Ignacio, 207, 208, 209
Ignacio–Bayfield Loop, 12, 206–210
Independence Pass, 12, 170–172, 271–274
Indian Peaks, 75, 98

IOOF Park, 189
Iron Horse Classic, 12, 216–219

J

Jacks Cabin Cutoff, 187, 189, 271, 274
James Canyon Drive, 75, 78, 83
Jamestown, 78, 79, 80
Julesburg, 256, 257
Juniper Pass, 46

K

Kansas, 259, 260, 261
Karval, 263, 264
Kawuneeche Valley, 68
Kebler Pass, 190, 197, 271, 272, 274

L

La Junta, 268–270, 279, 283
La Manga Pass, 12, 201–203
La Veta, 133, 136
Lake Catamount, 139
Lake City, 197–200
Lake City Town Park, 197
Lake Dillon, 157–160
Lake Dillon Loop, 11, 157–160
Lake Fork Campground, 195, 197
Lake Pueblo State Park, 124, 125, 127
Lake San Cristobal, 199, 200
Lamar, 279, 283
Landis, Floyd, 167
Laporte, 57, 61, 65
Larimer County, 23, 57, 60, 65
Leadville, 29, 160, 162, 167, 169
Leadville Trail 100 mountain bike race, 29, 167, 195
Lee Hill Drive, 75, 81, 83, 90
Lefthand Canyon, 10, 69, 73, 75, 77, 78, 80–84, 90
Leipheimer, Levi, 171
LeMond, Greg, 104, 108
Lions Park, 57, 59, 60, 61, 62, 64, 65, 67, 69
Little Church in the Pines, 89
Little Park Road, 13, 246–249
Little Park Road Loop, 13, 246–249
Lizard Head Pass, 12, 28, 223–225, 278

Lizard Head Peak, 28, 224
Lookout Mountain, 10, 34–36
Los Caminos Antiguos Scenic and Historic Byway, 201
Loveland, 62, 72
Loveland Pass, 157
Lyons, 68, 74, 77, 80

M

Magnolia Road, 10, 91–93
Mancos, 277, 278
Marble, 272, 273
Maroon Bells, 12, 29, 173
Maroon Bells Scenic Area, 173, 176
Maroon Creek Road, 12, 29, 173–176
Masonville, 59, 60, 61, 64, 67, 69, 72
McClure Pass, 271–274
Mesa, 253
Mesa Top Loop, 232
Mesa Verde National Park, 12, 229–232
Mesa Verde National Park Visitor and Research Center, 229
Million Dollar Highway, 226
Minturn, 163
Molas Pass, 219, 276, 278
Monarch Pass, 280, 283
Montrose, 281, 283
Morgul-Bismark Loop, 11, 103–107
Morrison, 37–39
Morrow Point, 196, 197
Mount Crested Butte, 185
Mount Evans, 11, 30, 149–153
Mount Garfield, 13, 200
Mount Princeton Hot Springs, 30, 177, 178
Mount Zirkel, 142
Mount Elbert, 162, 171
Mount Princeton, 30, 177, 178
Mount Princeton Hot Springs, 30, 177, 178
multiday routes, 271–283

N

Naturita, 232, 235, 238, 282, 283
Naturita Visitor Center, 232, 235
Nebraska, 256, 260, 261
Nederland, 98, 99, 100
New Mexico, 28, 111, 201, 203

New Raymer, 265, 266, 267
North Cochetopa Pass, 12, 192–194
Northern Rockies, 137–176

O

Oak Creek, 145, 146
Ohio Creek Road, 12, 29, 189–191
Old La Sal, 233, 234, 235
Olde Stage Road, 75, 77, 78, 81, 83
Ouray, 30, 226, 228, 229, 275, 276,
    277, 278
Ouray Hot Springs, 12, 226, 276
Ovid, 257

P

Pagosa Springs, 204, 205, 206
Pagosa Hot Springs, 204
Palisade, 13, 29, 249
Palisade Fruit and Wine Byway, 13, 29,
    249–252
Paonia State Park, 272, 274
Paradox Valley, 12, 232–235
Pawnee Buttes, 13, 264, 265
Pawnee Buttes Roubaix, 13, 264–267
Pawnee National Grassland, 266
Peak to Peak Highway, 24, 28, 74, 79,
    90, 98
Pikes Peak, 11, 16, 30, 121–124
Pikes Peak Greenway Trail, 11, 30, 111–114
Pinewood Reservoir, 61, 62
Pioneer Park, 128, 129
Placerville, 278
Plains to Pueblos, 13, 279–283
Platte River Trail, 10, 46–50
Pleasant Park School, 41
Pole Hill Road, 61
Poncha Pass, 182
Poncha Springs, 182, 280
Potter Park, 268, 269
Poudre River Canyon, 59
Powderhorn Mountain Resort, 252, 253
Prospect Road, 183, 185
Pueblo, 124, 125, 127
Pueblo Levee Mural, 125
Pueblo Nature and Raptor Center, 125
Pueblo Reservoir, 127

Puke Hill, 250

R

Rabbit Ears Pass , 11, 137–140
Race Across America, 279
Rattlesnake Ridge, 61
Red Cliff Arch Bridge, 163
Red Mountain Pass, 12, 30, 226–229, 277
Red Rocks Amphitheatre, 10, 37
Red Rocks Cruiser, 10, 37–39
Red Rocks Park, 37
Republican River, 260
Rico, 223, 275
ride locator map, 8
Ride the Rockies, 22, 206, 225
ride time, 25
rides-at-a-glance, 10–13
Ridgway, 226, 275
riding etiquette and safety, 18
Rio Grande Park, 172, 173
Rio Grande River, 198
Rio Grande Trail, 166, 273
Rist Canyon Loop, 10, 57–60
Riverside Park, 243, 246
Roaring Fork Valley, 273
Rocky Ford, 270
Rocky Mountain National Park, 28, 65, 67
Royal Gorge Bridge, 128, 129, 131
Runyan Lake, 124, 125, 127

S

Saguache, 192, 193
Salida Spinner, 12, 29, 180–182
Salida to St. Elmo, 12, 30, 177–180
Salina, 89
San Juan Range, 219, 255, 275, 281
San Juan Scenic Skyway, 13, 275–278
San Miguel River, 220, 222, 223, 225, 281
Sangre de Cristo Range, 130, 182, 192,
    280, 282
Santa Fe Regional Trail, 114
Santa Fe Trail, 269
Santa Fe Trail Scenic and Historic
    Byway, 269
Santa Fe Trail Triangle, 13, 29, 268–270
Santa Rita Park, 207, 208, 210, 212, 275

Segundo, 136
Silver Cliff, 131
Silverton, 216, 217, 218, 219, 226, 227, 228
Skyline Drive, 131
Slate River, 183
Slumgullion Pass, 12, 30, 197–200
Soul Crusher Hill, 135
South Boulder Creek Path, 101
South Platte River, 43, 47, 50, 256, 257
South Platte River Trail, 13, 256–258
South Platte River Trail Scenic and Historic Byway, 256
South St. Vrain Canyon, 10, 28, 73–77
Southern Rockies, 177–203
Southwest Colorado, 204–235
Spanish Peaks, 133
Spring Creek Pass, 197, 198, 200
Squaw Pass Road, 10, 44–46, 152, 153
St. Elmo, 177, 179
St. Francis, Kansas, 260
Stagecoach State Park, 145
Steamboat Springs, 29, 30, 137, 140, 142, 143, 144, 146
Steamboat Springs transit center, 137, 140, 143, 147
Stein Meadow overlook, 174
Stonewall, 135, 136
Stonewall Century, 136
Strawberry Park Hot Springs, 146
Sugarloaf Road, 91
Sugarloaf-Magnolia, 18, 91–93
Summit County, 157
Summit County Recreational Pathway System, 157, 159
Sunshine Canyon, 10, 84–87, 90
Super James Climb, 78
Super James Loop, 10, 77–80
Supermax prison, 129
Swan Mountain Road, 157, 159

T

Taylor Park, 186, 187, 188, 274
Taylor Park Trading Post, 187, 274
Taylor Park Reservoir, 187, 274

Taylor River, 185, 187
Telluride, 12, 28, 220–225, 275–278
ten essentials for cycling, 23
Ten Mile Canyon National Recreation Trail, 163
Tennessee Pass, 163
10th Mountain Division, 163
Texas Creek (town), 131
Texas Creek (body of water), 211
Texas Creek Loop, 12, 30, 210–213
Town Park (Cuchara), 133
Town Park (Lake City), 197
Town Park (Pagosa Springs), 204
Trail Ridge Road, 10, 28, 65–69
Trimble Hot Springs, 12, 215, 218
Trinidad, 133
Trout Lake, 224
Turquoise Lake, 168
Turquoise Lake Loop, 11, 29, 167–169
Twenty Mile Road, 144
Twin Lakes, 170, 171
Twin Lakes Historic Center, 170
Two Rivers Park, 164
Two Time Zones, Three States, 13, 258–261

U

Unaweep Canyon, 12, 236–239
Unaweep Divide, 237
Unaweep Tabeguache Scenic and Historic Byway, 238
Uncompahgre Gorge, 226
USA Pro Challenge, 61, 83, 94, 171
Utah, 233, 234
Utica Street Market General Store and Full Spectrum Fiber Arts, 83

V

Vail, 163
Vail Pass, 160, 161, 163
Valmont Bike Park, 27, 101
Veterans Memorial Park, 249, 250

W

Walsenburg, 133, 279, 280
Ward, 69, 74, 81, 83, 90

Washington Park, 55
West Elk Loop Scenic Byway, 194
Westcliffe, 131
Western Slope, 236–255
Wet Mountain Valley, 129, 131, 280, 282
Wetmore, 127
Whitewater, 236, 237
Wiens, Dave, 195, 197
Wilson Peak, 233
Wolf Creek Pass, 12, 204–206

Wolf Creek Ski Area, 206
Wonderland Creek Greenway Trail, 101
Wondervu, 98
Woodmen Road Park-n-Ride, 111
Wray, 258, 259, 261

Y
Yampa River, 138, 139, 147
Yampa River Core Trail, 138, 144, 146, 147, 149

If you like to climb—or even if you don't—Colorado is one of the world's truly great cycling destinations.

ABOUT THE AUTHOR

Courtesy Jason Sumner

Colorado native and avid cyclist Jason Sumner has been writing about two-wheeled pursuits of all kinds since 1999. He's covered the Tour de France, the Olympic Games, and dozens of other international cycling events. He also likes to throw himself into the fray, penning first-person accounts of cycling adventures in British Columbia, Belgium, Brazil, Costa Rica, France, Peru, and of course, Colorado, to name a few. Sumner regularly contributes to a variety of cycling titles. He is the features editor for RoadBikeReview.com and Mtbr.com, and the author of *Bicycling: 1,100 All-Time Best Tips*. He's also a marginally talented amateur bike racer, and once rode 220 miles in one day to celebrate a friend's fiftieth birthday.

MOUNTAINEERS BOOKS is a leading publisher of mountaineering literature and guides—including our flagship title, *Mountaineering: The Freedom of the Hills*—as well as adventure narratives, natural history, and general outdoor recreation. Through our two imprints, Skipstone and Braided River, we also publish titles on sustainability and conservation. We are committed to supporting the environmental and educational goals of our organization by providing expert information on human-powered adventure, sustainable practices at home and on the trail, and preservation of wilderness.

The Mountaineers, founded in 1906, is a 501(c)(3) nonprofit outdoor activity and conservation organization whose mission is "to explore, study, preserve, and enjoy the natural beauty of the outdoors." One of the largest such organizations in the United States, it sponsors classes and year-round outdoor activities throughout the Pacific Northwest, including climbing, hiking, backcountry skiing, snowshoeing, bicycling, camping, paddling, and more. The Mountaineers also supports its mission through its publishing division, Mountaineers Books, and promotes environmental education and citizen engagement. For more information, visit The Mountaineers Program Center, 7700 Sand Point Way NE, Seattle, WA 98115-3996; phone 206-521-6001; www.mountaineers.org; or email info@mountaineers.org.

Our publications are made possible through the generosity of donors and through sales of more than 500 titles on outdoor recreation, sustainable lifestyle, and conservation. To donate, purchase books, or learn more, visit us online:

MOUNTAINEERS BOOKS
1001 SW Klickitat Way, Suite 201 • Seattle, WA 98134
800-553-4453 • mbooks@mountaineersbooks.org • www.mountaineersbooks.org

OTHER TITLES YOU MIGHT ENJOY FROM MOUNTAINEERS BOOKS

100 Classic Hikes in Colorado, 3rd ed
Scott Warren
A full-color guide to Colorado's most
cherished landscapes and trails

Best Hikes with Dogs: Colorado
Ania Savage
80 hikes selected to delight your dog (and you) throughout
Colorado—many trails easily accessible from urban areas

Best Hikes with Kids: Colorado
Maureen Keilty
Colorado hikes that kids like—with lots of
features that will appeal to the whole family

**Outdoor Family Guide to
Rocky Mountain National Park, 3rd ed**
Lisa Gollins Evans
The top-selling family guide to magnificent
Rocky Mountain National Park—now fully updated!

More titles in the 75 Classic Rides series

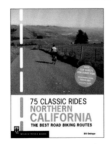